British White Water

Also by Terry Storry

Snowdonia White Water, Sea and Surf, Cicerone Press, 1986
Raging Rivers, Stormy Seas (with Marcus Bailie and Nigel Foster), Oxford
Illustrated Press, 1989

BRITISH WHITE WATER

A GUIDE TO THE 100 BEST CANOEING RIVERS

TERRY STORRY

FRANCES LINCOLN

Frances Lincoln Ltd
4 Torriano Mews
Torriano Avenue
London NW5 2RZ
www.franceslincoln.com

First Frances Lincoln edition 2005
First published by Constable 1991
Copyright © Terry Storry 1991

British Library Cataloguing in Publication data
A catalogue record for this book is available from the British Library

Printed and bound in Singapore

ISBN 0 7112 2412 9

9 8 7 6 5 4 3 2 1

Contents

Acknowledgements   9
The 100 best rivers of Britain   11
The river trips grouped by star quality   15
List of photographs   20
List of maps   21
Introduction   23
User guide   26
River grades   35
Access   39
The hydrology of white water rivers by Dave Williams   47

SCOTLAND
The Averon and other rivers of the Far North   61
The Findhorn and other rivers of the North-East Highlands   67
The River Roy   78
The River Spean and other tributaries of the Lochy   83
The Etive and other rivers of Glencoe and Ben Nevis   95
The Orchy and other rivers of the South-West Highlands   105
The Leny and other rivers of the Central Highlands   117
The North Esk and other rivers of the Eastern Highlands   125
The Nith and other rivers of the Western Border Country   135

ENGLAND
The Tyne and other rivers of the North-East   143
The River Tees and its tributaries   153
The Greta and other rivers of the Northern Lake District   160
The River Kent and its tributaries   165
The River Lune and its tributaries   173
The Duddon and other rivers of the Western Lake District   179
Great Langdale Beck and others rivers of the Central
    Lake District   187
The River Leven and its tributary the Crake   194
The Swale and other rivers of the Northern Dales   197

The Wharfe and other rivers of the Southern Dales   202
The Dart and other rivers of the South-West   211

WALES
The Ogwen and other rivers of Northern Snowdonia   227
The Afon Conwy and its tributaries   239
The Afon Llugwy and its tributary the Nantygwryd   248
The Glaslyn, its tributaries and other rivers of Tremadog Bay 257
The Afon Mawddach and its tributaries   267
The Tryweryn and other rivers near Lake Vyrnwy   276
The River Dee and its tributaries   285
The Twymyn and other rivers of Mid-Wales   290
The River Wye and its tributaries   299
The River Usk and its tributaries   308
The Tawe and other rivers of South Wales   316

Bibliography   321
Useful addresses and telephone numbers   322
Index   324

Acknowledgements

I cannot adequately thank all the people who have helped me while I researched this guide. On too many trips I have been guilty of putting camera before throw line. This was particularly so with members of the October Club: Marty Kelly, Gill Pile, Dave Luke, Ken Gowler, Harvey Collinson, 'Spike' Green, Stuart Hardy, Huw Evans, Piers Nesbitt and, above all, Dave Williams. Thanks also to Nick Warner and Mark Tweedie who developed the all too few pictures that resulted from these trips.

I owe an even greater debt of gratitude to those who have provided me with new information and corrected old: Ray Goodwin, Nick Doll, Nigel Lang, Dave Grant, Chris Dickinson, Kevin Danforth, Loel Collins, Stormont Murray, Tim Snaith, Chris Sladden, Sammy Crymble, Marcus Bailie and, again, Dave Williams and Harvey Collinson. If you find this guide useful it will be in no small measure thanks to them.

Finally I would like to thank my family for their tolerance of days spent canoeing, evenings wiping Tipp-Ex off the word processor, and nights asleep in the bath.

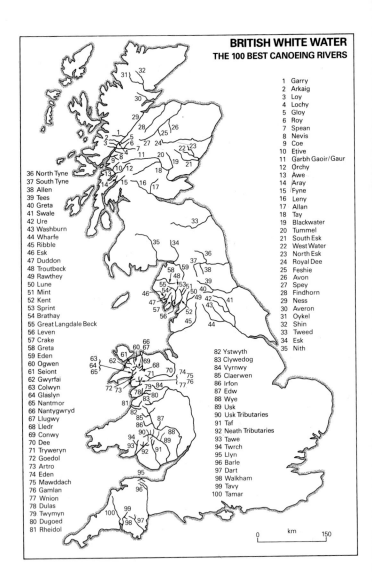

BRITISH WHITE WATER
THE 100 BEST CANOEING RIVERS

1 Garry
2 Arkaig
3 Loy
4 Lochy
5 Gloy
6 Roy
7 Spean
8 Nevis
9 Coe
10 Etive
11 Garbh Gaoir/Gaur
12 Orchy
13 Awe
14 Aray
15 Fyne
16 Leny
17 Allan
18 Tay
19 Blackwater
20 Tummel
21 South Esk
22 West Water
23 North Esk
24 Royal Dee
25 Feshie
26 Avon
27 Spey
28 Findhorn
29 Ness
30 Averon
31 Shin
32 Shin
33 Tweed
34 Esk
35 Nith

36 North Tyne
37 South Tyne
38 Allen
39 Tees
40 Greta
41 Swale
42 Ure
43 Washburn
44 Wharfe
45 Ribble
46 Esk
47 Duddon
48 Troutbeck
49 Rawthey
50 Lune
51 Mint
52 Kent
53 Sprint
54 Brathay
55 Great Langdale Beck
56 Leven
57 Crake
58 Greta
59 Eden
60 Ogwen
61 Seiont
62 Gwyrfai
63 Colwyn
64 Glaslyn
65 Nantmor
66 Nantygwryd
67 Llugwy
68 Lledr
69 Conwy
70 Dee
71 Tryweryn
72 Goedol
73 Artro
74 Eden
75 Mawddach
76 Gamlan
77 Wnion
78 Dulas
79 Twymyn
80 Dugoed
81 Rheidol

82 Ystwyth
83 Clywedog
84 Vyrnwy
85 Claerwen
86 Irfon
87 Edw
88 Wye
89 Usk
90 Usk Tributaries
91 Taf
92 Neath Tributaries
93 Tawe
94 Twrch
95 Llyn
96 Barle
97 Dart
98 Walkham
99 Tavy
100 Tamar

0   km   150

The 100 best rivers of Britain in alphabetical order

(E) England, (S) Scotland, (W) Wales

Allan (S)
Allen (E)
Aray (S)
Arkaig (S)
Artro (W)
Averon (S)
Avon (S)
Awe (S)
Barle (E)
Blackwater (S)
Brathay (E)
Claerwen (W)
Clywedog (W)
Coe (S)
Colwyn (W)
Conwy (W)
Crake (E)
Dart (E)
Dee (W)
Duddon (E)
Dugoed (W)
Dulas (W)
Eden (E)
Eden (W)
Edw (W)
Esk (S)
Esk (E)
Etive (S)
Feshie (S)
Findhorn (S)
Fyne (S)
Gamlan (W)

Garry (S)
Garbh Ghaoir/Gaur (S)
Glaslyn (W)
Gloy (S)
Goedol (W)
Great Langdale Beck (E)
Greta (E – Lakes)
Greta (E – North-East)
Gwyrfai (W)
Irfon (W)
Kent (E)
Leny (S)
Leven (E)
Lledr (W)
Llugwy (W)
Lochy (S)
Loy (S)
Lune (E)
Lyn (E)
Mawddach (W)
Mint (E)
Nantmor (W)
Nantygwryd (W)
Neath Tributaries (W)
North Esk (S)
North Tyne (E)
Ness (S)
Nevis (S)
Nith (S)
Ogwen (W)
Orchy (S)
Oykel (S)

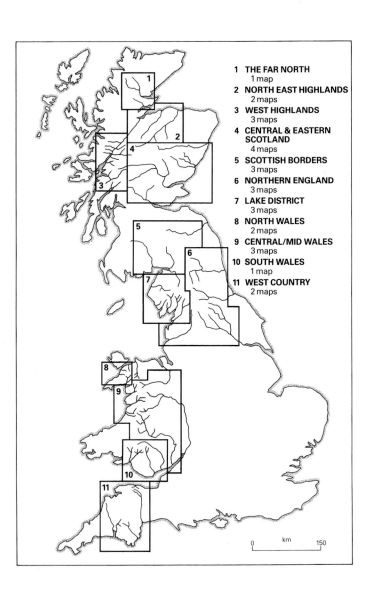

1 **THE FAR NORTH**
  1 map

2 **NORTH EAST HIGHLANDS**
  2 maps

3 **WEST HIGHLANDS**
  3 maps

4 **CENTRAL & EASTERN SCOTLAND**
  4 maps

5 **SCOTTISH BORDERS**
  3 maps

6 **NORTHERN ENGLAND**
  3 maps

7 **LAKE DISTRICT**
  3 maps

8 **NORTH WALES**
  2 maps

9 **CENTRAL/MID WALES**
  3 maps

10 **SOUTH WALES**
  1 map

11 **WEST COUNTRY**
  2 maps

km
0   150

Rawthey (E)
Rheidol (W)
Ribble (E)
Roy (S)
Royal Dee (S)
Seiont (W)
Shin (S)
Spean (S)
Spey (S)
Sprint (E)
South Esk (S)
South Tyne (E)
Swale (E)
Tamar (E)
Taf (W)
Tavy (E)
Tawe (W)
Tay (S)

Tees (E)
Troutbeck (E)
Tryweryn (W)
Tummel (S)
Tweed (S)
Twrch (W)
Twymyn (W)
Ure (E)
Usk (W)
Usk Tributaries (W)
Vyrnwy (W)
Walkham (E)
Washburn (E)
West Water (S)
Wharfe (E)
Wnion (W)
Wye (W)
Ystwyth (W)

Areas individually covered by separate maps

●━ = Access

○ = Egress

◐ = Access or Egress

[symbol] = Portage

[[symbol]] = Possible Portage

Rawthey   Underlining indicates that the access, egress
Bridge   or portage point is possible or necessary
          at that named place.

The above symbols indicate the position of the guidebook's recommended access, egress or portage points. They are by no means exclusive; nor do they necessarily indicate a legal right to land or embark. Reference should be made to any current access and usage agreements.

Key to symbols used in maps

The river trips grouped by star quality

Three Stars (***) = Excellent
Two Stars (**) = Very Good
One Star (*) = Good
No Stars = Quite Good

Within the star quality group the trips are in graded order, and within the grades by alphabetical order.

'Star quality' is defined in the User Guide and grades are defined in the chapter on River Grades (p. 29).

Three Star Trips (***)	Grade
Upper Swale	IIb (IVe)
Lower Roy	IIIc
Upper Conwy	IIIc (IVc)
Seiont	IIId (IVd)
Lower Tees	IVc
Upper Tryweryn	IVc
Averon (Alness)	IVd
Middle Dee (Wales)	IVd
Middle Ogwen	IVd
Lower Mawddach	IVd
Rawthey	IVd
Sprint	IVd
Lower North Esk	IVd (Ve)
Upper Duddon	IVd (Ve)
Lower Findhorn	IVd (Vf)
Ribble	IVe
Upper Roy	IVe
Lower Spean (Spean Gorge)	IVe
Tawe	IVe (Ve)
Upper Dart	Ve

Lower Glaslyn (Aberglaslyn Gorge)	Ve
Middle Orchy	Ve
Middle Etive	Ve (VIf)
Lower Conwy (Fairy Glen)	Vf (VIf)

Two Star Trips (**)

Upper Dee (Wales)	IIb
Lower Etive	IIc (IVd)
Dee (Royal)	IIIb
Upper Orchy	IIIb
Middle Tryweryn	IIIb
Lower Eden (Wales)	IIIc
Esk (Lakes)	IIIc
Lower Dart	IIIc
Greta (Lakes)	IIIc
Lower Usk	IIIc
Upper Wye	IIIc
Middle Wye	IIIc
Middle Llugwy	IIIc (IVd)
Lower Duddon	IIIc (IVd)
Lower Lune	IIIc (IVe)
Upper Spean	IIId
Twymyn	IIId
Greta	IIId (IVd)
Leven	IVc
Lower Nith	IVc
Lower Ogwen	IVc
Upper Ogwen	IVc (Ve)
Allen	IVd
Upper Findhorn	IVd
Gloy	IVd
Lower Kent	IVd
Wnion	IVd
Upper Ystwyth	IVd
Leny	IVd (Ve)

Colwyn	IVe
Troutbeck	IVe
Upper Irfon	Vd
East Lyn	Ve
Upper Nevis	Ve (VIe)

One Star Trips (*)

Spey	IIb
Lower Swale	IIb
Middle Findhorn	IIb (IIIb)
Lower Nevis	IIb (IVd)
Washburn	IIIb
Upper North Tyne	IIIb (IVd)
Artro	IIIc
Border Esk	IIIc
South Esk	IIIc
Feshie	IIIc
Grwyne	IIIc
Honddu	IIIc
Loy	IIIc
Lower Orchy	IIIc
Upper South Tyne	IIIc
Upper Usk	IIIc
Lower Wye	IIIc
Arkaig	IIIc (IVc)
Clywedog	IIIc (IVc)
Garbh Ghaoir/Gaur	IIIc (IVc)
Allan	IIIc (IVd)
Avon	IIIc (IVd)
Cilieni	IIIc (IVd)
Great Langdale Beck	IIIc (IVd)
Edw	IIIc (IVd)
Claerwen	IIIc (Ve)
Fyne	IIIc (Ve)
Lledr	IIIc (Ve)

West Water	IIIc (Ve)
Lower Dulas	IIId
Mint	IIId
Nantygwryd	IIId
Garry	IVc
Upper Tavy	IVc
Lower Tryweryn	IVc
Upper Wharfe	IVc
Upper Llugwy	IVc (Ve)
Middle Wharfe	IVc (Ve)
Blackwater	IVd
Upper Dulas	IVd
Lower Llugwy	IVd
Nedd	IVd
Upper Tees	IVd (IVe)
Aray	IVd (Ve)
Coe	IVd (Ve)
Taf-Fechan	IVd (Ve)
Middle Conwy	IVd (Ve/VIe)
Lower Wharfe	IVe
Upper Mawddach	Vd
Upper Rheidol	Ve
Lower Ystwyth	Ve
Lower Rheidol	Vf
Gamlan	VIf

Other Trips

Upper Glaslyn	IIb
Upper Etive	IIb
Lochy	IIb
Lower South Tyne	IIb
Middle South Tyne	IIb
Ness	IIb
Middle Tees	IIb (IIIb)
Lower Irfon	IIb (IIIc)

Upper Lune	IIb (IVd)
Senny	IIc
Tamar	IIc
Upper Kent	IId (IVd)
Awe	IIIb
Brathay	IIIb
Eden (Lakes)	IIIb
Lower Dee	IIIb
Tweed	IIIb
Barle	IIIc
Bran	IIIc
Crake	IIIc
Upper Nith	IIIc
Taf-Fawr	IIIc
Tarell	IIIc
Lower Tavy	IIIc
Upper Tay	IIIc
Upper North Tyne	IIIc
Walkham	IIIc
Ysgir	IIIc
Upper Eden (Wales)	IIIc (IVd)
Vyrnwy	IIIc (IVd)
Ure	IIIc (Ve)
Dugoed	IIIc (Ve)
Shin	IIIc (Ve)
Oykel	IIIc (Vf)
Gwryfai	IIId
Lower Tay	IIId
Garry	IVc
Upper North Esk	IVd
Hepste	IVd
Twrch (South Wales)	IVd
Tummel	IVd (Vd)
Middle Spean	IVd (Ve)
Mellte	IVe
Nantmor	IVe
Goedol	VIf

Photographs

Randolph's Leap on the Lower Findhorn	73
Wish You Were Here on the Upper Roy	79
Rooster Tail on the Upper Roy	80
Headbanger in the Spean Gorge	86
On the River Gloy	92
Eas a Chataidh on the Middle Orchy (*photograph by Dave Williams*)	108
Granite Falls on the River Fyne	112
The two-tier fall on the Lower North Esk	129
The second boulder garden on the River Allen (*photograph by Nick Doll*)	149
The Upper Tees	154
Rock Hop on the Greta	162
The Mint	170
Tebay Falls on the Upper Lune	174
The Upper Duddon	182
One of the final rapids on the Upper Duddon	184
Pillar Falls on Langdale Beck	188
The Brathay foot-bridge	190
Consiton Falls on the Wharfe	204
The artificial slalom course in Nottingham	214
Rescue on the Upper Ogwen	228
Fishermen's Gorge on the Ogwen	231
Bryn Afon Steps on the Seiont	234
Gates of Delirium on the Lower Conwy	244
Cobdens Falls on the Middle Llugwy	251
Pont Cyfyng Falls on the Middle Llugwy (*photograph by Andy Woodhouse*)	252
The wave (*photograph by Ken Fidler*)	262
Fedwrgog Falls on the Upper Tryweryn	278
Bala Mill Falls on the Lower Tryweryn	281
Glantwymyn Gorge on the Afon Twymyn	291
The last big drop on the Upper Usk	309

Unless otherwise stated all photographs are by the author

Maps

The 100 best canoeing rivers   10
Areas individually covered by separate maps   12
Key to symbols used in maps   14
Figure 1: the hydrological cycle   47
Figure 2: British average annual precipitation   49
Figure 3: the rain index   50
Figure 4: a flood hydrograph   52
Figure 5: a 'flashy' flood hydrograph   55

SCOTLAND
Rivers Averon, Shin and Oykel   62
Rivers Findhorn, Spey and Avon   68
Rivers Feshie and Ness   76
The tributaries of the River Lochy   90
The Etive and other rivers of Glencoe and Ben Nevis   96
The Orchy and other rivers of the South-West Highlands   106
The Leny, Garbh Gaoir/Gaur and surrounding rivers   118
Rivers Tay and Allan   121
Rivers North Esk, South Esk, West Water and Blackwater   126
The Royal Dee   132
The River Nith   136
The Border Esk   136

ENGLAND
Rivers North Tyne, South Tyne and Allen   144
The River Tweed   144
Rivers Tees, Greta, Swale and Ure   157
Rivers Greta and Eden   161
The tributaries of the River Kent and River Lune   166
The Duddon, Great Langdale Beck and Leven   180
Rivers Wharfe, Washburn and Ribble   206
Rivers Dart, Tavy, Walkham and Tamar   217
Rivers Barle and Lyn   220

WALES
The Afon Conwy, Lledr, Llugwy and Nantygwryd   241
The Afon Glaslyn and other rivers of Tremadog Bay   260
The Afon Mawddach, Twymyn and surrounding rivers   269
The Afon Tryweryn, Vyrnwy, Dugoed and River Dee   282
The River Wye and its tributaries   302
The Usk, the Tawe and other rivers of South Wales   313

All maps and figures drawn by Gary Haley

Introduction

In Percy Blandford's *Canoeing Waters*, the definitive 1960s guide to British inland waterways, 70 pages were devoted to the rivers Severn, Thames and Trent; 60 pages described waterways in South and East England; while 9 pages were considered sufficient for Wales (5 non-tidal rivers) and just 10 pages covered everything north of the border (6 non-tidal rivers). 'There are not', he boldly stated, 'a great many canoeing rivers in Scotland.' This guide, on the other hand, makes no mention of the Thames, Severn or Trent (the slalom course at Holme Pierrepont has made the Trent artificially white, but it cannot be classed a white water river), ignores the South and East, and has 34 Scottish rivers, 35 in Wales and only 31 in the England. This is a measure of the quiet revolution that has taken place over the last 30 years in canoeing (used throughout this guide as the generic word for canoeing *and* kayaking).

The quiet revolution – the change in the concept of canoe touring from long trips on calm water canals to short trips on white water – has been made possible by a revolution in manufacturing. At the beginning of the 1960s canoes were made out of plywood and canvas – many of them folding boats. This restricted the majority of canoeists to flat or low-graded water. Even the most experienced and talented paddlers were chary of risking their fragile hand-made craft on mountain streams, and only deep, wide, relatively mature white water rivers like the Spey, Royal Dee, Leven, Welsh Dee and Wye regularly saw canoeists paddling Grade III and above. First fibreglass and then plastic replaced wood and canvas. The new craft can take an almost infinite amount of punishment, far more indeed than the paddler. So now the intrinsically appealing but formerly expensive sport of white water canoeing is available to the brave and loony, skilled and incompetent alike.

Of course there will be many who still prefer canals, estuaries, lakes and flat rivers. There is no end of pleasure to be had pottering from pub to campsite or chasing reflections down a deserted loch, and there is much to be said for the sideways perspective on land gained travelling over water. Yet this is a different game to the one provided for in these pages. This book is a guide to the classic *white water* rivers of Britain, and the first national guide to be devoted to this branch of the sport.

Here (he boldly states) are 'The 100 Best in Britain' (with the Usk and Neath Tributaries counted as one each). In fact, of course there is no such thing as the 100 best anything; a selection being in the nature of things a reflection of the selector's bias. I have to admit bias towards Wales where I have lived for ten years and away from Scotland which is too far to travel every weekend. Being aware of this slant, however, I have tried to keep it within reasonable limits by consulting paddlers from other parts of the country; but I still could not resist including the Nantmor and Nantygwryd in the 100 Best. Perhaps I should have called the book *Possibly the 100 Best Rivers in Britain*, but then no-one else lets truth stand in the way of a good title.

Many of the rivers in this guide have more than one section worth canoeing. There are in fact 156 separate river trips described. This amounts to 1,189 kilometres of paddling. The rivers are grouped by proximity (rather than watershed) so that those on their holidays can base themselves in one part of the book as well as one part of the country. Each of the 31 chapters begins with the river I consider to be classic of the area; there follows a description of other good rivers in the vicinity. Sometimes the other rivers, the support rivers or 'also-rans', are as good if not better than the 'classic' rivers and this is indicated in the star-rating (the Rawthey, Ribble and Troutbeck, for instance, all receive more stars than the rivers heading their chapters); but wherever the 'supporting extra' comes away with the 'Oscar' it is still denied top billing because of the very limited number of days in a year that it is canoeable.

Although I have paddled most of the rivers in the guide I have not strayed far from the judgement of local paddlers when deciding their 'classification' and 'rateable value'. In the few cases where the descriptions are not based on my own paddling experiences, I have triple-checked them with local enthusiasts. If, despite this, I have not included your favourite river, or have undergraded your biggest thrill, or have dismissed a whole watershed in your back-garden, my apologies. Perhaps it will spur you on to write about your river/valley/rapid so that it can be included in the next edition.

Of course, a guidebook must always be an abbreviated listing of the facts and after reading the relevant description you must still 'read' the river. The guide may increase your enjoyment and ease your suffering on the way, but it cannot be followed from wave to eddy. Practitioners of other outdoor sports may find this unusual. Canoeing guides cannot be applied to water like, for instance, climbing guides can be applied to rock (and to a lesser extent ice). Water is too malleable to pin down exactly (as the chapter on river hydrology makes abundantly clear), canoe trips too long to describe wave by wave or eddy by eddy, and the sport too dynamic to permit 'on the job' reading.

Since few canoeists will carry the guidebook in their boats (like climbers do in their rucksacks), and even less ruin them in their buoyancy aids (as climbers do in their pockets), speed of use is not considered essential. Thus excessive abbreviation through the use of a guidebook 'coda' – letters, numbers, and symbols instead of words – is kept to a minimum, and I take space to describe the high country through which the rivers pass, to digress into the culture and history of the valleys below, and to comment on the antics of those who mess about in the white stuff. The odd titter of laughter and the occasional tut of anger will be a welcome reaction to the guide, more welcome indeed than a river tick or grading argument. To be read by the fire as well as used on the river bank would be praise indeed.

Feet up in front of such fire in the Bridge of Orchy Hotel I thought I had it cracked when a paddling friend called across, 'You know that guide you are writing?' He gestured with his pint at my 'Scottish file'.

'Yes.' I looked up, my academic smile oozing self-congratulatory smugness. It was surely the first of many fireside calls for stimulation, laughter, sensitization and learning.

'Can I borrow it to put under this table leg? It's a bit wobbly!'

User guide

The guide is written in longhand (as it were) but to make it more 'user friendly' summarized information is abbreviated into six lines at the head of each river section. These river section headings are standard throughout the guide. This User Guide explains the abbreviations and symbols, and the assumptions that lie behind them.

Example of six-line section heading:

Line 1: **Great Langdale Beck** *
Line 2: *Old Dungeon Gyll Hotel Bridge (285.060) to Elterwater Bridge (327.047)*
Line 3: *Grade IIc (IVd)*
Line 4: *No Portages*
Line 5: *6 Kilometres*
Line 6: *OS Sheet 90*

Line 1
Section name
None of the rivers in this guide are described in their entirety. If only one section of a river is described (as in the example above) then the full name of the river is used, but this does not mean it is described from source to sea. If more than one section is described then the prefix upper, middle or lower is used (Upper Dee, Lower Findhorn and so on). The prefixes are only 'upper', 'middle' and 'lower' in relation to each other and have no currency outside canoeing circles; there is no point in asking a policeman 'Where is the Upper Dee?'.

Many other sections of the rivers in this guide may be paddled but are not described, either because of the number of portages required, or because of the lack of white water. Typically these sections are either very high in the hills or very close to the sea. In a few cases there will be sections not described because they are not yet 'discovered'.

Star quality

A star (*) after a section name indicates that it is particularly 'good'. Two stars (**) are better than one, and three stars (***) better than two. 'Goodness' is defined primarily on the basis of continuity at the grade, which implies no large fluctuations in difficulty or seriousness, an absence of long flat sections and a minimum of portaging.

To a lesser degree 'goodness' is related to the river's general ambience. A river feels good if it takes the paddler through wild country, offers fine views, has stunning bank scenery, carves sculptures in the rock, and exhibits a profusion and variety of flora and fauna.

Difficulty and commitment are not qualities that affect the star-rating. The guide as a whole, as its name implies, has selected rivers that are *white*, but I have starred this selection irrespective of grade. Those enjoying open Canadian canoeing may find the guide somewhat biased towards closed decked canoes and kayaks, but if they like to paddle white water in open Canadians, they will be able to pick out plenty of good, even very good, sections of river for their sport.

Stars have not been scattered around like confetti. Even those sections with no stars are in some measure good – otherwise they would not be in the selection. Moreover a star indicates the quality or the river at the recommended water level – bank full. It does *not* take into account the fact that some rivers are more likely to be canoeable than other rivers. The Brathay, for instance, which has no stars is more likely to be bank full than its tributary, Great Langdale Beck, which has one star. The 'best' canoeing river in the area is not always the best river to go and canoe, particularly if you are up just for the weekend, so try to check conditions before you leave.

Line 2

Access and egress

Suggested put-ins and take-outs are based on common usage, but they are not exclusive. There may well be other suitable access and egress points – a few of the most commonly used alternatives are mentioned in the headings and the text. *Mention of access and egress does not imply a right to get on or off a river*, or even a lack of objection to that use, but most bridges and the land immediately adjacent to them are public rights of way. A few rivers have long-standing access agreements. For new agreements and more up-to-date details contact the British Canoe Union or their local access officer.

Wherever possible I have taken names of access and egress points from the appropriate Ordnance Survey Landranger Map of the area (see below). Precise details of the put-ins and take-outs (upstream or downstream of a bridge, left or right bank, and so on) are given in the description of each section. Please note that in a few cases sub-sections of the same river are not contiguous, so that the egress point from one section is not the same as the access point to the next (for instance the Upper and Middle Spean).

Grid reference

Every access and egress point given in the river section heading comes with a six-figure grid reference e.g. (285.060). The first three numbers are the Easting (a line parallel with the side of the map/sheet), the second three the Northing (a line parallel with the top or bottom of the map/sheet). These references are taken off the appropriate OS Landranger map/sheet for the river; the map/sheet number is given in Line 6 of the section heading.

Since most people, including some geography teachers (and a few guidebook writers), do not know how to give or use correct grid references, it is worth reminding readers that a grid reference is an area of land not a point on the map, and an object receives its grid reference from the area in which it lies, not from how close it is to a particular easting or northing. A six-figure grid reference on an OS 1:50,000 map indicates an area of land 100 metres by 100 metres east and north of the intersection of lines indicated. The access and egress point referred to lies somewhere within that area. Similarly a four-figure grid reference refers to an area of land 1 kilometre square.

Line 3

River grading

Grades are given for each section of the rivers described, e.g. IIIc. The grade refers to the hardest and most serious rapids on the section. It follows that much of the river will be easier than the grade given. Where there are one or two rapids that stand out as being *much* harder or *much* more serious than the rest of the rapids on the section, and where these rapids may be easily portaged, a grade is given in brackets which refers to these individual falls, e.g. (IVd). The individual harder or more dangerous falls are further identified by their name and grade in the main text, e.g. Pillar Falls (IVd). A very few rapids have a question mark after a grade (?); this means that I have not canoed the rapid, and have no knowledge of others canoeing it, but have inspected it from the bank.

Grades refer to the river when it is bank full, that is when the river is as high as it can be while still flowing between its normal banks. Grades may vary according to the water level. The grade of a river or rapid normally rises when the river does, and vice versa, but this is not always the case. For instance PTF on the Mawddach becomes washed out in very high floods and the Strid on the Wharfe becomes more dangerous in low water. Sometimes a river and its rapids – the Usk for instance – will be given a grade for normal bank full conditions and another grade for flood/spate levels – when the river is over its banks. Occasionally a river and its rapids – the Orchy for instance – will be given a grade for high water (HW) and low water (LW), as defined by a gauge or marker on the river. But there are many other rivers in this guide where the variations in difficulty and danger are less marked, or less well known or less well documented. The user should always take into account the level of the river or rapid *on the day*.

A definition of the grades will be found in the chapter on River Grades. The top grade (VIf) is only used four times in the guide. This is partly because I must have had evidence of someone having paddled a fall before grading it and canoeing at this level is a very recent phenomenon. More important perhaps is that there are just not, compared to other parts of Europe and the world, that many continous, canoeable Grade VIf rapids or rivers in Britain. The bottom grade (Ia) is never used because although this water always moves it is not white; and there are only a few rapids or rivers graded below IIb because continous sections of moderate white water are rare. Continuity at the grade is not the only reason for selection to the guide – the reasons are the same as for star-rating (see above) – but it is a very important one.

Line 4
Portages
The number of portages *at the grade* is indicated in the heading to each section, and their position on the river is indicated in the descriptive text. A question mark after a portage (?) means that it may, or may not, be necessary because of changes in the nature of the rapid. For instance, weir stoppers often become more dangerous in spate, while boulder chokes can become washed out in high water.

In point of fact there should be a question mark in the user's mind for every portage indication, including 'no portages', because winter storms, spring floods and autumn gales, farmers, anglers and canoeists can all change the nature of rivers and rapids. Boulders, trees, fences, scaffolding bars, fibreglass, plastic and all manner of broaching, pinning, trapping, ripping, tearing and drowning obstacles may enter the river after these descriptions have been written. The moral is clear; use the guide book and the grades in it as a guide not as a Bible; and always, but always, inspect what lies ahead before you paddle it.

Most of the rivers in this guide are 'young' upland rivers. Typically, therefore, they turn sharply, fall suddenly and are strewn with boulders. This makes the water highly technical to paddle; sometimes too technical. Bank inspection is essential whenever you cannot see what lies below. This will determine whether a rapid will 'go', and if so which is the best line.

Apart from the difficulty of the canoeing, there are two major hazards associated with 'young' rivers that should impress caution on the canoeist using this book. The first danger particularly associated with young rivers flowing through wooded country is a tendency to overflow their banks in spate causing the current to set through trees, bushes, branches and even fences. Occasionally, fallen trees and jammed logs can block the entire river. Inspection is vital and portaging may be necessary in these conditions.

A second lethal danger is the advent along the way of unsuspected waterfalls, weirs, sumps and siphons. A number of people every year do falls which they had no intention of doing, and with the increasing height of drops now being tackled, what lies under the water and on the bottom of the river bed is as important as what is on the surface. In the higher grades and in particular falls and weirs, prior inspection of rivers in drought conditions may be necessary before a sound judgement at canoeable levels can be made.

Whether to portage or not is always a difficult question. Camera or peer group pressure frequently leads to the wrong decision. Guidebooks too can have an effect. It is important that users realize that just because a river is described with no portages, or a certain number of portages (or given a certain grade), the guidebook is not necessarily right *on the day* or *for you*.

Line 5
Distances
All distances are in kilometres. For those still glorying in our imperial past, 5 kilometres is roughly equivalent to 3 miles. A few common words are used in the text in association with distances covered. 'Up' and 'above', 'down' and 'below' are respectively synonymous with upstream and downstream. 'Right' and 'left' are also used as if the paddler were facing downstream. 'River right' and 'river left' are also sometimes used as a way of reminding the reader which way (s)he should be looking.

Line 6
Maps
The best maps to consult when using this guide are the Ordnance Survey 1:50,000 Landranger Maps. There are 203 map/sheets covering the whole of Britain, and about 50 cover all the rivers in

this book. The number of the relevant map/sheet(s) for each section of river are given in the heading, e.g. OS Sheet 90. From the 1:50,000 map I have taken the names of key points of interest: access and egress points, tributaries, hills, forests, villages, towns and of course roads. Many of these features are not on road maps, and some are unnamed on the ground, so an OS map is often useful to make good sense of the guide.

It would be unrealistic to expect people to buy, or even borrow, every relevant 1:50,000 map/sheet, so I have included maps of each river to help locate access and egress points and portages. These guidebook maps are drawn to scale, but they are hand-drawn so the distance between the features cannot be relied on for absolute accuracy. Features like roads, rivers and bridges are intentionally exaggerated, while other features like towns and villages have been minimized, and yet others like vegetation and contouring have been excluded entirely. There is no distinction in line size between major and minor roads, although all the former and a few of the latter have been given their DOE number (A9, A5 etc.). Finally it should be noted that there is not always a direct relationship between rivers in the chapters and the rivers on the maps, so some cross-referencing is necessary. For instance the Lune and Kent are on the same map even though they are in different chapters, and the Rheidol and Ystwyth are on the same map as the Wye though they are included in the same chapter as the Twymyn.

The hidden 'bottom line': the environment
Pressure from the 'green' water lobby is now strong – justifiably so. Since the war there has been massive pollution of our rivers by farming, industry and local water authorities. In some parts of the country immersion sports are now a serious health hazard. The increased incidence of Weil's disease and the phenomenon known to users of the artificial slalom course at Holme Pierrepont as 'Trent belly' are symptoms of this. In the 1980s the government, while professing to be concerned, not only disregarded EEC minimum standards for drinking water, but actually proposed to reduce the legal standards of pollution to make the water

companies more attractive for privatization. Political and
economic change will be necessary to conserve our environment
and health, but on a small scale we canoeists should do our bit,
particularly since we want to be considered legitimate river users.

The river systems of Britain, particularly those of upland rivers,
are important not only for drinking water, but also for the
conservation of animal and plant life, to the extent that some are
designated as SSSIs (Sites of Special Scientific Interest). The
waterfalls and generally humid environment of white water rivers
tend to support good populations of mosses, lichens and ferns.
They are easily destroyed. Using paths on portages and access and
egress points will do much to minimize damage to these plants.

Many animals make their home along and in our fast flowing
rivers. Most cope better with canoeists than any other form of
human intrusion. Sometimes, however, canoeists forget the water
animals because they are passed unseen. The otter, for instance, is
adept at hiding from man, but their spraints can be found on
boulders along the river course. The less noise canoeists make, the
better chance the otter has of breeding and rearing young
successfully. We also do well to avoid dragging our boats through
dense growths of bushes and brambles along the river bank, for it
is here that otters often have their holts.

Mosses and otters are just examples of the flora and fauna which
share our rivers. Many humans too, apart from fishermen and
canoeists, share this fragile environment. Often it is their home
and they work and rest there long after we have gone. We should
respect their rights and privacy, avoid loud and aggressive
behaviour, paddle softly, play quietly and change discreetly,
leaving no physical or mental anguish in our wake. This probably
means travelling in groups of half a dozen or less, since above that
number a group of averagely sensitive individuals tends to become
an irresponsible mob.

In practice this advice will not seem too restrictive. Stopping on
white water rivers is not part of the game, except for inspection or
portaging, or in case of emergency. Camping and picnicking are
rare, as is extensive 'playing' in holes and on waves – the latter is
best done on the more mature rivers. White water canoeists do not

like regattas, preferring to rely on tight-knit groups for safety and speed. And the canoe itself causes no erosion, noise or pollution and leaves no trace of its passing. How simple it is for us then – compared to others working or playing on rivers or river banks – to take only pictures and leave only footprints.

River Grades

The dual grading system used in this guide, and defined below, is one I introduced in my *Snowdonia White Water, Sea and Surf* guidebook four years ago. It has since become widely accepted and used. It differs from the old International Grading System in dividing technical difficulty from commitment. The dual grading system became necessary because of the revolutionary effect of plastic boats on canoeing standards. The canoe will now go anywhere, irrespective of the technical ability of the occupant, so an assessment of danger (separate from difficulty) will be useful to those who like to 'push the boat out'.

Numerical grades indicate the technical difficulty of the canoeing while alphabetical grades indicate the degree of commitment. Another way to look at it is the Roman numeral indicates what the river or rapid is like to canoe, the letter suggests what it would be like to swim. 'I' and 'a' are the easiest and least serious grade; 'VI' and 'f' are the present upper limits of difficulty and danger. Whenever a river or rapid is graded the technical grading comes first followed by the grading for seriousness.

Usually the factors which make canoe manoeuvres hard also make for frightening water and normally a river or rapid which requires only a few paddle strokes will not worry those doing the breast-stroke (so I usually goes with a, II with b, IIIc, IVd, Ve and VIf). A significant minority of rivers and rapids, however, are only 'OK' if you stay in your boat (for instance Randolph's Leap on the Findhorn – Vf), while other rivers and rapids (also a minority but nonetheless significant) require a considerable level of skill but could be swum by a fit granny (for instance the Serpent's Tail on the Welsh Dee – IVc). The dual grading system assumes that canoeists, as well as deciding whether they can do a river or rapid, will want to know what might happen if they can't!

The definitions below are intentionally general to cope with a wide variety of river and rapid types. It is important to realize, however, that grades cannot cover all water conditions, and rivers and rapids may rise and fall in grade as they do in level. This point is amplified in the section on River Grading in the User Guide. I should remind people that in this guidebook rivers and rapids are graded when they are just *off the flood* or, in other words, when they are as high as they can be while still flowing between their normal banks.

Numerical grades of difficulty

I. Easy
Here are rivers with beautiful united waters, flowing in peaceful meanders down valleys. The canoe may float any way which it pleases down the channel.

II. Moderate
The river is already quicker. At moments there is a disturbance which the canoe sails over with disdain. An overhanging tree forces the canoeist into some adroit steering. A rock in the main channel must be avoided. But always the channel is clear and obvious.

III. Fairly Difficult
Now things are more complicated. The current is swift. Sometimes the river becomes narrow with big waves. The canoeist may have to manœuvre between rocks, stop in eddies, and cross currents. Nevertheless the best channel is easily recognized and remembered.

IV. Difficult
This is challenging water. Rapids follow each other in quick succession, or are continuous and difficult to read. Cushion waves build on obstacles and stoppers form below constrictions. The route is not obvious from the water, so inspection from the bank will be necessary to remember the way.

V. Very Difficult
Even after inspection from the bank, it is often difficult to recognize a route through Grade V water. There are pressure

waves, whirlpools, boils, waterfalls and holding stoppers. The water is always fast, often heavy, and the eddies are very sharp. A steep gradient, tight bends, and large boulders will hide the river from the canoeist on the water.

VI. *Extremely Difficult*
All previously mentioned difficulties are increased to the present limit of possibility. Grade VI water is a playing field of descents and foaming chaos. To all but the most experienced, and inexperienced, canoeist the river will appear impossible. It is runnable only at particular water levels. The paddler can expect at times to disappear completely, and at others to be hurled skywards by a prodigious force. The water sucks and surges unpredictably, often making route choice academic. Reactive skills must be of the highest order.

Alphabetical grades of seriousness

a. *Safe*
There are no obstructions in the river. It is always possible to swim to the bank with a boat.

b. *Little Danger*
The occasional rock, overhanging branch, or bridge pillar can cause problems, but rescue is simple and quick. Swimming to the bank is no problem, but a boat may have to be shunted.

c. *Some Danger*
Obstructions can pin or jam a boat, but a long and bumpy swim will hurt the pride more than the body. Ropes and lines are sometimes useful in rescues. An Eskimo roll can save problems.

d. *Dangerous*
The force of water can trap canoe and canoeist against obstacles. Stoppers may hold boats, but not swimmers. A swim is usually unpleasant and occasionally injurious, so the ability to roll is important. Rescues from the bank may be necessary.

e. Very Dangerous

Rescues from circulating stoppers, boulder chokes, jammed logs, and sumps are all very difficult. There is little another person in a boat can do to help; prepared bank security is normal. A swim is dangerous, so rolling is essential. There are committing ravines or gorges.

f. Extremely Dangerous

Mistakes may be dearly payed for; there is a definite danger to life and limb. Luck is more likely than rescue to be a saviour. Rolling is problematical in the turbulent water. Evacuation from the river will be difficult. Modern safety equipment in the canoeist's gear and the specialized wild water boat will improve the paddler's chances of winning.

Access

Under British law many non-tidal waters, which includes almost all the rivers in this guide, are privately owned, and owners may, or may not, give permission for canoeing. No canoeist has a legal right to paddle a river, unless it is public navigation or there is an access agreement. Neither the descriptions in this guide, nor the mention of access and egress are evidence of the right to put in, canoe, or land from a river. Moreover, nothing written here should be construed as advice or encouragement to commit the civil offence of trespass.

The very few variable and limited agreements that existed on English and Welsh rivers in 1989 were listed by Stuart Fisher in *Canoeist* magazine (April 1989). Out of a total of 19,144 kilometres on 656 rivers listed by Edwards in his book *Inland Waterways*, there were agreements covering 519 kilometres on 31 rivers. In other words anglers had agreed to share 2.7% of the available length of rivers in England and Wales with touring canoeists at some time of the year. The legal rights of landowners and riparian owners are less complete in Scotland, and Scottish paddlers have avoided making any national agreements.

More up-to-date information may be obtained from the British Canoe Union (BCU), the Scottish Canoe Association (SCA), the Welsh Canoeing Association (WCA), the Campaign for River Access for Canoes and Kayaks (CRACK), and local access officers – addresses from the BCU – but there is no sign of any radical improvement. Indeed at the time of writing agreements to paddle the Ribble, Tryweryn and Welsh Dee are being withdrawn by local landowners.

BCU members (there are about 20,000 in Britain) may obtain and use existing access agrrements on application to their local access officer. The four-fifths of practising canoeists who do not belong to the BCU are explicitly excluded from almost all the agreements. This is probably unjust, and certainly impolitic, but it makes sense for non-union members to stick to the agreements as well – if they can find out about them!

Whatever our affiliation, or lack of it, and whatever the river agreement, or lack of it, canoeists should get on and off rivers by a public right of way (most footpaths and bridges). If in doubt ask the landowner's permission. Canoeists should also be sensitive to the needs of anglers. After walking and swimming, fishing is probably the most popular sport in Britain. More than a million people do it every month, although only about a fifth of these are game fishermen. Anglers have as much right to be on the rivers as we do, and most of them are pleased to see others enjoying a river sport. If you meet a fisherman pass by quietly on the other side, or stop and ask when you can pass. This is natural courtesy and makes us good ambassadors for the sport.

THE POLITICAL DEBATE

For three decades British canoeists have been pressing, both formally and informally, nationally and locally, for legal recognition of the right of access to rivers. In a letter to the Minister of Land and Natural Resources, written on July 19th 1965, John Dudderidge, President of the BCU, pressed for 'legislation to secure public navigation rights, and provision of launching and landing points, and portage rights of way over land, since all these rights were in existence in EEC countries'.

In 1973 the BCU provided evidence to the House of Lords Select Committee on Sport and Leisure. Their report referred to the conflict of angling and canoeing interests, and recommended legislation to enable negotiations to take place equitably. There has to date been no progress on this.

In 1982 a Statement of Intent was jointly issued by the National Federation of Anglers, the Water Space Amenity Commission and the BCU. This stated that the broad aim should be:
a) To work actively towards and ultimately achieve a situation where canoeists can paddle all waters suitable for canoeing without challenge, but with reasonable consideration for other water users,

and with due regard for the law and the conservation of the environment.
b) To support fully the 'Sport for All' policy of the Sports Council and the principles of the Council of Europe 'Sport for All' Charter.

Over four years later, in January 1987, the BCU admitted that 'the anglers had not as yet responded positively' to the Statement of Intent. Then, three months later, the National Anglers Council recommended its members to suspend all access negotiations. By this time it seemed to many that the BCU had run out of steam in the fight for public access to British rivers.

Disillusioned by the lack of progress, canoeists inside and outside the BCU formed a pressure group calling itself the Campaign for River Access for Canoes and Kayaks (CRACK). Many canoeists had become concerned that the BCU were beholden to the government and the status quo by virtue of the annual grant (£350,000 in 1988/89) it received from the Sports Council. It further seemed that the BCU spent most of its time and budget organizing and promoting competition canoeing, and that any access work it did was for the sole benefit of union members. CRACK declared that because it was independent of the government, and wholly devoted to the interests of touring canoeists, it would be more vigorous in word and deed in pursuing the fight for access.

At a local level too, the cold war between anglers and canoeists was now beginning to catch alight. The advent of plastic boats, and the publication of white water guidebooks in the mid 1980s, meant that more people were canoeing upland game fishing rivers, formerly the preserve of a very skilled and knowledgeable few. Since this growth in numbers was limited to those few days in the year when the rivers were in spate, most anglers accepted the influx with equanimity. A few, however, took the law into their own hands, and in so doing for ever tarnished the image of game fishermen in the mind of the average canoeist.

One such incident occurred on 10th October 1987 on the River Seiont in North Wales. A local canoeist was paddling the river in spate with two friends when one of them swam. While effecting a rescue they were swept towards the anglers. Two anglers threw rocks at close range, splitting the rescuing canoeist's face open. While he was slumped over his deck, incapacitated and bleeding, the anglers continued to throw rocks at him and the swimmer. The canoeist required hospital treatment. The anglers were later identified but never prosecuted.

In March 1988 CRACK organized a mass rally on the Seiont as part of a campaign to get justice for the canoeist in question and to obtain an access agreement on the Seiont. The rally attracted mass media attention, mass support from canoeists, and a good deal of sympathy from the public. The BCU, however, felt they had to distance themselves from this 'provocative and illegal action', and, after a lengthy disciplinary process completed in January 1989, the BCU Council of Management expelled Geoff Wood, a leading spokesman for CRACK, and formerly BCU Access Officer for the Yorkshire and Humberside region.

CRACK were unrepentant. 'Was it right', they asked rhetorically in their Statement of Policy, 'for Ghandi to defy unjust laws in India, for Solidarity to break the law in Poland, Martin Luther King to cross lines of segregation in the United States, or Nelson Mandela to oppose apartheid in South Africa?'

'Legal rights', the Statement continued, 'should serve human rights.' When and where anglers refused to talk about any form of compromise, CRACK argued, then canoeists had the right to take the civil law into their own hands and canoe when and where they wanted at all reasonable times.

The BCU have always argued that they support the fight for river access provided it is carried out within the law. In the lengthy legal battle over access to the River Itchen, however, the BCU discovered that 'pursuing our objectives through the legal process is a method which required a level of financing out of all proportion to the subscription levels and the ability of the BCU to generate the necessary funds' (*Canoe Focus* May 1989). And when the Seiont anglers hit back in 1988 by prosecuting four paddlers for 'wilfully disturbing spawning-beds' on the River Seiont, the BCU showed a marked reluctance to become involved in the canoeists' court case and subsequent appeal, both of which the anglers won.

Canoeists involved in legal battles such as these have felt abandoned by their union, particularly since individual canoeists, both union and non-union, continue to demonstrate their support by contributing money to access funds (£1,500 was donated to the 'Seiont Appeal Fund' in a matter of months).

The BCU say their 'softly softly' approach reflects public opinion; CRACK argue that they should be leading public opinion from the front. The BCU, however, cannot afford to be too independent. Indeed political control over the BCU by the Department of the Environment through the Sports Council is becoming increasingly obvious. For example, in May 1989 two BCU instructors at a Sports Council National Centre were told by the Head of National Centres that they risked losing their jobs if they were found to be supporting CRACK – even privately. This sort of 'Big Brother' (or 'Big Sister') approach to political issues inevitably breeds resentment, and throughout the country in 1989 meetings were held with the aim of setting up an independent canoe body to represent touring canoeists. Whether this gets off the ground, only time and the attitude of the BCU will tell.

The political debate on river access is more intense now than it has ever been before. A generation has passed with no discernible progress. Even moderates are losing patience. The long, sometimes passionate letter from a respected canoe manufacturer in the January 1989 edition of the *Canoeist* magazine appeared to many to sum up the current mood. I quote from it here by way of conclusion:

'. . . I've no intention of talking here about the large sums of money paid for fishing rights, the supposed damage to spawning beds, the myriad of accusations that are levelled by fishermen and canoeists alike, but I am talking about a situation where the intransigence of fishermen has prevented generations of canoeists from practising their sport.

'Within my own personal experience I know that apartheid on rivers within the Peak Park is absolute. I first attended meetings with fishermen in my area in 1967. Now, twenty-one years later, not one scrap of river can be legally canoed and, in spite of all the lengthy negotiations at both national and local levels, there is no noticeable relaxation in the oppressive system . . .

'Custom and law concerning fishing rights go back to the days of serfdom. That doesn't make the law sacrosanct. How many laws we are supposed to uphold now were sneaked through Parliament centuries ago for the benefit of the Lord of the manor? . . .

'It is time the law was changed to allow multi-use of a scarce sporting facility. I doubt it will, because there is probably as much money being made from fishing rights as there is in our commercial dealings with South Africa.

'I've talked for twenty-one years, almost as long as Nelson Mandela has been in prison. I'm tired of talking. I haven't been able to practise my own sport and I'm approaching EPL (end of paddling life). My children have grown up. They have missed the fun. I would like my grandchildren to be able to enjoy their birthright. It won't come by talking. What is the reasonable thing to do?'

THE FUTURE

In the use of our natural sporting arenas – mountains, moorlands, the estuaries, coast and rivers – we British are faced not only with the problem of an archaic social structure but also with a large population seeking to use a limited area of 'wilderness'. Natural justice demands shared use, but even if river laws were to become based on this (instead of on the rights of ownership) mutual shared use would lead to conflict. The resolution of this conflict in other fields has been some sort of 'zoning' agreement based on space or time. Thus, following the campaign by the ramblers in the 1930s, a network of public footpaths and bridleways was set up in agreement with landowners, and public access was enshrined in the Access and Countryside Act of 1949. More recently rock climbers have voluntarily agreed to restrict their climbing on coastal cliffs during the nesting season following complaints from bird watchers and the RSPB.

An agreement between canoeists and game fishermen based around the closed fishing season (i.e. canoeists only allowed to paddle on upland rivers between the middle of October and the middle of March) is the obvious answer to many problems of access on young spate rivers. A few fishermen claim that canoeing disturbs spawning fish, but there is no evidence that a canoe upsets the breeding cycle any more than a passing tree or log brought down by the winter floods, and much evidence to show that fishing populations are greatly affected by other unconnected factors such as pollution and available food sources.

If agreements based around the fishing season are unsatisfactory to some fishermen (or canoeists) for whatever reason, year-round time sharing is an alternative (i.e. fishing permitted in the morning and canoeing in the afternoon as, for example, on the River Ubaye in southern France). Some fishermen claim that canoeing sends the fish to the bottom but others say 'a disturbed fish is a hungry fish'. If fishermen cannot agree on same-day use, an alternative year-round time-share could be based on spate levels as defined by a gauge (i.e. canoeists allowed to use the river only when it is above a certain level).

When it comes down to it the vast majority of fishermen on the bank only object to canoeists for two reasons. The first is that they sometimes interfere with their sport – tangle with their lines, obstruct their casting and so on. On a narrow river this is inevitable, so some sort of zoning agreement is necessary. The second reason is that, on game rivers at least, fishermen pay for their sport while canoeists do not. To most people the idea that an individual or group of individuals can own a stretch of water (or a mountain, crag, beach or moor) and make profit out of its use is outrageous, particularly when the user is taking nothing from the water (or land). Payment for 'stewardship' on the other hand is a different matter. Canoeists in large numbers do have an environmental impact and money is needed to maintain parking and camping areas, access, egress and portage trails. Ideally the 'steward' or regulator is a non-profit making body like the National Trust (as on the Conwy) or a White Water Centre (as on the Tryweryn), or possibly the new National Rivers Authority. It is unfortunate that in a radical, free enterprise, greed-motivated system, such as we have at the moment, regulation is habitually developed to private ownership.

Agreement between canoeists and fishermen is surely still possible. The vast majority on both sides remain reasonable people open to compromise. Many fishermen enjoy, or have sons and daughters who enjoy, canoeing, and many canoeists enjoy, or have fathers and mothers who enjoy, fishing. Even where these connections are not present it requires no great effort of imagination to perceive the interests of the other. It behoves the regulatory bodies – the owners, the National Parks Authorities, the National Trust, the Countryside Commission, the new Rivers Authority, and ultimately the Department of the Environment – to hammer out local and national agreements between the interested parties before this considerable goodwill and understanding disappears down a river of blood.

The hydrology of white water rivers
by Dave Williams

Every white water canoeist knows that the best sport is often obtained when the mountain streams and rivers are brimming with floodwater, although devotees of the more difficult gorges and falls will certainly disagree. But what are the reasons for high rainfall and how and why do rivers flood? A background appreciation of the factors responsible for both rainfall and flooding can only enhance the white water canoeist's chances of good sport.

The Hydrosphere
The earth's stock of water is contained entirely in an earth-atmosphere system known as the hydrosphere which extends from about 12 kilometres above the earth's surface to about ½

Figure 1: the hydrological cycle

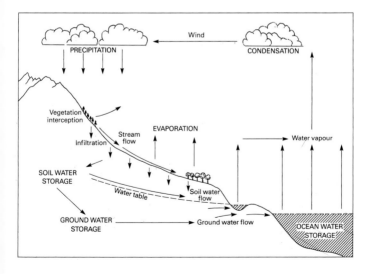

kilometre below it. The distribution and occurrence of this water at any one time is controlled by the hydrological cycle (Figure 1). In this cycle water moves between one part of the hydrosphere and another.

The input into the system is precipitation, and when this reaches the ground it immediately begins its return journey to the atmosphere either by evaporation or by means of run-off in rivers to the oceans. It is this latter part of the process that directly concerns the canoeist.

The influence of relief and climate

Precipitation itself is very variable, both in terms of time and distance. In Britain, for example, average annual rainfall can vary from as little as 50 centimetres in northern Kent to a staggering 500 centimetres plus in the mountain areas of Snowdonia and north-western Scotland. Figure 2 illustrates the pattern of average annual rainfall in Britain from 1916–50.

Much of the west and north of the country comprises the upland or mountain third of Britain. Geologically this is because the oldest and most resistant rocks are found here. It can be seen that there is a link between relief and rainfall. Here altitude is important because average annual rainfall increases by 8% for each 30-metre gain in altitude over sea level totals. A further contributory factor is the nearness of high ground to the Atlantic coast, where steep slopes directly exposed to the prevailing moist Atlantic winds will receive the most precipitation of all (Figure 3).

The vast majority of British precipitation occurs in relation to the fairly regular passage of frontal depressions from west to east over the country. These are the dominant feature of our climate since the depressions form in the north Atlantic where cool polar air meets warm tropical air. Areas of high relief intensify the precipitation from these depressions. From a canoeing point of view it is also worth noting that warm fronts, on average, result in much more intense rainfall than cold fronts.

Figure 2: British average annual precipitation 1916–1950

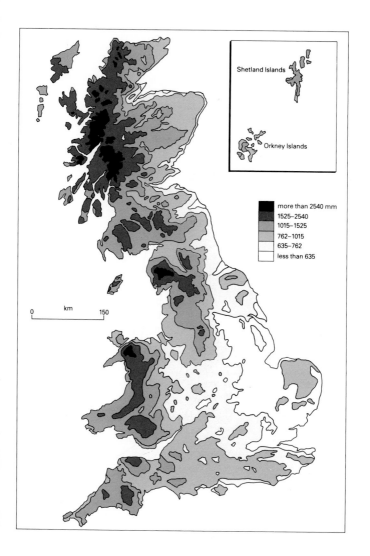

Shetland Islands

Orkney Islands

more than 2540 mm
1525–2540
1015–1525
762–1015
635–762
less than 635

km
0   150

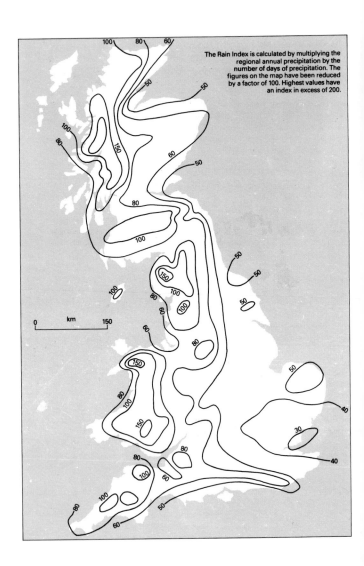

The Rain Index is calculated by multiplying the regional annual precipitation by the number of days of precipitation. The figures on the map have been reduced by a factor of 100. Highest values have an index in excess of 200.

km
0   150

The water balance
Once the precipitation has reached the surface, one of three things can happen to it, as shown by the following water balance equation:

precipitation = river discharge + loss through evapo-transpiration
                    − gains to storage

Discharge, or river-flow, is the amount of water in rivers, and it is always changing as different parts of the above equation change. It changes according to the weather. High rainfall makes water levels rise while high temperatures mean increased evaporation to the atmosphere and so river levels are lower. Water is not only stored on the surface in rivers and lakes but also in the soil, or in certain types of rock where it is called groundwater.

The hydrograph
Obviously, soilwater, groundwater and discharge represent the surplus water left from the inter-relationship of precipitation and evaporation, and since these will change from day to day, so therefore will the amount of surplus water. Such daily changes can be shown on a hydrograph although for the canoeist the storm or flood hydrograph is of greater interest (Figure 4). Rivers respond to heavy rainfall, as shown by the rising limb, but there is a time-lag from the start of the rain to the time of maximum discharge. This is due to river basin characteristics. After the rain stops, water goes on finding its way into the river system for some time so the flow becomes progressively rather than abruptly less. This is shown by the falling limb of the hydrograph.

Influences on river-flow
Although all river-flow eventually can be traced back to precipitation, the volume of water in a river at any particular time may originate from a complex and varied number of sources.

Figure 3: the rain index for Britain

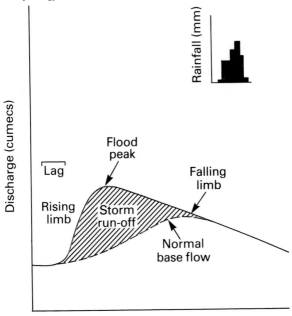

Figure 4: a flood hydrograph

1. Infiltration

Fairly intense, heavy rainfall may produce too much water to soak or infiltrate into the ground. The surplus water will run off into the rivers. The infiltration rate depends on the nature of the soil and, particularly in Britain, the fluctuation in the amount of water (infiltration capacity) in the soil due to previous weather conditions. In particular, the degrees of soil moisture can be linked to flooding, since saturated soil will be unable to absorb any more water, and so the ratio of run-off to rainfall will be high. In practical terms intense prolonged rain on a Friday following a week of wet weather could be expected to give some very high weekend river levels. On the other hand, intense rain after a long dry spell when much soil moisture storage will be available may produce little run-off to the rivers.

2. Seasonal factors

Despite the fact that intense and prolonged rainfall can occur at any time of year in Britain, there is a marked seasonal pattern of flooding. Over 75% of all floods occur in winter, with December and March having the highest flood frequencies (25% and 19% respectively), followed by November (12%) and January (11%). The March figure is clearly influenced by snow-melt, as those canoeing at Easter in Scotland will know well.

In fact, winter conditions are more likely to lead to flooding because of seasonal differences in infiltration capacity. Lower evaporation in winter will cause greater soil saturation and so lead to greater flood response in relation to heavy rainfall. In the case of most British rivers some two-thirds of the annual discharge occurs between October and March.

3. Aspect and snow-melt

Aspect is also important in relation to snow-melt. This is often the case in Scotland and other upland regions. The Tees, flowing eastward from the Pennines, can show a marked daily variation in flow levels during the spring melt period. In Scotland, snow tends to lie for longer and spring melting has a more marked and longer-term influence on flow levels. Rivers such as the Findhorn can be at a continuously high level for long periods of time, although much depends on whether the melting occurs during the day only, or whether it is continuous.

Without doubt snow-melt can be very important but it must be pointed out that little is really known of the exact nature of the link between it and flooding. Snow-melt comes as a result of a rise in temperature, usually accompanied by rainfall. Snow, though, seems to have a tremendous capacity to soak up rain when it first falls, and may not begin to melt for some time. But heavy rain with a frozen, and so impermeable, snow surface makes the story very different indeed for the canoeist.

However, snow rarely lies for long south of Scotland, and

melting causes a number of irregular flood peaks over several
weeks, related to falls of snow and subsequent melting. In Britain
snow-melt has little influence on rivers in comparison to Alpine
canoeing areas.

4. Localized rain

Another factor that the canoeist can do little to take advantage of,
unless he or she happens to be in the right place at the right time,
is localized rain. All too often a combination of relief factors and
synoptic conditions leads to intense flood – producing rain over a
relatively small geographic area. I have personally observed this
several times in North Wales where such an occurrence is quite
common. For example, one typical instance was the effect of
heavy rainfall over the Moelwynion mountains. This caused very
high flood-flows in all rivers draining radially from this area, the
Afonnydd Glaslyn, Goedol and Lledr, whereas other nearby rivers
such as the Conwy and Llugwy were so low as to be barely
canoeable.

5. Altitude

Other factors also affect how river-flow is related to rainfall.
British rivers, in comparison to rivers abroad, are short and steep.
Here again, altitude is important since slopes tend to steepen with
increasing height, but also because higher river drainage basins
tend to receive more rainfall. They are therefore more likely to
have saturated soils for a larger proportion of time.

6. The drainage area

The area of the drainage basin is also important since this
influences the size of the peak flood and also the time needed for
water to travel from the remotest part of the basin to the river.
Geology is also critical as impermeable rocks will produce a great
deal of run-off, which will be even greater if much bare rock is
exposed at the surface in the basin.

The Afon Artro in the Rhiniogau Mountains in North Wales is a
good example of a river where basin size, slope angles and geology
are all variously responsible for the river's response to heavy

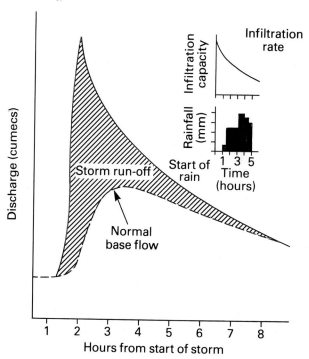

Figure 5: a 'flashy' flood hydrograph

rainfall. Here the catchment is small, the slopes steep, the soils thin and much rock is exposed at the surface. Consequently, the river responds rapidly to rainfall and its discharge rises and falls very quickly producing a 'flashy' hydrograph (Figure 5). The answer is to start paddling while it's still raining.

7. Drainage basin shape
The shape of the drainage basin is also important. Circular and/or compact basins result in more rapid water transfer from the

remotest part of the basin to the main river and if each tributary is contributing to the main river at the same time then, needless to say, the flood peak will be higher than that in an elongated basin.

Another factor of importance related to basin shape is the channel transfer time. This is well illustrated by the Afon Dyfrdwy (Welsh Dee) or the River Teme. In both cases the white water section is some considerable distance from the source and it takes time for floodwater to reach that particular section of river, thus giving good water many hours after heavy rain.

8. *The drainage network*

The complexity of the drainage network will also be crucial. Basins with a well developed river network, the Findhorn for example, will tend to produce greater flood peaks since surface run-off time will be cut down because water will have less distance to travel to find a stream channel. Also the time available for soil infiltration will be reduced. Artificial land drainage systems have much the same effect. For example, the upper Afon Gwy (River Wye) has become more 'flashy' due to both forestry and farmland drainage.

9. *Vegetation*

Vegetation also influences discharge since it intercepts rainfall. Woodland in particular delays water from reaching the rivers but heavy rain eventually breaks down this interception barrier.

10. *Baseflow*

Return of water to the river from soil and groundwater stores is also interesting. During dry periods, it is this baseflow water that accounts for river-flow and many canoeists will have noticed that discharge often increases downstream in many rivers, without the contribution of any major tributaries. This is due to springflow (a contributor to baseflow) from the bed and banks but is obviously less apparent in solid rock channels.

The baseflow characteristics of river drainage basins are highly variable. For example, the upper Afon Conwy and the Afon Twymyn in Wales are noted for retaining their water for many days after heavy rain. The Conwy gorge alongside the A5 can be canoed for several days after the flood peak, while the Fairy Glen, with the aid of the Afon Machno in part, can be canoed at a 'medium' level for up to five or more days after very heavy rain. Those familiar with the Fairy Glen will realize that channelling of water in a narrow gorge is also a contributory factor.

In comparison, the River Etive in Scotland and the upper River Dart on Dartmoor both have much more steeply falling hydrograph limbs and are often at a surpisingly low level in less than fifteen hours after the flood peak.

The reason for such contrasts lies in the dominance of certain different drainage basin characteristics over others. A final brief consideration of these can perhaps aid further understanding.

Firstly, the upper Conwy. This river has a very large basin area for a Welsh mountain stream and the drainage network is also well developed. More important though are the characteristics of the soil within the catchment area. The soil on most of the Upper Conwy basin on Mynydd y Migneint, east of Blaenau Ffestiniog, is composed of thick upland peat. Peat acts like a huge sponge with a tremendous capacity to store water and then release it slowly over a long period of time after rain. At the present time very little artificial drainage has taken place in the Upper Conwy basin, but if or when this occurs then the river will end up with a more flashy hydrograph. This change in behaviour would be rapid and noticeable.

On the other hand, the Upper Dart has both a much smaller drainage basin and drainage network. After the confluence of the East and West Dart at Dartmeet, no other major tributaries join the river upstream of Newbridge and the relatively thin and sandier soils here point to a reduction in the storage capacity of the drainage basin. Add a steep river gradient and you have all the necessary conditions for rapid run-off.

It is clear that a basic understanding of the hydrological characteristics of our white water rivers can be of immense benefit to canoeists wishing to paddle them. The enormous variety in river characteristics means that a knowledgeable canoeist will usually be able to find some water somewhere in any one of the upland areas of Britain.

Scotland

The Averon and other rivers of the Far North

The northern tip of Britain is a long way to go from anywhere, unless you work on the rigs, are a farmer or fisherman, or own a hotel. In that case you will probably want to escape to the Alps or Corsica, and get away from Scottish weather for canoeing holidays. Consequently, the canoeing potential of the region is relatively untapped. Tales have filtered south about the Helmsdale and Thurso (in the far north-east), but the only definite knowledge I have is of the River Inver flowing out of Loch Assynt in the north-west. Grade IVd rapids litter the Inver from lake (park by the loch) to sea (egress at the bridge at Lochinver after 8 kilometres) with a weir to portage in the middle and a gorge to inspect at the end. Other reports are sketchy, but perhaps it is a good thing that there is one part of the country where white water gems remain to be discovered.

As an introduction to the region, I can suggest three rivers, the River Averon (also called the Alness), the River Shin and the River Oykel. The first is a real classic – an amazingly continuous run at the grade, technical, moderately serious, but never desperate. The Shin and Oykel are too hard and easy by extremes to be excellent. However, they are major rivers containing much water, and, if only the Falls on the Shin are paddled, can be combined in a day's outing that will wet parts of your body that other rivers don't normally reach!

For those wanting a multi-day adventure, it is possible to start a trip on the Shin on the west coast at Loch Stack, continuing through Loch More, Loch Griama, Loch Merkland, and Loch Shin, thus crossing the entire country from west to east. This journey has been completed in a sail rigged open canoe in 14 hours.

RIVER AVERON (ALNESS)

The Averon, sometimes called the Alness, drains Loch Morie and the hills of Easter Ross into the Cromarty Firth north of Inverness.

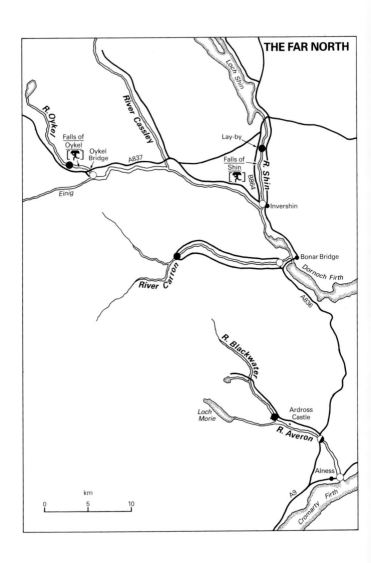

THE FAR NORTH

Loch Shin

R. Oykel

River Cassley

Lay-by

Falls of
Oykel
[🏛] Oykel
Bridge   A837

Falls of
Shin
[🏛]   R. Shin
B864

Einig

Invershin

River Carron

Bonar Bridge

Dornoch Firth

A836

R. Blackwater

Loch
Morie

Ardross
Castle

R. Averon

Alness

A9

Cromarty Firth

km
0   5   10

It requires heavy rain and/or snow-melt to bring it into condition, although the flow from Loch Morie can be artificially controlled by a sluice.

The level of the river may be judged from the egress point in Alness; there is a gauge downstream of the old A9 bridge on river left. If this reads 2.5 the river is Grade III with a few falls of IVd. If it reads between 3 and 4 the river will be continuous Grade IV, with some falls at the top end of the grade. A more general indication is given at the A836 'half-way' bridge. If the river is just canoeable here the rest of the river is also possible; if all the rocks are covered it will be continuous Grade IVd.

Averon ***
Blackwater confluence (591.747) to Alness (654.695)
Grade IVd
No Portages
12 Kilometres
OS Sheet 21

Access to the river is at the confluence of the Averon's major tributary, the Blackwater. A forest track leads down to this confluence from the minor road running parallel to the northern bank of the Averon. An alternative access point is 2 kilometres downstream by another forest track just west of Ardross Castle. The sight of Ardross Castle on the left bank coincides with the first of many Grade IVd rapids on the river. If you can resist the temptation of trying to find a Sleeping Beauty in this ornately turreted folly, continue for 2 kilometres to the first of Averon's two gorges.

There is a wooden fisherman's walk constructed precariously along the sides of the first gorge; a sign, if you have not guessed already, that the Averon is a good salmon river. The gorge is very impressive but not much harder, albeit more continuous, than the section above. It ends above a foot-bridge after a right-hand bend.

The second gorge is a kilometre below the A836 bridge but

there are many good rapids before, above and below the bridge to occupy the mind. A wide steep rapid (marked as a waterfall on the map) with a house prominent on the left bank marks the start of the second gorge. This continues for a kilometre. It contains two quite distinctive falls where the river is squeezed between bedrock walls. The Averon then relaxes for the last kilometre into Alness. Egress is below the road-bridge on the left bank by some steps.

RIVER SHIN

The Shin drains Loch Shin, the biggest loch in the far north, through a hydro-electric scheme. It remains canoeable for longer than most other rivers in the area and after heavy rain becomes an enormously powerful torrent. The main feature of the river is the awesome Falls of Shin, a 5-metre waterfall which should be inspected prior to any descent.

Shin
Lay-by (573.009) to Ivershin (574.975)
Grade IIIc (Ve)
No Portages
5 Kilometres
OS Sheets 16 and 21

The Falls of Shin are half-way down the river in a short gorge. The Falls, which are signposted from Invershin, are a noted tourist attraction and there is a café, car-park and well constructed path down to them from the road which runs parallel to the west bank of the river. Above the Falls the river is flat and it seems unduly tedious to paddle all the way down it from the power station at Lairg. It is better to start 5 kilometres below Lairg and a couple of kilometres above the Falls from a riverside lay-by on the west bank road (B864) or at the Falls themselves (557.991). In high water – when there are no rocks visible under the water on the top shelf of the fall – the Falls of Shin are very dangeous (Vf) due to the force of the water diving into the pool below. At medium to low levels – when there is an obvious eddy on the left at the top –

the Falls are somewhat safer (Ve). To portage the Falls get out in good time and carry over the rocks down the right bank. Between the Falls and Invershin are two or three lesser rapids (IIIc) which are enjoyable particularly in high water. Egress is at the junction of the B864 with the A837 where the latter bridges the Shin.

RIVER OYKEL

A series of small mountain streams flowing through wild hill country come together in Loch Ailsh to form the Oykel on the southern slopes of Ben More Assynt. The river then flows east for 50 kilometres to the village of Bonar Bridge on the Dornoch Firth.

From Loch Ailsh to just above Oykel Bridge the river falls as a series of big slow-moving pools. At Oykel Bridge the sandy bottom gives way to a series of steep rapids before the river is joined by the Eing to flow fast but flat down to the confluence with the River Shin.

It is a long drive for a short paddle, but, besides the Oykel, there is another river in the area worth checking out. This is the Carron (IVc). It meets the waters of the Oykel and Shin at Bonar Bridge. Access is below the Craigs road-bridge (480.920) and egress after 10 kilometres at Lower Gledfield road-bridge (585.910) a mile west of Ardgay (which is on the A9). Four short but difficult gorges provide the white water interest in between flat scenic stretches.

Oykel
Roadside field (371.012) to confluence with Eing (391.003)
Grade IIId (Vf)
No Portages
2 Kilometres
OS Sheets 20 and 21

Above and below Oykel Bridge – actually two bridges – is an obvious set of rapids, which are easy to inspect (IIId). Out of sight upstream, however, is a major drop: Oykel Falls (Vf). This can be taken down the right-hand side but it is an exceptionally serious rapid. This is partly due to the height of the fall (4–5 metres) partly to the long, quite difficult approach, but most of all to the faulting of the sandy rock on the river bed. Erosion has left fangs and shelves of rock pointing diagonally *upstream*, making pinning a distinct possibility, and swimming or even rolling very dangerous.

Access to the river is across the fields downstream of the school house, a kilometre above Oykel Bridge. It is well worth walking down to Oykel Falls to inspect this awesome drop. There was a fatal canoeing accident here some years ago – a poignant reminder that portage is sometimes the better part of valour. Egress is just above the confluence with the Eing either to a road on the right or to a track on the left (the latter is nearer but rougher). It would also be possible to get out at Oykel Bridge (385.008).

The Findhorn and other rivers of the North-East Highlands

The Findhorn, even more than the Orchy, has an awesome reputation south of the border. The Lower Findhorn, in particular, is famous for its serious section of hard canoeing in a deep gorge. The Lower Findhorn Gorge, however, is only 5 kilometres long and, while it is certainly continuous and committing, it is not desperately difficult, unless the river is in high flood. Do not, therefore, be unduly put off by stories of lost boats and paddles, or vertical walls of rock. A split paddle is a sensible spare but rescuing a canoe should always be possible and if the worst comes to the worst you can walk out of the gorge.

Sometimes, of course, discretion is the better part of valour. Most of the epics have happened to canoeists unable to cope with, or unrealistic in their judgement of, big volume water. When it rains or when the snow melts, the dark brown water running off the Findhorn's massive peat catchment backs up very quickly behind the sill of hard rock bordering the coastal plain and is then forced through the Lower Findhorn Gorge at a tremendous rate. In full flood you should perhaps consider the Middle Findhorn or one of the other rivers in the area. There is the broad and even Spey or one of its whiter tributaries, the Feshie or Avon; there is even the gentle Ness to run to in spate conditions. Whatever your decision you will soon be back to the north-east Highlands for more.

RIVER FINDHORN

A good place to judge the level of the Findhorn is Randolph's Leap. If only one side of Randolph's Leap is possible, the river is low. If both sides are possible (the left-hand exit being distinctly undesirable because of boils and whirlpools) the river is high. If the central rocks which divide the river at Randolph's Leap are anywhere near to being covered, say *au revoir*. In the beech wood on your approach to Randolph's Leap you may trip over a small

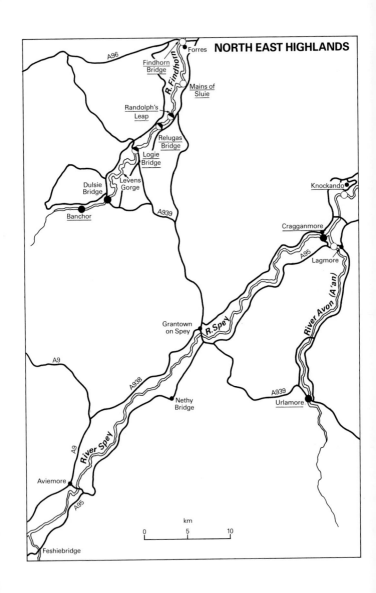

NORTH EAST HIGHLANDS

A96

Forres

Findhorn
Bridge

R. Findhorn

Mains of
Sluie

Randolph's
Leap

Relugas
Bridge

Logie
Bridge

Levens
Gorge

Dulsie
Bridge

Banchor

A939

Knockando

Cragganmore

A95

Lagmore

River Avon (A'an)

Grantown
on Spey

R. Spey

A9

A938

Nethy
Bridge

A939

Urlamore

River Spey

A9

Aviemore

A95

Feshiebridge

km

0   5   10

headstone placed there in 1829 to mark the height of the flood in that year. It is 50 metres above normal spate level. Was that when the Loch Ness Monster came in from the sea?

Upper Findhorn **
Banchor (907.402) or Dulsie Bridge (931.414) to Logie Bridge (959.462)
Grade IVd
No Portages
13 or 9 Kilometres
OS Sheet 27

Even more impressive than at the headstone at Randolph's Leap is the height which the 1829 floods reached at Dulsie Bridge. The water completely submerged the left-hand bridge arch and came to within a metre of the capstone on the main arch. That would have been some ride! Even in 'normal' spate conditions the rapids at Dulsie Bridge and Levens Gorge rise dramatically in level and difficulty (Grade Ve).

Dulsie Bridge (Grade IVd) is one of the harder rapids on the Upper Findhorn and rather than miss it or start in cold, it is perhaps better to drive up the left bank for 4 kilometres until just past Banchor and put in where the road comes back down close to the river. There are shingle rapids and small bedrock steps until a major tributary (Leonach Burn) enters from the right, swelling the river to twice its former size. Two kilometres below, at Dulsie Bridge, this new weight of water is squeezed between an overhanging wall and a large rock; an interesting problem!

From the Dulsie Bridge 3 kilometres of straightforward canoeing leads to Glenferness House (right bank), home of the Earl of Leven and Melville. This name has been given to the gorge which begins just round the next bend. Levens Falls (IVd) is the first and hairiest rapid in Levens Gorge. A look from the bank is essential to determine the best route here and since the river disappears from view there is little encouragement to run it 'blind'.

The next rapid should be run on the left, since the right-hand channel sumps underneath a gnarly boulder. This has been the scene of a number of epics in recent years. The whole section of 2 kilometres can become Grade Ve in flood.

Longer, easier rapids follow Levens Gorge leading after 4 kilometres to Logie Bridge and egress from the Upper Findhorn. So ends a long, exciting and beautiful section of river. It will be an appetizer, in the right conditions, for the Lower Gorge.

Middle Findhorn *
Logie Bridge (959.462) to Randolph's Leap (999.494)
Grade IIb (IIIb)
No Portages
6 Kilometres
OS Sheet 27

The quiet before the storm, here is a gentle and peaceful paddle in outstanding surroundings. It serves as a useful alternative to the upper and lower gorges when they are at ridiculous levels, or for the canoeist wanting a taste of the white stuff.

Access is at Logie Bridge. The current is swift and the occasional overhanging tree or submerged boulder can give problems but in all there is little to worry about. Two rapids near the end of the trip are a little harder than the rest. One comes near Daltulich after a sharp 'S' bend; the other, Carnage Corner (IIIb), is immediately above Relugas Bridge. This road-bridge (986.487) is an alternative access/egress point.

Randolph's Leap lies a couple of kilometres below Relugas Bridge. Lochead and Todd in their *Scottish White Water* guidebook nicely understate the case when they introduce this feature: 'Randolph, one of Bruce's Lieutenants at Bannockburn, is reputed to have jumped across the river here while fleeing from one of his (Scottish) enemies. Even allowing for the high degree of motivation on Randoph's part, one may deduce that the river is very narrow.'

The narrowest part of the river lies 200 metres above the rapid of the same name; here the gap is so narrow that a canoe may not pass through it sideways. It can hardly be missed – by the eye at least! Dead Thing Eddy (DTE) recirculates detritus in majestic slow motion just upsteam and to the right of the narrows. Get out in it to reach the steep bank and path above.

Lower Findhorn ***
Randolph's Leap (999.494) to Mains of Sluie (005.527) or
Findhorn Bridge (011.581)
Grade IVd (Vf)
No Portages
5 or 13 Kilometres
OS Sheet 27

Access to this famous section of river is from DTE (see above) or, more often, by a small eddy below Randolph's Leap (Vf). Randolph's is a very serious proposition due to the undercut walls on entry and exit. It is easier in low water but becomes progressively harder and more serious as the river rises. Entry on the right and exit on the left, through the Punch Bowl, is the only way in low water. In higher flows you will want to keep to the right at the bottom but the water tries to drag you into the horrible whirlpool that forms next to the Punch Bowl on the left.

Below Randolph's, the Findhorn is much easier for a while, and is a suitable warm-up for the Gorge. A big gravel island divides the river and then 2 kilometres further on a bouncy Grade IIIc on a left-hand bend (next to a large mansion on the right) warns of bigger things to come. The rapids are now close together and bank inspection is often necessary to identify route and difficulty. Corkscrew (IVd) is obviously harder than the rest whether you see it from the river or the bank. The tortuous line(s) through Corkscrew vary somewhat according to the effects of the most recent flood and the current state of the rapid can be surveyed from a massive rock on the left, against which much of the water piles. The technical paddling in heavy water and the stoppers which form near the bottom make this rapid Ve in high water.

There is not much of a breathing space before Triple Steps (IVd). The gorge is tight all around and it is with some difficulty that you will get to the best eddy on the right. A short scramble gives a good view over the rapid. It is very technical in low water and you may be grateful to be in a plastic 'ball' in this pinball machine. In high water a more direct line is possible through large stoppers.

You must have a strong feeling of commitment in the Gorge here, for even a cursory look at the towering banks of rock and shrub will convince you that the easiest way out is down. Two easier rapids lead to the Slot (IVc) – sometimes called Fishladder. This innocuous little drop has many people over and in. In low to medium water it must be taken through the middle where every effort to keep away from the undercut right wall seems to be thwarted by the river. In high water it is possible to take the slab on the left.

The hardest part of the river is now over and there remain 7 kilometres of easy canoeing down to Findhorn Bridge. The last flat section of river is a long drag after the excitement above and some will want to take out at the Mains of Sluie. This collection of farm buildings, a little way below the Slot on the right bank, cannot be seen from the river (the way up is just above an obvious large red cliff) and access to it is over private land. You may prefer, therefore, to drift quietly down to the A96. If you do, and the weather is warm, your lazy paddle strokes may disturb what looks like a couple of wet cats – they are in fact otters practising a different sort of sport in the afternoon sun.

RIVER SPEY

Speidh is the Gaelic word for speed or strength and certainly the Spey, with all the power of the melted snow of the Cairngorms behind it, is probably the fastest-flowing major river in the British Isles. This makes it an easy touring river for kayaks and canoes. Unfortunately for the white water buff, the gradient of the Spey is relatively even and only the short section described below offers much in the way of excitement.

Randolph's Leap on the Lower Findhorn

Spey *
Cragganmore (168.368) to Knockando (195.415)
Grade IIb
No Portages
8 Kilometres
OS Sheet 28

At Cragganmore access is from the right bank by a disused railway-bridge (now part of the Speyside Way) 3 kilometres upstream of the B9138 bridge. There are two good play rapids, one ½ kilometre below the confluence with the Avon, Blacksboat Rapid; and the other right at the end of the trip, Knockando Rapid. Egress (and access for playing on the Knockando Rapid) is just below on the left with a path leading up to an old railway station.

Tomdhu distillery at Knockando is one of many along the river. The Lower Spey has more distilleries per square mile than any other part of Scotland and the two Speyside valleys of Glenlivet and Glenfiddich are bywords for malt whisky. Recalling the trip in a bar, it can be sobering to think that the expensive bottle from which you are drinking is made out of the water through which you have paddled.

RIVER FESHIE

The Feshie is a tributary of the Spey and is only canoeable in high water – the long, upper, braided section is extremely tedious otherwise. The level of the river can be judged from Feshiebridge. If the final rocky rapid above the bridge is possible, so is the rest of the short gorge upstream; if most of the rocks are covered, the whole river can be run and the gorge will be worth inspecting.

Feshie *
Achlean Farm (849.975) to Feshiebridge (851.043)
Grade IIIc
No Portages

7 Kilometres
OS Sheets 35 and 36

Access to the river at Achlean Farm is via a path through the steading. The first 6 kilometres are Grade IIb but the last is in a small gorge and is a grade or more harder depending on the level of the river. Egress is below the bridge at Feshiebridge or continue down the Spey to Aviemore.

RIVER AVON

Like the Feshie, the Avon is a spate tributary of the Spey. A boulder strewn stream, the Avon is at its best in high water.

Avon *
Urlarmore (149.201) to Lagmore (182.358)
Grade IIIc (IVd)
No Portages
17 Kilometres
OS Sheets 36 and 28

Access is near Tomintoul where the A939 crosses the river and egress is 2 kilometres before the confluence with the Spey where the A95 crosses the river – both these bridges are called the Bridge of Avon. The B9008 follows the river the whole way so this long trip may be reduced by getting in from the road lower down the rirver. A large rapid called Distillery Falls (IVd) is worth inspecting. This is heralded by a large group of factory buildings on the right bank about 1 kilometre upstream of a small road-bridge (146.255).

RIVER NESS

Like the River Lochy which drains the other end of the Great Glen, this well-fed, easy river offers the unshuttled driver the opportunity of a round trip using the neighbouring Caledonian Canal.

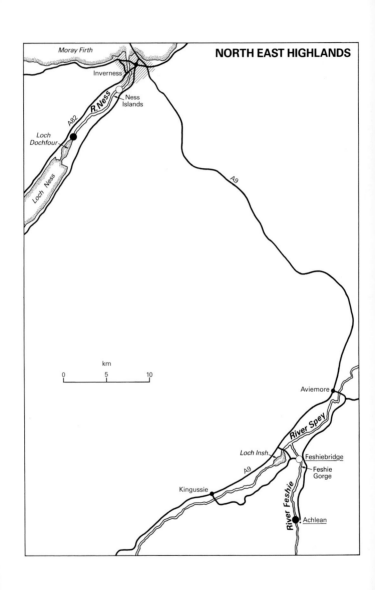

Ness

Loch Dochfour (612.395) to Ness Islands (660.435)
Grade IIb
No Portages
9 Kilometres
OS Sheet 26

Access is from the A82 where the road runs next to the canal and river, and egress to a minor road (off the A82) at some large islands where the Ness enters the city of Inverness. A shorter (round) trip can be arranged by getting out (or back into the canal) at Ness Castle on the right bank (A862) after 5 kilometres. The river can flood quite dramatically when a storm coincides with a high flood tide in the Moray Firth. On one such occasion in early February 1989 the Inverness railway-bridge was washed away by the river.

Rivers Feshie and Ness

The River Roy

Glen Roy is a national nature reserve – a huge, beautiful, wild country little visited or inhabited. Once you have turned up the narrow winding road from Roybridge into the Glen, you will often be alone in this spectacular landscape of 'parallel roads' – mountain terraces left by the slowly sinking waters of an ice-dammed loch which once filled the valley. Then look down and you will see a narrow ribbon of white disappearing into the trees. This is the Roy, a classic run down an isolated valley, and in high water it is undoubtedly one of the finest white water trips in Britain.

The Roy is naturally divided into two sections by the wooden bridge at Cranachan farm, known locally as Stone Bridge. The Upper Roy is forced into tight gorges and steep drops by metamorphic rock, and the technical difficulty, while nowhere extreme, is prolonged and continuous. After Stone Bridge, softer sedimentary rock has allowed the Roy to expand to double its width, erode a more even gradient, and provide a leisurely paddle. The level of the river may be judged by looking upstream from the A86 at Roybridge. If all the bedrock in the river bed is covered, the Lower Roy is canoeable. The Upper Roy needs more water than this to make it worth doing at all, and indeed you will have a better run on the Lower Roy when it too is higher.

Upper Roy ***
Brae Roy Lodge foot-bridge (330.909) to Stone Bridge (297.845)
Grade IVe
1 Portage (?)
10 Kilometres
OS Sheet 41

The road from Roybridge to Brae Roy Lodge climbs steeply

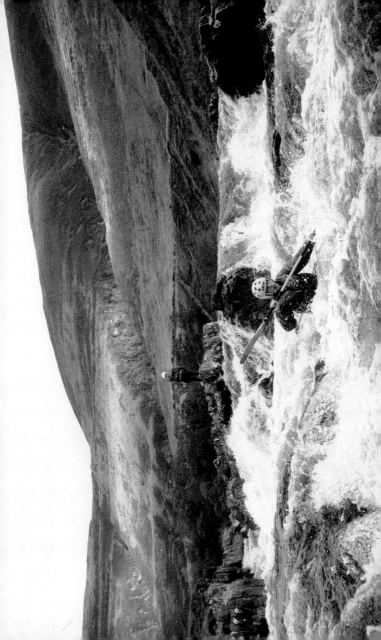

beside the river for 11 kilometres before emerging into the upper glen. The last 5 kilometres are largely flat but to put in at Brae Roy foot-bridge (1 kilometre below the Lodge) is a useful warm-up. If time is pressing, the river may be reached at a large bend at the top of the steep section, 4 kilometres below Brae Roy Lodge foot-bridge (thus reducing the Upper Roy to 6 kilometres).

After paddling gently down the glorious upper glen, the big right-hand bend, mentioned above, leads into the first and relatively open gorge section. This drops pleasantly over a number of steps and ends dramatically with the wide rocky fall Wish You Were Here (IVd) – well worth inspecting. The next big drop, Rooster Tail (IVd), also needs a look to assess the line past the central rock. None of this, however, should come as a great surprise for this section of river is partially visible from the road.

Subsequently, the Roy starts to fall more steeply in a series of narrow gorges. Trees grow thickly to hide the river from the road and continue to do so all the way to the end of the river. The first narrow section, Archavady Gorge, named after the house high on the river bank, is the most serious (IVe) and deserves bank inspection. The first step in the gorge is dramatically undercut and, although it has been paddled in favourable conditions, it is normally portaged (Vf). A few metres downstream is an entertaining double fall on a sharp 'S' bend – the Brothers Grimm (IVd). The Upper Roy continues with a number of difficult rapids, some of which are awkward to inspect from the bank and therefore tempting to shoot 'blind'. In very high water, large stoppers and waves bar the way and the river can reach Grade Ve. This superb stretch of white water is one of the most continuous in Scotland.

The Upper Roy ends dramatically with a metre-wide gash through a 10-metre high cliff. Below, the valley sides fall back, grass takes over from rock on the banks and there is a choice of routes down the water. Stone Bridge is 1½ kilometres downstream.

Rooster Tail on the Upper Roy with the 'parallel roads' in the background

Lower Roy ***
Stone Bridge (297.845) to Roybridge (270.813)
Grade IIIc
No Portages
5 Kilometres
OS Sheet 41

Stone Bridge was built for wheeled vehicles, but now, its timbers rotten and collapsing after years of rain and neglect, will take only pedestrians. Little wonder then that the track down to the bridge is overgrown and hard to spot from the road (if you reach the tourist car-park you have gone too far). Fortunately, once found, the rutted path is soft enough to allow canoes to be dragged on the 200-metre 1 in 4 incline down to the river.

The river starts with a couple of interesting rapids on 'S' bends and continues at the same grade as far as Roybridge. Although they are not very hard the rapids keep on coming at you, and a major tributary, the Gleann Glas Dhoire which enters from the left shortly below Stone Bridge, ensures that, despite the greater width and more gradual gradient, the river is still very fast-flowing. Egress is on the left bank below the railway-bridge to a parking spot next to the camp-site entrance, or you can continue down the Spean as far as Spean Bridge (see chapter on the Spean).

The River Spean and other tributaries of the Lochy

Between the Lochs Laggan and Lochy, the River Spean gurgles, chatters and roars its way down 23 kilometres of valley and gorge. It only escapes from the attentions of the Aviemore–Fort William road (A86) towards the end, and, with dams at top and bottom and copious roads, tracks and footpaths in between, it could never be described as unexploited or unexplored. But the quality of the white water will draw canoeists back again and again from the wildest glens and, especially in the Gorge, there is almost always sufficient water to tickle the most jaded palate.

Should you have had a surfeit of the Spean then you might consider four other tributaries of the Lochy – the loch and river which, together with the Ness, divide the Highlands in two. These are the Gloy and the Loy which are spate rivers *par excellence*, but share with their more famous sister, the Roy, an excellence of continuity at the grade. Shorter but with more reliable waters are the Arkaig and Garry – the latter actually enters Loch Oich just up the road from Loch Lochy – both of which drains long lochs and a huge area of the wet western Highlands.

The Lochy itself is included not so much because of its white water, of which there is very little – although it does contain the local 'hot-doggin' rodeo site – but because if everything else is too low it is a last recourse for the water-hungry.

RIVER SPEAN

The level of the Spean may be judged from Spean Bridge. If the rocks below the bridge are showing the Gorge will be something of a scrape and you can forget about the Upper or Middle Spean. If the rocks are covered but the gauge on the bridge shows less than 2, the Gorge will be Grade IVd. Between 2 and 4 the Gorge becomes more difficult and the Upper and Middle Spean are at their best. If the gauge reads above 4 some of the difficulties in the Gorge are ironed out but the Upper and Middle Spean become quite frightening.

Upper Spean **
Laggan Dam (372.807) to Inverlair Bridge (340.805)
Grade IIId
No Portages
4 Kilometres
OS Sheet 41

At least one, preferably two and frighteningly three pipes or more should be releasing water from Laggan Dam to make this trip worthwhile. Perhaps fortunately the last alternative is rare, but even the first two are not common even when the wipers are doing a tap dance on your windscreen.

 Access is down the steep right bank from the A86. Put in immediately below the dam. The river hereabouts is fast and technical with long, bouncy rapids reminiscent of the Alps. Unused to this quantity of water, the undergrowth on the banks is swamped and bushes and saplings sway to and fro in the flow. They could cause problems if you are swimming but in your boat you will enjoy the helter-skelter of small haystacks and friendly stoppers.

 The railway line passes overhead and then, on the left, the trees give way to fields just before the confluence with the Treig (a dam-controlled river canoeable from Loch Treig at Grade IVd). The best of the Upper Spean is now behind but the added weight of the Treig makes the few remaining rapids surprisingly powerful. So take care to get out in good time above Inverlair Bridge (left or right bank) because the falls below are *terminal!*

Middle Spean
Monessie Gorge (298.810) to Spean Bridge (222.817)
Grade IVd (Ve)
No Portages
8 Kilometres
OS Sheet 41

The section between Inverlair Falls and Monessie Gorge (5 kilometres) will not interest the white water paddler unless you want to try the Grade VIf falls that delineate this quiet stretch. So put in below Monessie Gorge (park on the A86 just before Glenspean Hotel on a sudden bend in the river) or, if you have had part of your brain removed, put in on the falls themselves, and continue through a long Grade IIId rapid. A short flat section precedes another fall where a good line is crucial to miss a large stopper on the right (IVd). It is important to stop below this rapid as an even harder one follows.

A line down the left of the next fall is possible but the consequences of blowing it are not pleasant (Ve). Many will prefer to portage this rapid even though climbing out of the steep valley and back in again is awkward, to say the least. A narrow gorge spanned by a high iron foot-bridge lies immediately below, the last of the difficulties before Roybridge.

Roybridge (270.813) is an alternative access point for those wanting a quieter (or shorter) trip. Between Roybridge and Spean Bridge the river is broad and even; a gently pleasant passage apart from the short excitement of Railway Bridge Falls (IIIc). A bend or two after the railway passes over the Spean, a ledge bisects the river producing a powerful stopper. Railway Bridge Falls are normally shot by a 'staircase' on the right. The egress point is 2 kilometres below – just above Spean Bridge to a minor road or, lower down, to a public car-park (both on the left bank).

Lower Spean (Spean Gorge) ***
Spean Bridge (222.817) to Mucomir Power Station (183.838)
Grade IVe
No Portages
6 Kilometres
OS Sheet 41

The Spean Gorge has been described as the 'poor man's Verdon' and, like the latter, it is more serious than it is difficult although not without its share of technical problems. The water sumps, disappears round blind corners and pushes under overhangs. It is not the place to practise the breast-stroke. Occasionally trees will and, at the time of writing do, block the line down a rapid. The

Spean Gorge deserves respect at whatever water level you paddle it.

The level and thus the nature of the Gorge can change dramatically even during the space of a day. Since the water is constricted in a narrow channel it goes *up* rather than out, sometimes rising a metre in an hour. High water progressively irons out the technical twists and drops, but the powerful flow creates boils, whirlpools and big waves, and reduces the number of eddies. At radically different heights it hardly seems the same river.

Access at Spean Bridge is upstream on the left bank and is most easily approached from a lay-by on a minor road running parallel to the river. Easy water leads down to a dismantled railway bridge high above the gorge. Downstream of this bridge, just as another dilapidated bridge with a fir tree growing out of its buttress comes into view, is the first rapid of note – The Fairy Steps (IIId). A line down the right, presently obstructed by a tree, is obvious in most levels.

Beyond the second bridge there are two drops – the second noticeably harder than the first, except in high water when they are both washed-out. The best line on the first drop is left of the central boulder on the lip. The second drop, Headbanger (IVd), is worth inspecting and protecting as it is very 'hit or miss'.

The Spean now becomes further constricted by multi-storey boulders in its bed. One such boulder hides a big fall – the Cauldron (IVd) – until it is almost too late to stop. Follow-my-leader is not a good strategy as the available eddy on the left, just after the distinctive narrow approach gap, only holds about 1½ boats. The famous Constriction lies below, forcing the canoeist in drought conditions to keel her boat over on one side to get through. This is a much harder rapid in big water (IVd). Two rapids remain, the second in low water rewarding the over-relaxed with a pin if attempted on the left.

The river gently meanders down the final kilometre and into the

On the edge of Headbanger in the Spean Gorge in low water

Lochy. In fact, because of the management of that river through the Caledonian Canal and the Mucomir Power Station, the Lochy normally appears to be the tributary. When the heavens have really opened, however, you can't paddle into or past the outflow from the power-house. This doesn't matter as far as egress from the Spean is concerned because the B8004 (which incidentally follows and gives good, if distant, views of the Gorge from the right bank) can be reached from immediately upstream of the power station.

RIVER LOCHY

The Lochy emerges from Loch Lochy via Mucomir hydro-electric station and flows into Loch Linnhe (the sea) at Fort William. It is an easy paddle on a wide river with good views of Ben Nevis. It is suitable for kayak novices and competent open canoeists. The neighbouring Caledonian Canal offers the possibility of a two-way trip. To do this put in above the locks of Neptune's Staircase and get out at Gairlochy.

Lochy
Gairlochy (196.839) to Victoria Bridge (124.756)
Grade IIb
No Portages
13 Kilometres
OS Sheet 41

Access is at Gairlochy and involves a short carry from the road (B8004) to the river. The only rapid of note comes after about 9 kilometres at Torcastle. The Lochy constricts and bends sharply left, producing some quite large standing waves. Flatter water then leads down to Fort William. Egress is opposite the Ben Nevis distillery at Victoria Bridge on the outskirts of the town.

Should you be desperate for moving water in a dry spell, the outflow from the aluminium smelter produces a 100% reliable, polluted, standing 'play' wave (IVa) surrounded by fishermen –

southerners will feel at home. This is a little way below Victoria Bridge and can be reached by car from the A82.

RIVER ARKAIG

The Arkaig is a short 'one rapid wonder'; it is, however, in beautiful surroundings isolated from the road and it stays 'up' for longer than other rivers in the area. Its huge source, Loch Arkaig, is famous for ospreys and for the trout on which they feed.

Arkaig *
Loch Arkaig (170.884) to Bunarkaig (187.878)
Grade IIIc (IVc)
No Portages
2 Kilometres
OS Sheet 41

Access is at the outflow from Loch Arkaig. The biggest fall on the river (IVc) is a little way below round a left-hand bend. The adrenalin is hardly out of your system before you are at Bunarkaig Bridge. The Arkaig's last little fling is a good play rapid just before the river collapses into Loch Lochy.

RIVER GARRY

The Garry, like the Awe, is a useful river to have up one's sleeve when all else is dry, since it is dam-controlled. At the time of writing Loch Garry Dam was releasing every Tuesday – but check with local canoeists for up-to-date information. The easier upper section between Loch Quoich and Loch Garry is not described here but may be worth doing for the scenery alone.

Garry
Loch Garry Dam (276.018) to Invergarry (307.010)
Grade IVc
No Portages

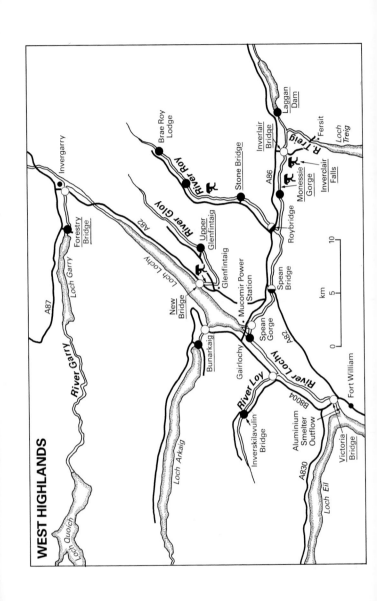

WEST HIGHLANDS

6 Kilometres
OS Sheet 34

Turn off the A87 onto a forestry track and park where it crosses
the river – White Bridge (283.013). Carry up the right-hand bank
by a footpath, inspecting the rapids on the way, and put in below
the dam. Apart from one rapid soon after White Bridge, the
section you have seen constitutes the sum of the difficulties. White
water prangsters may prefer, therefore, to take out at White
Bridge rather than continue down the easy lower stretch to
Invergarry. Here then is another good river for the one-car-
canoeist (see also the Lochy and Ness) providing of course that the
dam is releasing.

RIVER GLOY

For really exciting canoeing the Gloy should look like it sounds – a
runny, chocolate-brown glue. In that flooded condition it provides
a serious and continuously interesting trip down an isolated glen.
Access to and from the river is not easy and in the narrow stream
there is the ever present danger of jammed tree trunks which may
force the occasional portage.

Gloy **
Upper Glenfintaig (258.887) to New Bridge (225.879)
Grade IVd
Occasional Portages (trees)
8 Kilometres
OS Sheet 41

Turn off the A82 at Glenfintaig Lodge and immediately cross the
Gloy by a narrow bridge. This is a possible egress point for a
shorter and easier trip. The single-track road continues steeply up
the right bank some 50 to 100 metres above the river. Access is at
the top of the road where it crosses the river at Upper Glenfintaig.

The tributaries of the River Lochy

A short little gorge leads from the bridge to the confuence with a major tributary coming in from the left. The Gloy is then continuously interesting (IIIc) to Glenfintaig Lodge with many narrow falls and rapids.

Below the Lodge, the Gloy parallels and then passes under the A82 in a steep gorge to gush into Loch Lochy by the Invergloy hostels. This superb sustained section is a grade harder (IVd) than the river above. Egress is recommended at the A82 New Bridge – 'newer' than the one carrying General Wade's military road – since the gorge between there and the loch is impassable in places and the road down to the Invergloy hostels is private. A steep haul up on the left bank just upstream of New Bridge leads to a lay-by some way back on the same (south) side.

RIVER LOY

Like the Gloy, the Loy is only canoeable during or just after heavy rain. Unlike the Gloy, it can be readily inspected from the road from which it is at all times easily accessible. It is shorter, less confined and less continuous than the Gloy.

Loy *
Inverskilavulin Bridge (125.831) to B8004 bridge (147.818)
Grade IIIc
No Portages
4 Kilometres
OS Sheet 41

On the drive up the Glen the road crosses from left to right bank at Inverskilavulin's Bridge. Put in here. The first kilometre is quite gentle, if fast. After a stream comes in from the right, things get more interesting. There are four notable drops, each one big enough to bury your boat and the last quite technical. The river then eases off for a while. Towards the end of the trip there are three or four more rapids which will exercise muscle and mind.

Pop out at the get-out on the River Gloy

The B8004 road-bridge is obvious but do not get out just yet. Below the bridge is a 50-metre tunnel taking the Lochy underneath the Caledonian Canal. Enter the tunnel if you dare for there is not enough light to see whether a stopper lurks inside! A subsidiary tunnel on the right provides a watery way back to the road.

The Etive and other rivers of Glencoe and Ben Nevis

Ben Nevis and the mountains of Glencoe are some of the first and certainly the highest bits of land to be hit by the warm, moisture-laden south-westerly winds that prevail upon the United Kingdom. Forced upwards by the 1,000-metre high landmass the air cools and drops its load. So the big, bad Ben and its satellites stream with water and Fort William nestling on its western slopes is 'Spate City UK'.

If you want reliable wet weather in the UK go to Fort William. For example, between the 5th and 7th February 1989 125 millimetres of rain fell in 36 hours, and in the six weeks of the New Year up to that date Fort William had had 800 millimetres of rain. This is more rain than most places in Britain get in a year.

So close are the mountains to the sea that there is no chance for a major river to develop between the Spean to the north and the Orchy to the south. All the rivers in this area are spate rivers, rising and falling as quickly as a change in the weather. One section of one river alone is best in dry conditions and it is the best of them all – the Middle Etive. The Upper and Lower Etive, Coe and Nevis must all be paddled in monsoon conditions and they provide excellent, sometimes the only, sport to be had in a region as famed for its 'bad' weather as its beauty. And there are many other smaller streams not described here – for instance, the Kiachnish and Scaddle which face each other across Loch Linnhe – that are worth a look when the mountains are lost in mizzle.

RIVER ETIVE

The Etive rises in Rannoch Moor on the 300-metre contour and after just 20 kilometres flows into the sea at Loch Etive. This enormous height loss is achieved through a series of rapids and waterfalls concentrated in the middle section of the river. Due to the ferocious nature of the Middle Etive one should avoid it when there is much surface run-off. Indeed one of the attractions of this

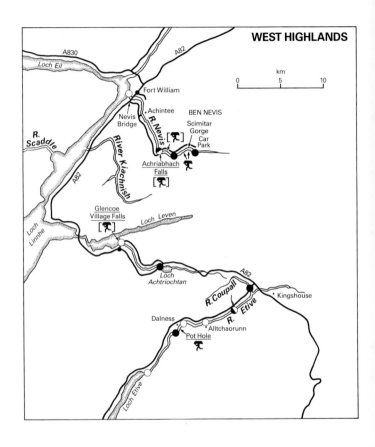

WEST HIGHLANDS

A830

Loch Eil

A82

Fort William

Achintee

BEN NEVIS

Nevis
Bridge

R. Nevis

Scimitar
Gorge
Car
Park

R. Scaddle

River Kiachnish

Achriabhach
Falls

Glencoe
Village Falls

Loch Leven

Loch
Linnhe

Loch
Achtriochtan

A82

R. Coupall

R. Etive

Kingshouse

Dalness

Alltchaorunn

Pot Hole

Loch Etive

km

0   5   10

The Etive and other rivers of Glencoe and Ben Nevis

section is that it provides technically difficult canoeing when other rivers in the area are dry.

In the Upper and Lower Etive, however, the more gentle gradient demands high water to make canoeing worthwhile. The short distance from source to sea means that the Etive rises and falls very quickly. It is best therefore to wait until the rain arrives before canoeing the upper or lower sections.

The level of the Etive can be judged at the Triple Fall, the first rapid on the hard section. If the first drop on this three-tier waterfall can *only* be shot on the right (between the midstream rock and the wall) then the middle section is at a good level. If on the other hand this drop can be shot anywhere, it will probably be too high for comfort – better to go for the Upper or Lower Etive or the Orchy.

Even if you are disappointed by the level of the river, the Glen is an experience in itself. Towering, heathery, sometimes snow-capped hillsides drop at a gradient of 1 in 2 from Buchaille Etive Mor (1022 metres), Meall a Bhuiridh (1108 metres) and Chasaig (862 metres) into this narrowest of valleys. The perspective is quite daunting and few other landscapes in this country will make you feel so small and insignificant.

Upper Etive

Confluence with River Coupall (243.542) to road-bridge (219.520)
Grade IIb
No Portages
3.5 Kilometres
OS Sheet 41

The road down Glen Etive crosses the Coupall just above its confluence with the Etive. This is the recommended access at normal levels but in high water the Coupall adds an enjoyable although somewhat harder 3 kilometres from Lagangarbh (IIIc). Just above the confluence with the Etive, the Coupall thunders over a difficult fall (Ve). This is easily seen from the road and should probably be portaged. There is an even harder fall on the

Etive above its confluence with the Coupall which has probably been paddled but, to normal mortals, militates against starting that river at the Kingshouse Hotel.

Below the Etive–Coupall confluence, the Upper Etive passes over shingle beds and through shallow gorges without too much fuss or froth. Most of it can be seen from the road on the way down. If you have bumped and scraped a plastic smear down this section, you may want to continue over the first waterfall on the Middle Etive and so on down that section of river. If the river is up, however, you will want to stop well before this. A warning is given by a sheep trolley over the river 200 metres above the waterfall. The actual get-out is marked by the road-bridge over a small subsidiary stream coming in from the right. You can leave your car in a passing-place obvious from the river; obvious too to passing sheep who like to nestle against the warmth of the engine block.

Middle Etive ***
Road-bridge (219.520) to Dalness Falls (172.511)
Grade Ve (VIf)
No Portages (?)
5 Kilometres
OS Sheet 41

This is a very beautiful section of river, both in terms of scenery and canoeing. The rock resists the river with all its strength, the land closes in around it and the river has to run the gauntlet of plunge and drop, squeeze and overhang, gorge and gully, in the fight to escape to the sea. To follow the river on its weaving and dodging flight requires the utmost cunning and strength, and just a pinch of idiocy, for there, beside you all the way, is the road.

The track was built by a nineteenth-century entrepreneur who wanted this wild and narrow place for his own. Fortunately he was a few centuries too late for his fantasies to achieve reality. Fortunate too that the river is too small and steep for trout or salmon, otherwise perhaps money would still try to buy the excitement and splendour of the water.

The Middle Etive is characterized by a series of big falls interspersed with smaller, less defined rapids. Reference to the larger, named falls will help you to keep track of your position on the river. If in doubt, drive down the road and 'suss' them out beforehand. This section should only be attempted in low water and it is described and graded for those conditions. The character of the drops changes dramatically as the river rises during and immediately after heavy rain.

The first rapid Triple Fall (Ve) is very obvious from the road. It contains a number of glutinous eddies and stoppers, so close bank support is recommended. The next big fall, Letterbox (Ve), is very ragged at the top and at the bottom! A line tight to the left bank, left of the weird slot on the lip – the Letterbox – offers the best chance of avoiding a crash-landing. A short way downstream is Ski Jump (IVd), a pleasant chute into a plunge pool. Easier water then leads down to the next big one, Crack of Doom (IVe). The entrance to this fall is a very narrow channel about a metre wide leading into the froth-filled gully between the large central rock on the left and a rock wall on the right. Once through the gully with a couple of tight turns, an easy although quite big drop leads into the large pool below.

The next fall, Crack of Dawn (Ve), has been the scene of a number of pinning incidents in recent years. The 'pool' beneath the drop is very shallow, a fact that cannot be ascertained from the bank. Careful probing of the pool will help you decide whether it is worth the risk. A relatively easy section of 100 metres follows. The Rock Slide (IVd) provides a wild ride down the left-hand side of a rock ledge into a big pool. Care should now be taken as the next section ends in a very big drop (6–7 metres). It is worth checking the location of the Waterfall (Ve) from the car, although the appearance of trees on the bank gives an indication of its approach from the river. The run-in to the fall is more difficult, although much less scary, than the drop itself and many people prefer to launch off the rock immediately above the lip. The boils in the plunge pool can push you up against the wall on the left.

A series of easy boulder fields follow the Waterfall, with one harder rapid ending in a constriction (IVd). This fairly long section of easier water ends just above Alltchaorunn with a difficult rapid ending in a vertical drop of 2 metres (Vd). Rescue above and below the final fall is comparatively easy because, by now, the river and valley have opened out considerably. The bridge at Alltchaorunn (197.512) is a good a place to get out if you anticipate portaging the Grade VIf at Dalness since a long flat section lies ahead.

Just above Dalness the river breaks away from the road and a series of waterfalls drops steeply under a bridge. This rarely-canoed series of drops is appropriately named the Pot Hole (VIf) for it has the atmosphere of a subterranean river. The three falls taken in sequence, culminating in an 8-metre plunge, are extremely technical and serious. One look over the bridge into the Pot Hole will be enough to persuade all but the stoutest hearts and keenest minds to portage.

Lower Etive **
Dalness (166.508) to Loch Etive (116.455)
Grade IIc (IVd)
No Portages
10 Kilometres
OS Sheets 41 and 42

Because of its length, this is preferred to the upper section as a day trip. It lacks the Etive's distinctive narrow gauge feel: the hills have drawn back and the river floods and braids. But the scenery remains outstanding, and there is the odd blind corner and the occasional short gorge to remind you of the water's tumultuous history.

Access is most convenient ½ kilometre below the Pot Hole at Dalness where the road comes close to the river on a bend. From there 2 kilometres of straightforward canoeing lead to Lake Falls (IVd), a big rapid requiring some technical ability to get the best line. The Lake Falls are visible from the road just upstream of a lake perched above the river. Below Lake Falls is a small, placid gorge. In very high water this disappears, and Lake Falls becomes Ve.

Enjoyable, easy water continues down to the loch. A few little surprises, all of them pleasant, keep the paddler on his toes; the higher the water, the better. Egress is to the road on the right just before the river enters the loch. Strong south-westerly winds blowing up the loch can make the last 2 kilometres less of a placid float than the gentle gradient promises.

RIVER COE

The valley of Glencoe is infamous in Scottish history as the site of the massacre of the Macdonalds by the Campbells. It is famous to tourists for its outstanding beauty and a mecca for climbers for its winter ice and summer rock. But the river in the valley floor has been largely ignored by canoeists which is understandable because of its extreme level of difficulty. With the advent of ultra-short plastic boats this section of the Coe will no doubt become fashionable territory. For the moment, however, it remains the preserve of a very few and I have no first-hand knowledge of descents.

Below Loch Actriochtan, where the hills drop back and the valley bottom flattens out, there is a more amenable section of river. The Lower Coe is still hard but only in parts, and the two hardest falls may be easily portaged. The upper section is obvious on the drive up the A82 but although the road follows the river lower down many of the falls are hidden from view. Frequent bank inspection is recommended. Like the Upper and Lower Etive, the Coe needs heavy and continuous rain or snow-melt to bring it into condition.

Coe *
Loch Achtriochtan (140.568) to Loch Leven (098.592)
Grade IVd (Ve)
1 Portage (?)

7 Kilometres
OS Sheet 41

From Loch Actriochtan bouncy rapids (IVc) lead under the A82 bridge and on down to Backdoor Man (Ve). This is obvious from both the A82 and the backroad down to the Clachaig Inn, but not all that obvious from the river. Inspection is vital here to avoid the no-go area on the left. A small, slightly worrying slot follows the main fall and then easier water, with one bigger rapid (IVd), leads down to the start of Coe Gorge (IVd).

Coe Gorge begins just below the Glencoe visitor centre (perched high on the left bank). It is ½ kilometre long with vertical sides and is quite scary in big water. Prior inspection is necessary to check for trees. The gorge peters out before a major tributary, the Fionn Ghleann, enters from the left.

The Coe swings away from the A82, below the confluence with the Fionn Ghleann and there are two more difficult drops (IVd) which need inspecting. The river then becomes broad and flat as far as Glencoe village. To avoid this less interesting last 4 kilometres it is possible to get out where the river again comes close to the A82 opposite the Glencoe camp- and caravan-site (113.576).

The Coe has a final spurt of energy below Bridge of Coe. An easy rapid succeeds the bridge and then a stratum of harder rock forces the whole river over, through, and *under* a little narrow gorge – Glencoe Village Falls (Vf). This has been responsible for at least one drowning and the jutting fins of rock and bubbling siphons demand a measure of respect not obvious from casual inspection. Canoeists are recommended to portage this rapid. Egress is at the road-bridge downstream where the Coe collapses into the salty arms of Loch Leven.

RIVER NEVIS

The Nevis is a powerful spate river of extreme contrasts. At the limit of road access (and above) it is exceptionally difficult and rarely paddled in its entirety. Below the first foot-bridge downstream it is still difficult, but less serious and continuous, and below the bridge at Achriabhach the river settles into a leisurely scenic paddle.

Upper Nevis **
End of road (167.691) or foot-bridge (158.684) to Achriabhach Falls (145.684)
Grade Ve (VIe)
Some Portages
2.5 or 1.5 Kilometres
OS Sheet 41

Access to this classic spate run is either from the end of the Glen Nevis road, or from the foot-bridge lower down – just before the road starts climbing steeply into the upper valley. The second access provides easier canoeing by avoiding Scimitar Gorge (VIe) which includes two drops that are usually portaged.

   Below the foot-bridge a 'mad mile' of continuously exciting but gradually easing water finishes at a difficult rapid with a narrow final slot. Some 300 metres downstream is Achriabhach Falls (Ve), the waterfall under the road-bridge. Many will want to portage this waterfall although it is sometimes paddled. It marks the end of the difficult upper section of the river.

Lower Nevis *
Achriabhach Falls (145.684) to Nevis Bridge (112.742)
Grade IIb (IVd)
No Portages
8 Kilometres
OS Sheet 41

Access to this section is from the right bank below the exit gully of Achriabhach Falls. A more exciting start to the run can be made by putting into the gully immediately below the Falls and canoeing the little rock shelves (IIIc). Below this the Nevis is straightforward with only a few shingle beds and sharp bends to create the odd minor disturbance. The only exception is a rapid near the bottom, Roaring Mill (IVc). This is obvious from the road and river, and is easily portaged by beginners. Egress from the Lower Nevis is on the outskirts of Fort William to the Achintee Road on the right or, with more difficulty, on the left at Nevis Bridge.

The Orchy and other rivers of the South-West Highlands

If water is plentiful and you only have time to paddle one river in Scotland, it must be the Orchy. It is the classic big water river of Britain, with something for everyone: long rolling rapids with play holes and surfing waves, challenging heavy falls that test the best reactive skills, and awe-inspiring waterfalls where some will paddle and more will take pictures.

If you are on holiday or living in the area it is also worth taking in three excellent rivers further south. The Awe is a dam-controlled river which is bouncy fun in full flood. The Fyne and Aray are parallel tributaries of Loch Fyne and share a more technical character. The latter has gained something of a reputation as a test-piece.

RIVER ORCHY

Despite its reputation as a scary ride, the Orchy is a friendly river. The glaciers of the West Highland ice-cap carved a broad path for the river and its tributaries, so the glens are wide open and share beautiful moorland vistas across to the uplands of Lochaber and Argyll. More important for the canoeist, the banks are usually low and access is therefore easy for inspection, rescue or portage.

The middle section of the Orchy is the one to which everyone aspires. The Bridge of Orchy which marks the put-in has a useful river level gauge (downstream side, right bank). The river can be run when it is above 0 on the gauge, while 2 and above indicate high water with some rapids increasing in difficulty by as much as a grade. In high water the upper section of the Orchy is recommended and, even at moderate levels, both upper and lower sections provide good entertainment for the intermediate paddler.

Upper Orchy **
Loch Tulla (291.418) to Bridge of Orchy (297.396)
Grade IIIb

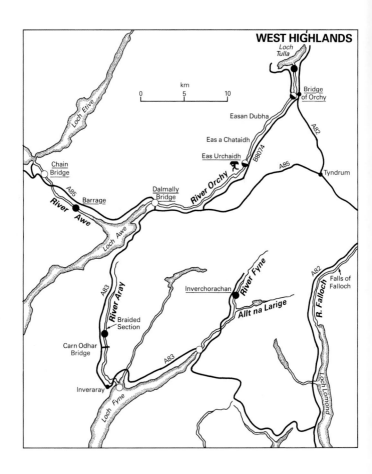

The Orchy and other rivers of the South-West Highlands

No Portages
3 Kilometres
OS Sheet 50

Described by local paddlers as one of the best Grade IIIb sections in Scotland, it has certainly suffered by comparison with its more prestigious successor. In high water this is a great stretch with some particularly fine surf waves and at the end, just above the bridge, a meaty rapid with powerful stoppers half-way across the river.

Access to Loch Tulla is easiest from the West Highland Way (B8005) which follows the right bank of the river. This part of the Glen is even more open than the rest of the river and the drive up and paddle down the Upper Orchy offer fine views of dark waterlogged Rannoch Moor to the north, and the often snow-capped Beinn an Dothaidh (1,000 metres) and Beinn Dorain (1,074 metres) to the east. Egress is below or above the rapid at the Bridge of Orchy where there is a handy pub and bunkhouse.

Middle Orchy ***
Bridge of Orchy (297.396) to Eas Urchaidh (242.321)
Grade Ve
No Portages
10 Kilometres
OS Sheet 50

The Middle Orchy varies in character perhaps more dramatically than any other river in this guide, so it seems appropriate on this very popular section of river to give two grades for each rapid: one for low water (LW) and one for high water (HW). Low water is defined as when the river level is less than 1 on the gauge at the Bridge of Orchy, while high water is more than 2. There are three rapids which are Ve at any canoeable level, but the 'married-with-two-children-and-a-mortgage' paddler should not be put off since they can all be easily portaged.

To begin with you will wonder what all the excitement is about.

There is little of consequence for 1½ kilometres, even after a major tributary, Allt Kinglass, enters from the left (the B8074 first joins the river here, also on the left, and remains comfortably close for the rest of the trip). Shortly thereafter, however, there is clearly something different on the menu. A huge rocky ledge stretches from right to left across the river and the water cascades over it in an impressive mantle of white. This is the first of many pool-drop rapids in the steepening glen (IIIc LW, IVc HW).

The subsequent rapids in order of descent are Big Rock (IVc LW, IVd HW), sometimes called Chicken Shoot if the main difficulty is avoided by going down the left (IIIc LW, IIId HW); Sheep Trolley Gorge, a long rapid ending in a big hole on the right towards which the paddler must work – good 'enders' below (IIIc LW, IVd HW); and Easan Dubha, the first of the meanies (Ve LW/HW). Easan Dubha has been run every which way and at all levels, but in low water a line down left (watch out for boils and underwater ledges) or over the central rock seems sensible, while in high water the evil-looking right-hand channel goes well if you can control your nerves on the run-in.

In high water there is a danger of swimmers from Easan Dubha being washed down the next big rapid, Sore Tooth (IIId LW, IVd HW). In any event, it is worth inspecting this long, ragged rapid before you shoot Easan Dubha because the high adrenalin levels generated in the successful descent of the Grade Ve will urge you down anything 'easier' without delay. In Sore Tooth a line down the left is easiest in high water because it avoids the big curling stoppers, but in low water you are forced right.

Sore Tooth is followed by Roller Coaster (IIIc LW, IVc HW) and, after a braided section away from the road, the End of Civilization (IVc LW, IVd HW). This is the longest rapid on the Orchy, but don't be too put off by the name – there are no neolithic stoppers round the corner. The best line is down the left bank through two big waves and some fast bouncy water. A big island follows and then about a kilometre of easier water leads to

The gripping lefthand run at Eas a Chataidh on the Middle Orchy

Eas a Chataidh (Ve LW/HW). Get out in plenty of time to inspect when you hear its roar, for here the end of civilization is a more distinct possibility.

Eas a Chataidh can be shot right or left, or in high water by a channel over the huge central rock. Opinions differ about which of the two sides is best and there is no reason why my opinion should be preferred so I will refrain from giving it. The choice is between a 5-metre drop into a sucking backtow (right), or a 2-metre drop followed by a long curving ramp over jagged rocks (left). The high water central line is fairly straightforward (when it is possible) but has awesome consequences if you miss the entrance channel. Those who have portaged can seal launch on the left into the narrow gorge below.

Witches Step (IVc LW/HW) is the next rapid, preceded by an excellent play stopper on the left. Witches Step is also on river left, and the stopper below it flushes through nicely. The fall on the right is incomplete except in very high water. The road has now rejoined the river, and offers a way out to the egress point at the bridge below Eas Urchaidh. You will certainly want to inspect and probably portage this massive drop, so get out on the left in plenty of time when the bridge comes into view.

Eas Urchaidh, otherwise known as the Falls of Orchy, are only regularly shot on the extreme right by a narrow, rocky and quite steep 'chicken' chute (Ve LW/HW). Taken through its guts, the waterfall would have to be VIf if anything. Whether canoed or just viewed, these falls are a suitably awe-inspiring finish to a brilliant section of river.

Lower Orchy *
Eas Urchaidh (242.321) to Dalmally Bridge (165.276)
Grade IIIc
No Portages
10 Kilometres
OS Sheet 50

This is an excellent run for intermediate paddlers, particularly in high water when a fast flow eats up the considerable distance and gives big waves in a number of rapids. It can be extended by another 4 kilometres to Loch Awe, where the best egress is Lochawe village hall (131:281) on the west shore. However this last section is largely flat (Grade Ib) and very open to the wind, and is therefore not recommended.

Put in just below the bridge at Eas Urchaidh, just above a weir which is taken through the centre. A number of bouncy rapids – relatively easy in a kayak but quite intimidating for open canoes – lead down to the old suspension bridge at Catnish. Here is another river gauge. If it reads more than 3 the Orchy is high; if it reads 0 or less it is low.

The next 4 kilometres are very easy, mainly shingle rapids but the superb scenery more than makes up for it. A kilometre after the Catnish bridge, the forest, which has been following the right bank of the river ever since Loch Tulla, finally gives out. Two kilometres of open glen and hill on the other bank are vouchsafed before the forestry commission does the dirty again.

Shortly after the forest starts there is a lonely house, also on the left bank (202.284). An obvious braided section follows and then a long set of rapids with some powerful stoppers forming over ledges in high water. This is the last of the difficulties before Dalmally Bridge. Whether you get out here or in Loch Awe, take five minutes to look around the remains of Kilchurn Castle (132.276) built in 1440 and occupying the spit of land jutting into Loch Awe's north-eastern arm.

RIVER AWE

The Awe is not one of the great touring rivers of Scotland but nevertheless useful to have 'up one's sleeve' because a (canoeable) release from the barrage is guaranteed by statutory limits. The Awe improves with a high release or after heavy rain because of in-fill from the side streams. There is a gauge under the old bridge 2 kilometres downstream of the barrage. If this reads 20 the Awe is at a reasonable minimum level (Grade IIb) – a level which is maintained by releases even in dry summer weather; at 25 the river is quite a bit better (reaching Grade IIIb in the slalom site);

and at 40 (flood level) there are haystacks through the slalom site and fast chunky water elsewhere (IIIb).

Traditionally access to the Awe has been hassle free, but when the BCU Wild Water Racing Committee paid £1,900 to the Awe Fishery Board to secure access for the 1988 Europa Cup Final, it created quite unrealistic expectations amongst local landowners and fishermen about the value of canoe access on the Awe. It will take a generation before this erroneous impression is finally changed. Meanwhile local clubs, centres and individuals are regularly denied access to the river because they cannot match the southern medal-hunters' gold. Such is the long-term price of meeting the anglers' short-term price. Beware the paying precedent!

Awe
Grade IIIb
Barrage (045.288) to Chain Bridge (018.314)
No Portages
5 Kilometres
OS Sheet 50

The Awe flows from the Awe Barrage at the end of Loch Awe to Loch Etive a distance of 6 kilometres. Access is from a lay-by at the barrage. The river is a fast, bouncy ride with a few harder sections. After 2 kilometres there are road and railway bridges and beneath them the slalom site. This is the best of the Awe providing big big waves in flood. A short open gorge section follows and then more rapids. The river eases over the last kilometre of the run.

The egress point, a chain bridge across the river, could not be more obvious. Get out on the left bank and walk across a field for about 100 metres to a track. To reach this point drive along the A85 in the direction of Oban, keeping an eye out for the track (on the right) which leads off from a fast left-hand bend.

The last drop on Granite Falls on the River Fyne in low water

It is possible to continue down the Awe into Loch Etive to get out at the jetty on the left. There is a succession of dangerous weirs below the chain bridge all of which should be portaged (left bank). A sign below the chain bridge reading 'No boating beyond this point' warns of the danger.

RIVER FYNE

This small spate river offers tight, technical canoeing in splendid wild country. The road that runs beside it is privately owned and permission to use it should be sought from Glenfyne Estate; it is most likely to be granted outside the fishing season.

Fyne *
Inverchorachan (228.179) to Loch Fyne (193.125)
Grade IIIc (Ve)
No Portages
8 Kilometres
OS Sheet 50

The hardest and best of the Fyne is above Glenfyne Lodge but so is the toughest driving and where you get in may be determined as much by the state of your vehicle as your paddling ability. If you can make it put in near a solitary white cottage at a flattening in the valley called Inverchorachan.

In the kilometre from Inverchorachan to the confluence with the Alt na Lairige (entering from the left) the Fyne is a superb mountain river. The opening triple Granite Falls (Ve) are technical and spectacular with the 15-metre deep 'black hole' waiting with open arms below the middle fall. A short way below Granite Falls is the difficult and serious shallow ramped Salmon Ladder (Ve) with boulders blocking the exits.

After the confluence with the Alt na Lairige, the Fyne is continuously difficult but never desperate down to the bridge below Glenfyne Lodge (214.148). Egress here or continue on flat water to Loch Fyne where the A83 crosses the river's tiny estuary.

RIVER ARAY

The Aray is part of a very efficient drainage basin and therefore rises and falls very quickly. In high flood the river is a brown, churning channel of liquid excitement and its three major falls become portages (or VIfs). In medium flow, for which this description is written and graded, all the falls are possible. In low water the Aray is not canoeable.

   The Aray has one great advantage over its eastern neighbour the Fyne; it has a main road running parallel to it (A819) so access problems are minimized. It is possible to canoe from a higher point than described here but low branches and trees may well rearrange your face.

Aray *
Braided section (086.144) to Inveraray Pier (091.085)
Grade IVd (Ve)
No Portages
6 Kilometres
OS Sheet 50

Access is at the braided section (marked on OS map) next to the road. This is 1½ kilometres above a wire foot-bridge opposite the small summit of Carn Odhar (166 metres).

   An easy section, sometimes blocked by trees, lasts for about 1 kilometre. This is followed by the lead-in to the Falls of Aray (Ve) under the Carn Odhar foot-bridge. An eddy on the left above the Falls allows inspection and, if necessary, portaging (carry over bridge and put in below on the right). The Falls are difficult and serious down the right, and terminal on the left.

   The Aray is now more straightforward for a kilometre down to Three Bridges. The difficult fall (Ve) of the same name just below may be run on the right or portaged on the left. On the excellent subsequent 2 kilometres down to Carloonan Mill Falls the white water is continuous but not too hard (IVc).

   Carloonan Mill Falls (IVd) should be inspected for it is awkward

at any level, particularly the shallow top-drop which can pin
canoes. From here the Aray could be described as a pool–weir
river, for there is a succession of weirs (all safe) preceded by open
pools where the river has ponded. Egress is to Inveraray Pier after
passing under two bridges into Loch Fyne.

The Leny and other rivers of the Central Highlands

Three routes lead north through the Central Highlands of Scotland. The A82, the western route out of Glasgow along Loch Lomond, will take you past the impressive Falls of Falloch. The central route is the A84 out of Stirling through Callander; it passes the Falls of Leny, and, by a small extension (the A827), the Falls of Dochart at Killin. These three rapids are well known to paddlers specializing in 'one-offs' but the Leny is the most attractive of the three as a canoeing river. The Falloch, including the Falls, is Grade VIf with portages from the Elbow (370.238), while at the other extreme the Dochart, apart from the Falls (IVe), is Grade Ia.

The third route is the skiers' way up the A9, on the east coast; from this road the rivers Allan, Tay, Tummel and eventually the Garbh Ghaoir/Gaur are accessible. The Allan, and more especially the Tay, will appeal to those looking for more gentle white water. The Tummel and its tributary the Garbh Ghaoir/Gaur are more continuous which, in the case of the Garbh/Gaur, is fortunate because their white water is at the end of a long and tortuous drive.

RIVER LENY

It is only a short paddle from Loch Lubnaig to Callander but it will seem a lot longer than 5 kilometres. The Falls of Leny alone are worth thirty minutes of inspection and protection and the rapids above and below will detain any who like to 'play'. The river is best in high water, and indeed may not be canoeable in a drought.

Leny **
Loch Lubnaig (585.092) to Callander (626.079)
Grade IVd (Ve)
No Portages
5 Kilometres
OS Sheet 51

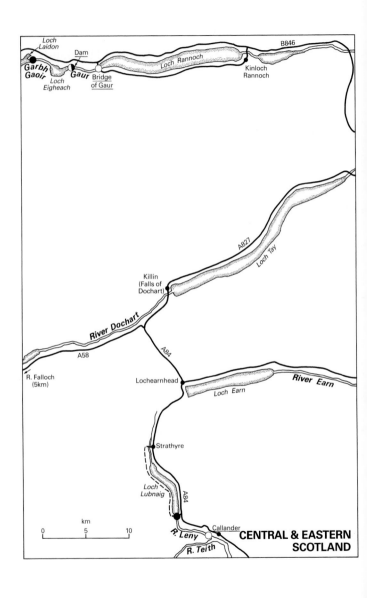

Loch
Laidon
Dam
Garbh
Gaoir
Loch
Eigheach
Gaur
Bridge
of Gaur
Loch Rannoch
Kinloch
Rannoch
B846

A827
Loch Tay

Killin
(Falls of
Dochart)

River Dochart

A58
A84

R. Falloch
(5km)

Lochearnhead
Loch Earn
River Earn

Strathyre

Loch
Lubnaig
A84

km
0   5   10

R. Leny
Callander

R. Teith

**CENTRAL & EASTERN
SCOTLAND**

Access to the Leny is from the public car-park at the foot of Loch Lubnaig. The river is immediately big and bouncy and the first rapids provide a good warm-up for the Falls of Leny below.

The approach of the Falls of Leny (Ve) is indicated by the second broken bridge and a spume of spray. They may be easily inspected from a catwalk on the left-hand side, and portaged on either bank. They are usually shot on the left of the central island, since the right-hand side consists of a big drop. The two channels reform below the island to run down a gully ending in a very worrying and unpredictable stopper.

Below the Falls there are two meaty rapids (IVd) with plenty to shout about for those who have chosen the portage above. The Leny then gradually eases off until it joins the River Teith for the run into Callander. In high water it is the Teith that looks like the tributary, not the Leny, and the lasting impression that most people take from the swamped pavements of the Leny's Callander shore is of the amazing power and weight of this short river.

It is possible to continue down the Teith for a further 8 kilometres or, indeed, begin an easy trip from the above recommended egress point – Callander car-park. The Teith here is a good novice river (Grade IIb) except for two weirs (inspect). The whitest natural water is at Torrie Rapid about half-way down; it is used for slaloms. Egress is at Deanston distillery on the right bank ½ kilometre above the A84 bridge.

RIVER TUMMEL

The River Tummel is a short tributary entering the Tay just south of Pitlochry. Access to this section of the Tummel north-west of Pitlochry is from the B8019. The river is dam-controlled and if there is only compensation water flowing, the rapids become technically easier although a few become so rocky that they must be portaged.

The Leny, Garbh Gaoir/Gaur and surrounding rivers

Tummel
Clunie Dam (883.604) to Loch Faskally (913.498)
Grade IVd (Vd)
No Portages (?)
5 Kilometres
OS Sheets 43 and 52

Two hundred metres east of the road to the Clunie Dam a gap in
the forest leads down to the north bank of the river (follow the
power lines). The river begins easily but becomes progressively
harder down to Sawmill Falls (IVd). The Tummel is then
somewhat easier before another even harder section at the end of
the run – the Linn of Tummel (Vd). This should be inspected and
if necessary portaged.

RIVER GARBH GHAOIR/GAUR

The Garbh Ghaoir flows out of the great wetness that is Rannoch
Moor. It does not depend on man to make it canoeable and can
sometimes be run when the Gaur Dam is not releasing. It is a
beautiful start to the Gaur.
    Unlike its tributary, the Gaur cannot be paddled unless its dam
is generating. To find out whether the Gaur Dam is releasing,
phone the Tummel Valley hydro control centre at Tummel Bridge.
Heavy rain tends to encourage a release.

Garbh Ghaoir/Gaur *
*Loch Laidon (418.577) to Loch Eigheach (447.578) or Bridge of
Gaur (501.567)*
Grade IIIc (IVc)
No Portages
4 or 9 Kilometres
OS Sheet 51

Rivers Tay and Allan

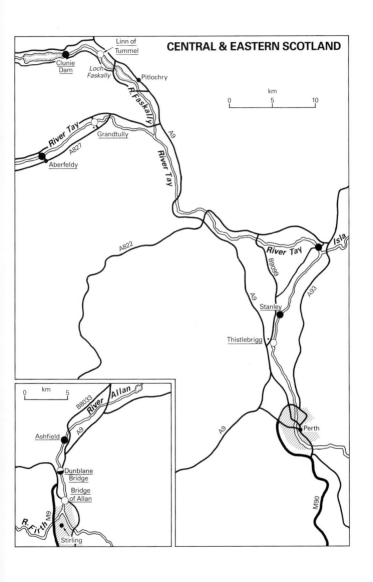

CENTRAL & EASTERN SCOTLAND

Linn of Tummel

Clunie Dam

Loch Faskally

Pitlochry

R. Faskally

River Tay

A827

Grandtully

Aberfeldy

A822

A9

River Tay

River Tay

Isla

B9099

A93

A9

Stanley

Thistlebrigg

A9

Perth

M90

km
0   5   10

km
0   5

River Allan

B8033

A9

Ashfield

Dunblane Bridge

Bridge of Allan

R. Firth

M9

Stirling

The River Garbh Ghaoir runs for 4 kilometres from Loch Laidon to Loch Eigheach. A short carry from Rannoch station will bring you to the remote and beautiful Loch Laidon. Paddle south-west down the lake for about a kilometre until the river leads out. After 2 kilometres the Garbh Ghaoir runs under the railway and from there follows interesting and quite continuous white water. Egress either to the north shore of Loch Eigheach or, if the Gaur is running, carry round the dam.

The first rapid on the Gaur is the hardest (IVc) on either river and is easily seen from the road 1½ kilometre below the power station. The rest of the river is remarkably continuous at the grade and, if a big release is on, you may well want to go back for more.

RIVER TAY

The Tay is not a great white water river but it does have the advantage of almost always being canoeable in low water. There are two sections worth considering and both are good introductions to white water. Grandtully Rapid is the best rapid on either section and famous as the site of national slalom competitions, while the easily accessible Stanley to Thistlebrigg section is the most frequently paddled river trip in Scotland.

Upper Tay
Aberfeldy (851.491) to Grandtully (915.533)
Grade IIIc
No Portages
10 Kilometres
OS Sheet 43

Grandtully Rapid (IIIc) is the site of major slalom competitions and has been canoed by most Scottish paddlers at one time or another. The rest of the section is much more straightforward but not without interest. Access is in Aberfeldy on the upstream side of Wade Bridge on the south bank. Egress is to the lay-by east of Grandtully on the south bank.

Lower Tay
Stanley (119.337) to Thistlebrigg (108.320)
Grade IIId
No Portages
4 Kilometres
OS Sheet 53

Access is from the caravan-site at Stanley (reached from the B9099 8 kilometres north of Perth). It is also possible to put in further upstream at the Bridge of Isla thus taking in the notorious whirlpools of Campsie Linn (IIIe) but this is not recommended.

The only hazard on the section below the caravan-site is a partially destroyed weir – Stanley Weir (IIId). The weir has a large number of metal spikes in it and should be inspected – avoid the easy-looking shoot on the far left. Below the weir there is fairly continuous white water with the best rapid (IIIb) just above the take-out. Egress at Thistlebrigg is up some steps to a lay-by (B9099) on the right bank.

RIVER ALLAN

The River Allan is a small tributary of the River Forth, joining the latter just north of Stirling. Due to its small watershed it requires heavy rain to make it canoeable. In that condition the section near Dunblane described below provides a continuously enjoyable run.

One other stretch of white water is worth mentioning for those in the vicinity of Perth and Stirling. This is on the River Earn which flows mostly flat from Loch Earn to the sea. The stretch between the A822 Crieff Bridge (858.209) and the B8062 Kinkell Bridge (935.166) has a series of weirs difficult enough (up to Grade IIId) in flood to provide excitement for the white water paddler.

Allan *
Ashfield (786.039) to Bridge of Allan (788.976)
Grade IIIc (IVd)

No Portages (?)
6 Kilometres
OS Sheet 57

Access is from a small road leading down to the river at Ashfield.
If you are travelling north on the A9 turn off onto B8033 towards
Kinbuch and take the first left. The hardest fall, Mill Falls (IVd),
is near the start just below a 3-metre weir (some will want to
portage the latter). The water runs alongside the mill walls and
then drops steeply over a shelf. There are a number of other
shootable weirs on the way down to Dunblane Bridge which is the
half-way spot and an alternative access and egress point (781.010).
The lower part of the river consists of a number of long rapids in a
wooded section and then a harder fall (IIIc) a little way above the
finish.

The North Esk and other rivers of the Eastern Highlands

The Lower North Esk provides the best white water canoeing of a handful of good spate rivers in the eastern Highlands of Scotland. These other rivers are well worth considering if you have done the Lower North Esk, or on that particular day it is judged to be too high. If the North Esk is canoeable in its upper reaches, so will the best of its tributaries – the West Water. The two together provide an excellent day out.

Like its northern neighbours, the South Esk is a spate river. It is canoeable from Acharn to the sea at Montrose (60 kilometres) but only a short stretch in the middle is of interest to white water buffs. The most southerly of all these rain dependent rivers, the Blackwater, is perhaps the most serious. A number of good paddlers have run away from its gorge in high water.

All these rivers suffer the disadvantage of low summer levels. Those frustrated by a week of dry weather may want to consider an 8-kilometre section of the Royal Dee near Banchory. The river here is big and mature in the style of Middle and Lower Spey. It is tame by comparison to the twisting, falling, spate streams to the south and north but provides satisfying water in flood.

RIVER NORTH ESK

The North Esk is canoeable from Loch Lee to the sea, a distance of 40 kilometres. Below Gannochy Bridge, however, it is of little interest to the white water canoeist. He or she must wait for heavy rain or snow-melt to bring the river in Glen Esk into condition. But it is worth the wait for then the Esk provides two sections of exciting canoeing, of which the second and harder gorge is particularly good.

Upper North Esk
Loch Lee church (445.804) to Dalhastnie Bridge (542.787)

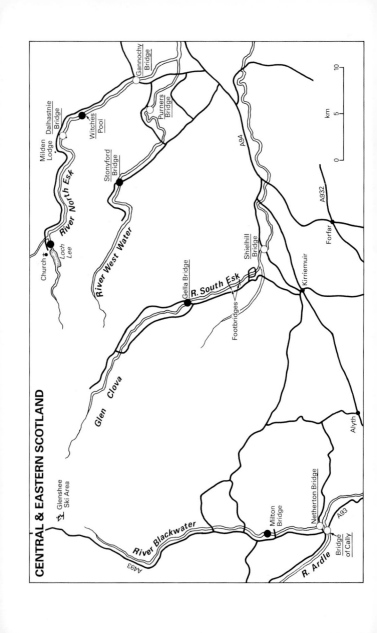

CENTRAL & EASTERN SCOTLAND

Glenshee
Ski Area

River North Esk

Loch Lee

Church

River West Water

Glen Clova

Gella Bridge

R. South Esk

Footbridges

Shielhill Bridge

Kirriemuir

Forfar

A932

A94

Gannochy Bridge

Purners Bridge

Dalhastnie Bridge

Witches Pool

Milden Lodge

Stonyford Bridge

Alyth

River Blackwater

Milton Bridge

Netherton Bridge

Bridge of Cally

R. Ardle

A93

A93

0   5   10
km

Grade IVd
3 (?) Portages
13 Kilometres
OS Sheet 44

A car-park at Loch Lee church provides access to the River Mark, 400 metres upstream of its confluence with the North Esk. If this tributary is canoeable, the rest of the river will be too.

There are four rapids of IVd to watch out for in the first 3 kilometres. The first is about 300 metres downstream of the confluence and is best shot on the left through a series of stoppers. The second is just below the foot-bridge at Whitehillocks, a very shallow drop which can pin and may have to be portaged. A kilometre downstream the Effock Burn enters from the right. This is a warning of the approach of the third fall which has two separate shoots often blocked by trees (possible portage). The fourth fall is at Dalbrack Bridge and is a straightforward plunge into a narrow pool.

The North Esk now becomes easier for 6 kilometres as far as Keenie Farm, where the river falls through a difficult bedrock step (IVe? or portage). The river then picks up speed, forming many sets of standing waves over the 4 kilometres to Dalhastnie Bridge (near Milden Lodge). The fall above the bridge is something of a boat-gobbler (IVd). It is possible to continue into the Lower North Esk by paddling the 8 kilometres between Dalhastnie Bridge and Witches' Pool but most will want to miss out this easy middle section (IIb).

Lower North Esk ***
Witches' Pool (573.754) to Gannachy Bridge (600.709)
Grade IVd (Ve)
No Portages
6 Kilometres
OS Sheet 44

Rivers North Esk, South Esk, West Water and Blackwater

Between Witches' Pool and Gannochy Bridge vertical schists of rock force the river through two narrow gorges. This provides the best canoeing on the river, continuous and quite hard. There is one major rapid – the Rocks of Solitude (Ve) – and a number of other sizeable drops. The Rocks of Solitude may be inspected by a path through the Burn on the left bank. If there is enough water to canoe the Rocks of Solitude, then the Lower North Esk is up.

The first gorge, which provides the best section of canoeing on the river (IVd), starts about a ½ kilometre below Witches' Pool. Access to the river can be made down through birch woods (vague footpath) where the road comes close to the right bank between Haughend and Craigoshina. The entrance to the gorge is guarded by a difficult two-tier fall which is followed by a constriction which can usually be taken either side of a rock in high water. Below is another awkward constriction which at most levels will force the paddler left. This is followed by a series of smaller drops. The last rapid on this section is some way below, consisting of a long shoot down into and through a smooth-sided rocky gorge.

The river now eases off for a couple of kilometres, giving the canoeist a chance to savour the lush green fields and shimmering copses of silver birch. The second gorge is guarded by the hardest fall on the river, the Rocks of Solitude (Ve), which should be inspected and if necessary portaged on the left. In medium water the river is funnelled into an enormous haystack on the right. This 'explodes', on average, every 9 seconds, so there is an element of luck in running the rapid. In my albeit limited experience, the haystack has never failed to spit people out into the narrow cleft below, so I hesitate to call it a stopper! In high water the 'wave' is even bigger but there is a shoot down the fish ladders on the left. In these conditions the lead-in is quite tricky and so inspection is even more crucial.

Below the Rocks of Solitude is a longer but easier rapid leading to a very narrow constriction (IIIc). A few more interesting rapids with small play stoppers lead to Gannachy Bridge. The steps next

The two-tier fall on the Lower North Esk

to the bridge on the left lead up through a door and on to the road. It is an unexpected but apt finish to a river full of surprises.

RIVER WEST WATER

The best place to check the level of the West Water and to inspect the hardest fall on it – the Loups – is to walk upstream from the picnic-site at the egress point. If the river is very high it may be better to finish above the Loups where the road comes close to the river (570.696). If the river is only at medium level you may want to start at Bridgend (536.683), thus shortening the trip by 6 kilometres. Whatever your decision you can always change your mind about the Loups when you get there.

West Water *
Stonyford Bridge (505.726) to Purners Bridge (579.688)
Grade IIIc (Ve)
No Portages
13 Kilometres
OS Sheet 44

The West Water from Stonyford to Bridgend is Grade IIIc with the hardest section near the top in a little gorge. Below Bridgend the river is easy for a couple of kilometres but then descends into a high, wide gorge for the last 5 kilometres to Purners Bridge. This gorge is not too hard apart from a two-tier waterfall at the top of a very narrow section towards the end – the Loups (Ve).

The Loups are dangerous because of the shallow plunge-pools and copious quantities of fish-netting in them. Egress to the road on the left above the Loups is possible. Immediately below the Loups, however, there is an interesting and enjoyable section of gorge which should not be missed. Egress is to the picnic-site below Purners (foot) Bridge.

RIVER SOUTH ESK

The South Esk is an excellent run on continuously hard but never desperate water.

South Esk *
Gella Bridge (372.652) to Shielhill Bridge (426.580)
Grade IIIc
No Portages
12 Kilometres
OS Sheets 44 and 54

Access is at the picnic-site beside the bridge at Gella. After 2 kilometres is a long, bouncy section of 300 metres in a small gorge. After 4 kilometres there is Elly foot-bridge. Between here and the next foot-bridge (1½ kilometres) is the Wall of Death, a left-hand bend where the main flow runs into some large boulders. From the second foot-bridge one can inspect the difficult ledge downstream which is the trickiest fall on the river – Sawmill Dam (IIIc). Below the *Dam*, the South Esk continues with less tension but much rocky interest all the way to Shielhill Bridge.

RIVER BLACKWATER

The appropriately named Blackwater (sometimes known as Sheewater) runs beside the A93 out of Glenshee (latterly famous for its ski runs). Its huge catchment area ensures that after heavy rain or indeed snow-melt, the Blackwater remains white (and black) for longer than neighbouring rivers. Near spate conditions are necessary to canoe the river, while in full flood some sections will need close inspection. The best place to judge the level is at Milton Falls. If these are shootable then the river is up; if the four falls have merged into one rapid the river is in flood.

Blackwater *
Milton Bridge (137.570) to Netherton Bridge (144.521)
Grade IVd

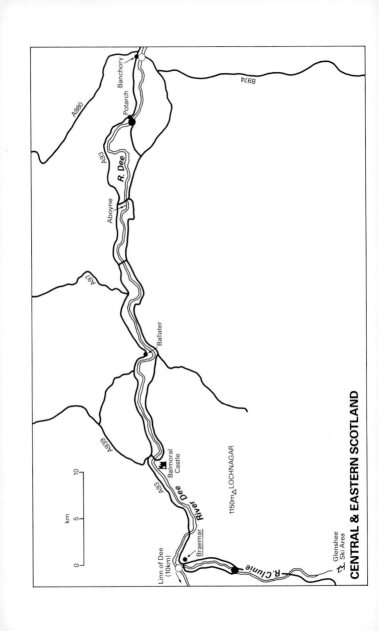

CENTRAL & EASTERN SCOTLAND

No Portages
6 Kilometres
OS Sheet 43

The access point is just above Milton Bridge which takes a minor road into Alyth Forest from the A93. Milton Falls (IVd), just above the bridge, are a difficult start to the day and will be a grade harder in flood. The Blackwater becomes much easier down to the small bridge near Persey House. A kilometre of blind, twisting drops (IIIb) leads to the short but excellent Ashmore Gorge (IVd). This is very difficult and serious in flood (Ve). The gorge soon opens out and easier paddling takes the canoeist down to a last exciting rapid at Netherton Bridge – Netherton Rapid (IVc).

Egress is downstream of Netherton Bridge on the left bank. Alternatively, it is possible to continue to the confluence with the Ardle, taking care to inspect a nasty 2-metre weir on the way. Egress is then from the Bridge of Cally ½ kilometre upsteam on the Ardle. For reasons unknown the river below the confluence of the Blackwater and Ardle is known as the Ericht. Whatever its name, the combined river is canoeable for a further 3 kilometres before a horrendous and hitherto uncanoed gorge bars the way.

ROYAL DEE

The Dee, called 'Royal' because it passes Balmoral Estate, is a classic, easy, big water, kayaking and canoeing river. It is also a major salmon fishing river and, if you don't want to be sent to the Tower of London for disturbing the Queen Mother's flies, it is best to canoe between October 1st and February 1st or on Sundays.

Given suitable water levels it is possible to canoe from the Linn of Dee above Braemar to the sea, a distance of 112 kilometres. This is a longish paddle in one day so a shorter section is recommended below: it takes in the best rapids on the river.

The Royal Dee

Dee **
Potarch Hotel (607.973) to Banchory Bridge (697.952)
Grade IIIb
No Portages
8 Kilometres
OS Sheet 45

Take a turning off the A93 for Potarch Hotel, 5 kilometres west of the Bridge of Canny. Above the bridge by Potarch Hotel is an excellent rapid – put in above or below. The river is easy for 3 or 4 kilometres below Potarch Hotel and then gradually increases in difficulty. Two notable rapids are Cairnton and Invercanny. The latter is good for playing and, having completed one run, it is a simple matter to carry up the bank for another. Below Invercanny Rapid it is straightforward down to the egress point at Banchory (and beyond).

Should the Dee be very high there will be white water sport near Braemar above the Linn of Dee. The Linn itself, however, is too dangerous to canoe. Another spate canoeing possibility which finishes in Braemar is the River Clunie, a tributary of the Dee. Access is near the ski area of Glenshee from a single-track road on the west bank of the river (turn west on the A93 and cross the Clunie by a petrol station in the village) or lower down the river. Egress is in Braemar below six good rapids of IIIc.

The Nith and other rivers of the Western Border Country

The English–Scottish border country between Carlisle and Glasgow (Dumfries and Galloway) is relatively unknown to canoeists apart from two rivers: the Nith and the Border Esk. Both are described below. Two other rivers are worth mentioning. The Ayr flowing out of the western hills is largely flat but provides a pleasant introductory trip from Stanlane to Mainholm (9 kilometres, Grade IIb). On the other hand the Mouse Water north-east of Lanark is harder, with two difficult gorges between Cleghorn Bridge and Mousemill Bridge (6 kilometres, Grade IVd).

Clearly this large area of hill country over 900 metres has many other white water possibilities. Local activists will have more information but whether they will (or should) part with their secrets is open to question. A minority response to my research for the guide particularly in Scotland has been chary. 'I do have reservations about passing the information on,' one paddler wrote. 'The correct place to put the information is in the hands of the SCA [Scottish Canoe Association].'

I mention this because I am aware of the respectable body of opinion which questions the value of guidebooks, either because they encourage insensitive use of 'local' rivers by 'outsiders' (however defined), or because they diminish the experience of canoeing 'unknown' stretches of river. I believe, however, that parochialism is no safegurd of the environment and although it may prolong the status quo over access this is not necessarily a good thing. As regards the 'adventure experience' canoeists do not have to read guidebooks and, even if they do, there are always more rivers and new levels of water to canoe.

RIVER NITH

The Nith rises in the hills of South Ayrshire, and flows south through the towns of New Cumnock, Sanquhar, Thornhill and

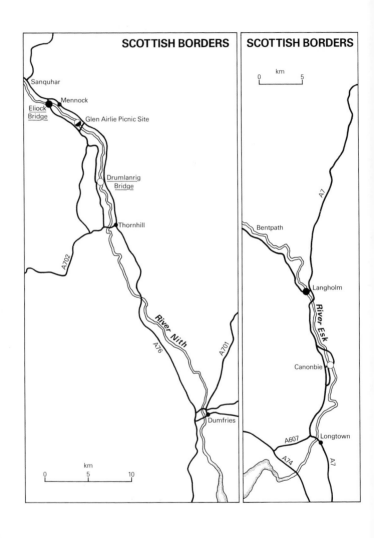

SCOTTISH BORDERS

Sanquhar
Mennock
Eliock
Bridge
Glen Airlie Picnic Site

Drumlanrig
Bridge

Thornhill

A702

River Nith

A76

A701

Dumfries

km
0   5   10

SCOTTISH BORDERS

km
0   5

A7

Bentpath

Langholm

River Esk

Canonbie

A607
Longtown

A74
A7

Dumfries, some 64 kilometres from source to the Solway Firth. Above Sanquhar and below Thornhill the river is flat and of no interest to white water canoeists. In between, however, there is an excellent 12-kilometre stretch of medium-grade water. It is easy for access (paralleled by the A76 Dumfries to Cumnock road) and frequently used as a white water race course. It is undoubtedly the best section of white water in the southern uplands.

The Nith is similar to the more mature rivers of the Lake District and North Wales, such as the Lune and the Dee, in that it is largely flat with only a short hard section of interest to the white water enthusiast. It requires heavy rain to make it worth paddling, often being uncanoeable in the summer. On the other hand, because it flows through a narrow gorge, the quality of the canoeing rises as fast as the water. A good indication of the river level is given by the gauge at Drumlanrig Bridge (the egress point for the Lower Nith). If it reads between II and III the river is up, and most would say 'the higher the better'

Upper Nith
Eliock Bridge (803.082) to Glen Airlie picnic-site bridge (834.056)
Grade IIIc
No Portages
5 Kilometres
OS Sheet 78

Eliock Bridge, 5 kilometres south of Sanquhar, is reached from the A76 just north of Mennock. The best rapids on this section are immediately below the bridge, the most notable being Hotel Fall (LW IIIc, HW IVc) named after the neighbouring Mennockfoot Lodge Hotel on the left bank. There are two possible options here: left is best in flood but in low water it is too tight; so go right but watch out for the big boulder at the bottom.

After Hotel Fall the river is much easier all the way to Glen Airlie picnic-site, although in high water there are interesting standing waves. The picnic-site is situated 100 metres upstream of

Left: The River Nith.   *Right:* The Border Esk

the Glen Airlie Bridge on the left (A76) side of the river. Parking and toilets abut the river. Just above is the most popular starting-point for white water races and for tours.

Lower Nith **
Glen Airlie picnic-site (834.056) to Drumlanrig Bridge (859.998)
Grade IVc
No Portages
7 Kilometres
OS Sheet 78

Starting above the picnic-site and finishing at Glen Airlie Bridge (stopper below the bridge in flood) is Start Rapid (IIIc). There is then flat water for ½ kilometre before S Bends (IIIb) – such evocative names! A further kilometre of easy water leads to the Graveyard (LW IIIc, HW IVc) – every good river should have one. The river eases again for a kilometre to Campbell's Island – in the early 1970s a goods train loaded with a well known brand of soup popular in Scotland shed its load from the high embankment into the river, giving the rapid a name and keeping the fish population fed for a week.

The rapid is split by the island of the same name. The best line is down the right-hand side but the left-hand channel has an exciting 1-metre drop. Dodd's Folly (IIIc) is the next rapid after ½ kilometre, with a distinctive boulder at the bottom forming a whirlpool in high water. The white house (left bank) at Enterkinfoot is a little over a kilometre below and offers an escape route for those who have found the river testing enough already. Below lie the Jaws O' Neath – at last a name to set the blood racing – otherwise known as Drumlanrig Gorge (IVc).

There are only two different rapids in the kilometre-long gorge. The first is a 1-metre drop, immediately after an obvious narrowing in the rock walls; the second, some way below, is a more technical twist and turn. At 'normal' levels (between II and III on Drumlanrig Bridge gauge) the banks can be traversed for inspection, rescue or portage. The road, however, is now some distance away and in very high flood the banks become inaccessible, so these two rapids can give the gorge a higher grade; but anyone going to the Nith for continuous Grade V water will be disappointed. The gorge is not in the same league as, for instance, those on the Findhorn or Spean.

This is not to say that Drumlanrig Gorge cannot be relished for what it is: a scenic and technically interesting paddle that will 'stretch' the medium grade canoeist. It is also of great interest to fly fishermen – and presumably to the fish whose jaws they are trying to 'stretch'. However, the expected conflict of sporting interests does not occur because canoeing is allowed on Sundays and throughout the spawning season, or in other words outside the fishing season. Scottish salmon and trout are obviously more randy than their English or Welsh counterparts, since apparently the latter can't procreate when there are canoes passing overhead.

Egress from this excellent section of the Nith is on the right bank at Drumlanrig Bridge, a kilometre of flat water below the gorge. The bridge is named after the castle overlooking the river on the right. This was built by the Duke of Queensberry but, after the sandstone turrets were finally finished in 1680, he was so shocked at the cost of the building that he spent just one night in the castle before settling in Sanquhar.

BORDER ESK

The River Esk rises in the southern uplands of Scotland and crosses into England just north of Carlisle. It is canoeable from Benpath Bridge (311.902) but the 11 kilometres from there to Langholm will only be of interest to novices (Grade Ia). Langholm is therefore recommended as the put-in. A large rock adjacent to the sewage works at Langholm can be used to judge the level of the Esk. If this rock is showing the river is low; when it is covered the river is at a good level.

Esk
Langholm Bridge (363.849) to Canonbie Bridge (395.765)
Grade IIIc
No Portages

10 Kilometres
OS Sheet 79

Access is from the bridge in Langholm and cars may be left in the town car-park. After a kilometre you pass the marker-rock (see above) and this is followed by the first set of rapids, Skippers. Skippers is just above the A7 road-bridge. The pool below Skippers provides a good 'collecting' point.

A kilometre of easy water brings you to Dog Island This is normally started on the right, followed by a cross over to the left before the final run into the pool. Another island, 2 kilometres below near Irvine House, provides the next section of difficulty. The island is taken on the right and a large rock shows in low water half-way down the rapid – Irvine Rapid.

After 6½ kilometres the reinforced concrete breakwaters at Hagg Island appear. It is possible to egress here to the A7 on the right bank (376.794) but if you have coped so far it is worth continuing. About ½ kilometre below Hagg Island is Hollow Weir which should be inspected prior to shooting, followed immediately by Hollow Mills Rapid. The combination of rapid and weir gives an exciting run in high water.

A bridge and flat water succeed Hollows Mill and then, after ½ kilometre, there is the somewhat easier although extremely rocky Byreburnfoot Rapid. The paddling from Byreburnfoot to Canonbie is straightforward, although for the energetic there remains the Hush. This is a good rapid for practising technique – including rolling! Egress at Canonbie is immediately below the bridge on the right bank. Suitable parking is available at the public hall 100 metres away.

England

The Tyne and other rivers of the North-East

Paddlers who reach EPL (end of paddling life) without venturing into the north-east of England are missing a treat. It may not be the easiest place to get to and it may not have the Lake District's outstanding beauty or the Welsh and Scottish density of white water rivers but you'll never feel the arrogant cold shoulder of wealth in a pub or the sense that you are an intruder into a foreign land. An interpreter may be useful to understand what's going on but to ask twice for help is an insult and to want for companionship on a river an impossibility.

Considering the early history of the place, it is perhaps surprising that there is such a warm welcome in the North-East. The Tyne was (and still is by some) regarded as the northern limit of civilization. The Romans fortified the ridge above the Tyne valley by building their most comprehensive defence system – Hadrian's Wall. The Roman wall had seventeen forts along its length, and one of the best preserved is the cavalry fort at Chesters beside the North Tyne. Later inhabitants of this unstable region between England and Scotland built castles and peel towers, many of them near the Tyne, to guard themselves against raids from across the border.

The River Tweed further north now performs the function of a border between England and Scotland, and castles like Norham and Neidpath testify to the violence that this riverside has seen. Berwick-upon-Tweed, the town which guards the mouth of the river, changed hands thirteen times before it was finally claimed as English territory in 1482. In point of fact the Tweed acts as a border for only 27 kilometres, and the upper section recommended below is entirely in Scotland. It is perhaps the least exciting but most scenic of the rivers in the North-East.

The Tyne has two major branches: the North Tyne and the South Tyne. Both are canoeable in varying degrees of quality; the former most famous for Warden Gorge, and the latter best in its upper reaches. The north and south tributaries meet near the town of Hexham. Below Hexham the mature river is of no interest to

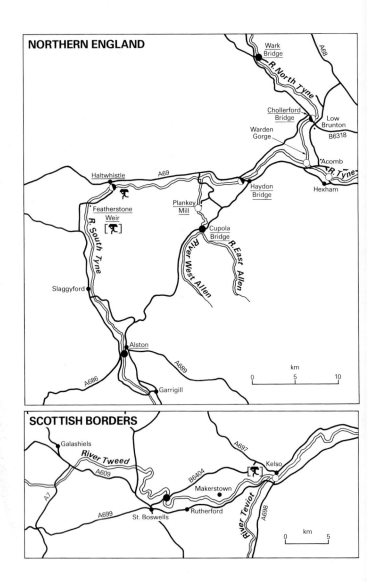

NORTHERN ENGLAND

Wark Bridge
R. North Tyne
A68
Chollerford Bridge
Low Brunton
Warden Gorge
B6318
Acomb
R. Tyne
Hexham
Haltwhistle
A69
Plankey Mill
Haydon Bridge
Featherstone Weir
[🎣]
Cupola Bridge
River West Allen
R. East Allen
R. South Tyne
Slaggyford
Alston
A689
km
0 5 10
A686
Garrigill

SCOTTISH BORDERS

Galashiels
A697
River Tweed
A609
B6404
Kelso
A7
Makerstown
River Teviot
A699
St. Boswells
Rutherford
A698
km
0 5

white water canoeists but 8 kilometres above Hexham, flowing
into the South Tyne down a steep wooded gorge, is the superb
little Allen. If there are wet umbrellas in the street and rivers on
your windscreen, go to the Allen for it is the best that the North-
East has to offer.

RIVER NORTH TYNE

Although national white water races are held on the North Tyne,
the only outstanding section of white water is the short Warden
Gorge. The discharge down the River Tyne has been greatly
affected since the war by aforestation and the construction of the
Kielder dam and reservoir. To some extent the river level is
dependent on overflow or release from Kielder dam. The hydro-
electric station normally generates power at peak times but there is
a time lapse of about six hours before the release affects the level
in Warden Gorge. The best level indicator is Chollerford Weir
(Lower North Tyne access); if this is canoeable then the river is
up.

Upper North Tyne
Wark Bridge (862.770) to Chollerford Bridge (919.705)
Grade IIIc
No Portages
9 Kilometres
OS Sheet 87

This section begins at Wark, once the capital of Tynedale and the
place where Scottish kings held court. Dippers bob on the rocks
just above the water as the Upper North Tyne sets off with fairly
continuous small rapids. This promise is not kept, however, and
the river flattens off past Barrasford down to Chollerford. Care
should be taken to shoot the broken weir at Barrasford on the
right. The Upper North Tyne is best canoed in high water.

Above: Rivers North Tyne, South Tyne and Allen.   *Below:* The River
Tweed

Lower North Tyne *
Chollerford Bridge (919.705) to confluence with South Tyne
(919.660) or Hexham (940.646)
Grade IIb (IVd)
No Portages
5 or 9 Kilometres
OS Sheet 87

Access is down the left bank below the bridge to get in above
Chollerford Weir, a straightforward 1½ metre sloping drop usually
shot just right of centre. Slackwater follows for 1 kilometre before
a minor rapid runs past the famous Roman garrison fort of
Chesters. Then, also on the right bank, Walwick Grange is passed
which is an imposing country residence. Below the house is
Imagine, a small rapid with a good little play stopper – this is
washed-out in high water.

A rather tedious flat stretch now intervenes before Mill Race
Rapids on a right-hand bend. Another half kilometre of flat water
leads to Warden Gorge (IVd). This is only ½ kilometre long but a
completely different kettle of fish, so to speak, from the rest of the
river.

The first rapid in Warden Gorge is formed by an angled ridge of
bedrock reinforced on the right by concrete and timber to direct
water down an old mill race. This rapid ends in a cliff on the right
– grief to the inexperienced and unwary. A 100 metres of flat
water then precedes the main section of gorge. It is best to get out
at Private Notice Rock and inspect.

Many ways down the gorge have been tried with varying degrees
of success. An upright in-boat approach is recommended. There is
a constriction about half-way down the gorge which in high water
produces a carnivorous stopper. In full spate most of the gorge is
washed out except for a monstrous hole at the bottom which can
increase the grade to Ve. Warden Gorge finishes about ½
kilometre above the junction with the South Tyne. Egress is to the
sandy beach on the left which is reached from a small track leading
down from Acomb. Alternatively, continue down the Lower South

Tyne and egress in Hexham (see below). The latter is the normal finish for the long race courses on the North and South Tyne.

RIVER SOUTH TYNE

The South Tyne has its source high in the North Pennines to the south of the market town of Alston, a few miles to the east of Cross Fell where the Tees rises. The river falls steadily north through the attractive valley of South Tynedale and then swings east from Haltwhistle to join with the North Tyne just upstream of Hexham. The combined river then continues east to reach Newcastle and the North Sea.

The South Tyne's steady fall means that, unlike its tributary the River Allen (see below), it has no individual rapids of great difficulty. When it is running high, however, it does offer a long run of virtually continuous white water in its upper reaches. The section from Alston to Haltwhistle is especially recommended in high spate when it provides kilometre after kilometre of powerful bouncy water of no great difficulty. If the whole river bed is covered at Alston Bridge then this is a good level to paddle the Upper and Middle South Tyne. The Lower South Tyne, which is suitable for introducing novices to white water canoeing, can be paddled at any level outside drought conditions.

Upper South Tyne *
Alston (717.461) to Haltwhistle (699.633)
Grade IIIc
1 Portage (?)
9 Kilometres
OS Sheet 87

In very high water it is possible to get in above Alston. There are several narrow and inescapable gorges but no major falls. There are the usual obstructions to be found on forested rivers – trees, branches and jammed logs. There is also a pipe to look out for below the bridge at Garrigill; it spans the river, sometimes at garrotting level! Garrigill is one of the alternative higher access points for the Upper South Tyne (744.415).

Access at Alston is upstream of the bridge on the west bank. There are no sudden drops on this section but there are two long stretches of continuous rapids. A shorter trip may be had by finishing at Slaggyford; egress is immediately below the bridge on the west bank (680.519).

Below Slaggyford the South Tyne becomes progressively larger as more streams flow in. In spate there are some very impressive waves, especially where the river is squeezed between high bluffs. There are no particular dangers apart from the weir at Featherstone some 5 kilometres above Haltwhistle. This should be inspected and if necessary portaged. It can be shot down the right in low water but in high water the stopper is vicious.

Middle South Tyne
Haltwhistle (699.633) to Haydon Bridge (843.642)
Grade IIb
1 Portage
14 Kilometres
OS Sheet 87

Access/egress at Haltwhistle is under the bridge on the south bank. The weir under the old bridge further down has a nasty concrete sill and is portaged on the right. The river now consists of easy rapids with flat stretches in between. After 10 kilometres the River Allen enters from the right. At Haydon Bridge there is a weir which can be shot at all levels through the far left-hand arch. The access/egress point is below the new bridge on the south bank.

Lower South Tyne
Haydon Bridge (843.642) to Hexham (940.646)
Grade IIb
No Portages
12 Kilometres
OS Sheet 87

The second boulder garden on the River Allen

Access is below the new bridge on the south bank. This is the
normal start for river races. This section of river is good for
training and teaching novices. There are many easy rapids and no
problem areas. Some 4 kilometres above Hexham the North Tyne
enters from the left.

It may be worth walking a kilometre up the east bank of the
North Tyne to paddle Warden Gorge (see above). A kilometre
above Hexham is Tyne Green, a deep flat stretch much used by
rowing boats, windsurfers and recreational canoeists. Egress in
Hexham is just above the bridge on the south bank. The weir
below the bridge is shootable (inspect) but should be avoided in
the fishing season.

RIVER ALLEN

The Allen is a small and continuously technical river which needs
spate conditions to make it worth paddling. Woods line the river
and fallen trees can be a problem, occasionally blocking the whole
river. Nevertheless, the trees combine with the ivy and lichen-
covered rock to add to the wilderness feel of the river.

In high flood the river increases in difficulty and seriousness by a
grade. There are two river level indicators. If the rocks and ledge
under Cupola Bridge are three-quarters covered then the Allen is
up; when they are all covered it is a superb run. At the egress
point if the foundation ledge of Plankey Mill foot-bridge (right
bank) is covered then the river is worth canoeing; if it is covered
by 30 centimetres of water, all the better.

Allen **
Cupola Bridge (799.591) to Plankey Mill (794.621)
Grade IVd
No Portages
4 Kilometres
OS Sheet 87

Access to this section of the Allen is just below the junction of the
East and West Allen (the latter is canoeable from further up at

Grade IIIb). Cupola Bridge, carrying the A686, crosses here. There are two boulder gardens in the first 2 kilometres making for continuously interesting canoeing with a number of 'blind alleys'. Several fast rapids follow until, after another kilometre, there are the Rock Steps. The stoppers at the base of both steps are good for 'enders' but watch out for white water racers doing a training run.

About ½ kilometre below Rock Steps a meadow appears out of the dense forest on the left. This gives a warning of the approach of Hog Bank Weir, a 2-metre natural sloping drop, some 300 metres downstream. At most levels this is easily shot but in flood conditions a dangerous stopper forms below the drop and it should be portaged.

That safely negotiated, there are only two smaller stoppers round the next bend before easier water leads down to Plankey Mill (easier water then leads down to the confluence with the South Tyne). At Plankey Mill a foot-bridge crosses the river. Egress is on the right bank just below this bridge which can be reached by car from a small road leading off the A686 at Langley.

RIVER TWEED

The Tweed is a long and very beautiful river. It rises in the Scottish Tweedsmuir and Lowland Hills, and the sheep that graze there are the source of the woven cloth that is milled in the valley and named after the river. The Tweed continues in Scotland for most of its 160-odd kilometres and rarely rises above Grade I. However spring snow-melt and autumn storms can produce big waves where formerly there were peaceful meanders, and this is particularly true in the section described below. It is a satisfying coincidence that the Tweed also looks its best in the rising greens of spring and the falling rusts of autumn.

The Tweed is a big salmon river. Scottish fishermen are generally very generous and charitable towards canoeing interests and this has been notable on the Tweed. Canoeists should therefore take the trouble to find out local access agreements currently in force on the section of river they intend to paddle.

Should the Tweed be in spate it will be worth checking out an exciting northern tributary, the River Whiteadder. The Whiteadder drains the Lammermuir Hills to join the Tweed just west of Berwick. The best section of white water (IVd) is from Abbey St Bathans to Preston, but go carefully for there are a number of steep falls along the way!

Tweed
B6404 road-bridge (610.320) to Kelso Bridge (727.336)
Grade IIIb
No Portages (?)
14 Kilometres
OS Sheet 74

Put in at the B6404 bridge north of St Boswells. The river is flat and easy down to and some way below the bridge and islands at Mertoun. About 2 kilometres below the bridge is Rutherford Cauld (IIIb). This weir carries the river to the left and is straightforward down that side. In fact inspection would probably be more difficult to negotiate than the fall.

There are more islands below Rutherford and then a long and quite intimidating rapid, Mackerstoun (IIIb) – a family of three. The middle and lower falls can be frightening for the uninitiated so inspection is recommended (right bank). The so-called Goat-Hole through which the paddler finishes the last fall has a nasty 'kick' if approached the wrong way.

Below Mackerstoun the Tweed relaxes into its more normal leisurely pace as far as Kelso Junction, a weir just above the confluence with the River Teviot. After the confluence is a road-bridge and then Kelso Cauld. Extreme caution is necessary at Kelso Cauld as the only route down the weir is by a channel close to the right bank. If the water level is too low for this route Kelso Cauld is a recommended portage. Egress is soon afterwards on the left bank where the A698 runs close to the river.

The River Tees and its tributaries

The black-faced sheep have made skinheads out of the rolling hills of Teesdale. Of shrub and brush there is none, and the grass is crew-cut short. Unless it is covered by a decorative quilt of snow, the eye is invariably drawn away from this barren landscape to the big moorland sky over Cross Fell, the highest peak in the Pennines, or down to the tributaries and waterfalls of the Tees.

The River Tees is one of the most famous canoeing rivers in the north of England, and justly so. It has a large and relatively 'untapped' catchment area and therefore remains canoeable for longer than other rivers in the area. Despite gaining an over-ample girth during its swift rush to maturity, it retains, particularly in high water, an abundance of white water. It is no surprise to find that 'Tees' means boiling or surging in Celtic.

For continuity of interest, a tributary of the Tees, the River Greta, is probably a better bet. The problem is that it needs very heavy rain to bring it into condition. The alternative in a dry spell is to travel south into the Dales (to the Swale and Ure) or east to the coast in the hope of finding surf. If you do the latter and it suddenly rains, there is always the lonely little River Esk to lead you down to the North Sea at Whitby, with a kilometre of rough water (IVd) between Houlsyke railway-bridge and Lealholm – a section referred to locally as Crunkley Gill.

RIVER TEES

The Tees emerges from Low Green Reservoir in a flurry of activity over the 60-metre volcanic staircase of Cauldron Snout. 10 kilometres downstream is the even more impressive High Force, pouring 30 metres over a dolerite sill into a cauldron of bubble and spray. Both are popular with tourists but neither with canoeists. There is a canoeable stretch in between and no doubt someone some day will launch themselves over both, but it is normal to begin the Tees below High Force.

At first the river runs through the broad Force Gorge with a

number of difficult rapids over bedrock steps. This section
culminates with Low Force. Then there is a long easy stretch
before Eggleston Gorge, a wild water racing site. The river then
becomes progressively easier after this second gorge, with only the
occasional burst of activity below Barnard Castle.

The Tees in spate is an impressive run but because it is
immoderately wide for an upland river, it becomes a tiresome
bump and scrape after a spell of dry weather. Both upper and
lower gorges are possible in moderate water, but most people will
prefer the whole river in flood.

Upper Tees (Force Gorge) *
High Force (882.285) to Wynch Bridge (903.278)
Grade IVd (IVe)
No Portages
3 Kilometres
OS Sheet 92

Access to the broad and leafy gorge below High Force is down a
footpath opposite High Force Hotel. This huge waterfall is visited
by thousands of people every year and the landowner has cashed
in on this natural asset by charging for parking and access. It is
possible to put in at Holwick Head Bridge a kilometre downstream
but in doing so you miss a good stretch of river.

Force Gorge is very open and the difficulties are caused more
often by bedrock steps than constrictions. There are a number of
excellent rapids, some requiring inspection. Low Force can be
inspected from the right or left banks but there can be little doubt
that the right side is the easiest run (IVe). Low Force is just
upstream of Wynch Bridge which is accessible by footpath from
Bowlees on the B6277 (this road follows the river as far as Barnard
Castle). It may be worth inspecting Low Force before starting the
trip.

The Upper Tees between High Force and Low Force

Middle Tees
Wynch Bridge (903.278) to Eggleston Bridge (996.232)
Grade IIb (IIIb)
No Portages
13 Kilometres
OS Sheet 92

This long trip is well worth doing in high water. The difficulties are never intense and all very safe, but the rapids are continuous and the water fast-moving. This section may be shortened by using Middleton Bridge as an access or egress point. Do not, however, consider paddling the Middle Tees in low water. In this condition only the bank wildlife and scenery (including a well preserved waterwheel) are of any interest.

Access at Wynch Bridge is by the footpath from Bowlees. Between Wynch Bridge and Middleton there are three weirs which need inspecting in high water. At Middleton Bridge access is on the right by a gate near the shingle beds. The 6-kilometre stretch below Middleton is perhaps slightly more technical than the 7 kilometres above. In particular there is the slalom site at Leekworth Farm, just above the confluence with the Lune entering from the right, which can be exciting in big water. Access and egress at Eggleston are upstream of the bridge on the right bank.

Lower Tees (including Eggleston Gorge) ***
Eggleston Bridge (996.232) to Cotherstone Bridge (012.201) or
    Whorlton Lido (144.168)
Grade IVc
No Portages
5 or 18 Kilometres
OS Sheet 92

From Eggleston Bridge the river digs a deep broad valley. The numerous rapids are formed by bedrock steps and sharp turns in

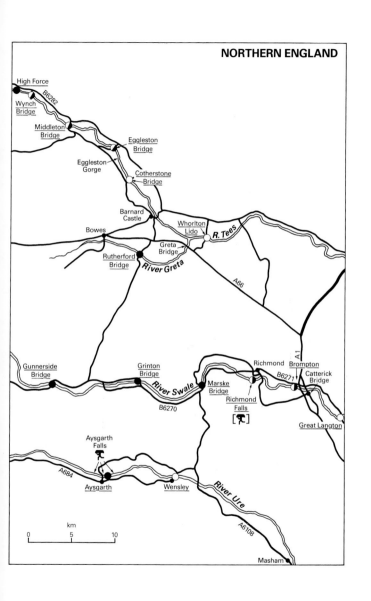

NORTHERN ENGLAND

High Force

Wynch Bridge

B6282

Middleton Bridge

Eggleston Bridge

Eggleston Gorge

Cotherstone Bridge

Barnard Castle

Whorlton Lido

R. Tees

Bowes

Greta Bridge

Rutherford Bridge

River Greta

A66

Gunnerside Bridge

Grinton Bridge

River Swale

Marske Bridge

B6270

Richmond

Richmond Falls

[⚓]

Brompton

B6271

A1

Catterick Bridge

Great Langton

Aysgarth Falls

A684

Aysgarth

Wensley

River Ure

A6108

Masham

km

0   5   10

the course of the river. The twisting river hides its difficulties from the canoeist and in some water conditions inspection is advisable. Eggleston Gorge is canoeable in low water (Grade IIIc) but it is much better and quite daunting at higher levels. The Gorge ends at Cotherstone Iron Bridge (land left) which is used to reach a small road leading to the B6277 and Cotherstone (right bank). Eggleston Gorge is the best of the Tees – a classic middle-grade run in attractive surroundings.

If you want a longer trip at the same, but much less continuous, grade, there are a number of widely-spaced rapids downstream of Eggleston Gorge. After 3 kilometres Towler Hill Rapid is notable; so are Wren's Dam in Barnard Castle (do not shoot in the centre), Abbey Rapids 2 kilometres below Barnard Castle (harder than they look), and Whorlton Falls ½ kilometre below Whorlton Bridge (inspect). If you get out at Whorlton Falls you will have paddled a total of 18 kilometres from Eggleston Bridge. Land left and with whatever strength you have left carry through the Lido.

RIVER GRETA

The Greta is a tributary which enters the Tees 5 kilometres below Barnard Castle. The Greta needs a heavy downpour to bring it into condition and it should not be left too long after the rain has stopped. The section described is continuously technical, with difficult falls at the beginning and end, and can be serious due to the number of fallen trees in the river. It is to be highly recommended to the experienced white water paddler.

Greta **
Grade IIId (IVd)
No Portages
10 Kilometres
OS Sheet 92

Access is at a small road-bridge 2 kilometres south of the A66. It is possible to get in at Bowes 5 kilometres upstream but the paddling on this upper section is a little tedious.

Below the recommended access point the river immediately begins to steepen and narrow. An awkward 1½-metre drop (IVd) leads you into the gorge which is continuous Grade IIId. The deciduous woodland hides what little habitation there is close to the river, increasing the sense of isolation. There is a foot-bridge after 2 kilometres and tributaries which enter from the south after 3 and 4 kilometres, but little else to judge your position on the river. Then after 7 kilometres the woodland starts to thin.

The river now relaxes for 2 kilometres as it passes under Greta Bridge (A66) and into Rokeby Estate. Within its ultimate kilometre, just before the Greta enters the Tees, is Mortham Tower Bridge with a gatehouse next to it. The bridge is a landmark for Rokeby Falls (IVd). The exit to this 1-metre rocky drop is almost completely blocked by a large rock, so it should be inspected. There is a good eddy on the right just above the Falls.

Below Rokeby Falls are only a small stopper and a cluster of rocky slabs before the Greta spills into the Tees. Unfortunately, it is only possible to walk out from here, since Mortham Tower road-bridge is privately owned. It is better therefore to continue down the Tees for 2½ kilometres to Whorlton Falls and get out above or below them on the left to Whorlton Lido.

The Greta and other rivers of the northern Lake District

Formed by the confluence of two tributaries at Threlkeld, the Greta drains the southern slopes of Skiddaw and the northern slopes of Helvellyn to flow into the Derwent at Keswick. Despite its shallow overall gradient the river is remarkably continuous at the grade and in high water gives a superb white water run. The fact that it flows through a picturesque and seemingly isolated valley confirms its reputation as the best river in the northern Lake District.

Apart from the Greta, the rivers of Northern Cumbria are not noted for their white water. The Eden in the east and its two tributaries – the Eamont (Pooley Bridge to Brougham Castle, 11 kilometres, IIb) and the slightly more interesting Lowther (Askham Bridge to Brougham Castle on the Eamont, 6 kilometres, IIIb) – are disappointing unless you are training or racing. The Eden is probably the best of the three and certainly has the most reliable water. In the west is the Derwent which, although almost flat, has superb scenery through Borrowdale (confluence with Stonethwaite Beck to Grange Bridge, 3 kilometres, IIb) and below Bassenthwaite Lake provides a good introductory trip (Ouse Bridge to Cockermouth, 10 kilometres, IIb).

RIVER GRETA

Given the extensive watershed of the Greta one would expect it to be canoeable for three or four days after heavy rain. Unfortunaely, St John's Beck, one of two major tributaries of the Greta, flows out of the dam-controlled Thirlmere from where the water is piped to Manchester, so the full benefits of high autumn and winter levels are not felt in the river. However, if there is water enough to paddle the Greta through Keswick at the

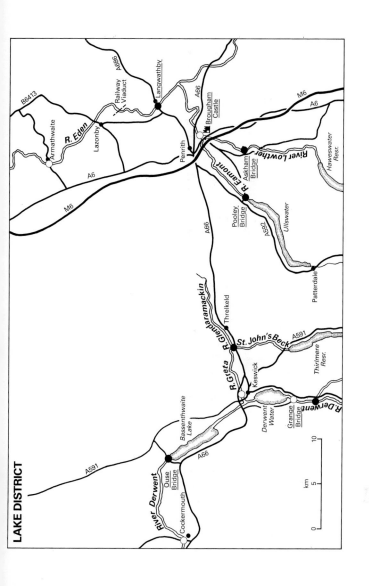

LAKE DISTRICT

suggested egress point then the more channelled river upstream is worth a visit. Another measure of water level is given by the weir at the road-bridge further into Keswick (264.237). Here the concrete overflow channel will be in use if the river is up.

Greta **

Confluence of Glendaramackin/St John's Beck (315.247) to Keswick (247.237)
Grade IIIc
No Portages
6 Kilometres
OS Sheet 90

The river is characterized by a series of bouldery rapids over rocky ledges. There are four notable rapids. The first, Rock Hop (IIIc), is about a third of the way down the river and has some sharp eddies and big boulders. The second is a long section of haystacks and stoppers about half-way down; an excellent and scenic stretch of river. The third and fourth are weirs, both broken and quite safe. There is an entertaining sharp right-hand bend above the second weir; this should be taken on the right down a bouldery rapid.

The Greta is followed by a disused railway line. It crosses and recrosses the river seven times on the way to Keswick but it is only when the river nears the town that you are reminded that the A66 is also somewhere up there beyond the woods. The road by-passes Keswick and crosses the Greta as a dual carriageway. Continue for another kilometre until you see a swathe of grass running down to the river opposite a filling-station. This is the best place to get out. There is nothing of interest further into Keswick although it is possible to continue for a couple of kilometres to the confluence with the Derwent and so to the A66 bridge over that river.

Rock Hop on the Greta

RIVER EDEN

The Eden, if nothing else, gives a measure to the quality of the Greta. Famous in the canoeing world only because it is a race course, it is a better training-ground for marathons than white water races. It does have a few rapids, but in between there are more boring flat stretches than a royal baby has names. However, it is well-supplied with water and stays up longer than many other rivers in the area.

Eden
Langwathby Bridge (566.336) to Armathwaite Weir (503.453)
Grade IIIb
No Portages
17 Kilometres
OS Sheets 90 and 86

From Langwathby Bridge the Eden is flat for 7 kilometres. After it passes under the railway there is Eden Lucy Falls (IIIb). This proves that you are *not* somewhere between Devizes and Westminster. The river is then flat again as far as Lazonby (550.404). This is where most people get in – upstream of the bridge at a lay-by – and where the white water race starts.

The river below Lazonby improves. Sandstone buttes prevent the river from becoming too civilized and one particularly big cliff stands proudly beside its creation – a long rapid with good play waves (IIIb). Small rapids and sandstone outcrops continue and one cliff on the right bears the following carved inscription:

'Oh the fisher's gentle life, happiest is of any, void of pleasure, full of strife and beloved by many. Other joys are but toys and to be lamented, only this a pleasure . . .'.

Armathwaite Weir finally appears 10 kilometres below Lazonby. This is usually shot on the right, but to avoid hassles with those enjoying 'the only pleasure' it is best to get out above on the left by a stone shed (the end of the river race course).

The River Kent and its tributaries

The River Kent and its two biggest tributaries, the Sprint and Mint, provide some of the best paddling in the Lake District. The Sprint is clearly the best of the three but, like its sister the Mint, is only canoeable after heavy rain. The Kent, on the other hand, drains a massive catchment area, particularly in its lower reaches where it benefits from the water brought in by the Sprint and Mint. It is the most reliable of the southern Lakeland rivers.

RIVER KENT

The Kent flows from Kentmere Reservoir through Kendal to the estuary at Arneside. The Upper Kent is alternately tedious and dangerous (due to the numerous weirs) and needs more rain than the Lower Kent to bring it into condition. Far better is the Lower Kent where the river flows through two unique narrow undercut gorges and over a number of spectacular falls.

Upper Kent
Elfhowe Bridge (467.995) to Alavna Roman Fort (516.906)
Grade IId (IVd)
Some Portages
14 Kilometres
OS Sheet 97

This section of river is quite easy apart from two falls but is serious because of the number and state of the weirs. The first difficult fall (IVd) is at the put-in. It is followed by easy water down to two weirs (*inspect*) just above Staveley. 3 kilometres downstream of Staveley at Cown Head there is a difficult rapid *underneath* a factory, with a weir just above (IVd).

A nasty weir splits the river a kilometre downstream at Bowston and there is another one just above Burneside. These should be

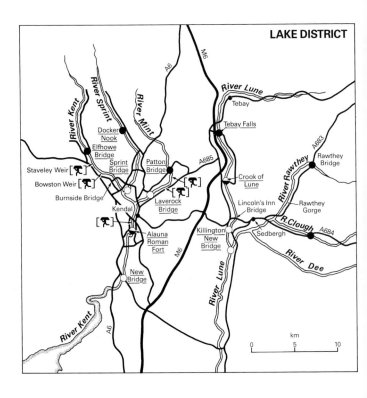

The tributaries of the River Kent and River Lune

inspected and probably portaged. Below Burneside, the Kent is
joined by first the Sprint and then the Mint before entering the
town of Kendal. You may need some 'sprint' power if you shoot
the next weir in the town. The river is canalized right through
Kendal and forms little stoppers and waves over the man-made
shelves. Egress is on the left just after you have passed the last
buildings (the K Shoe factory) on the left bank.

Lower Kent **
Alavna Roman Fort (516.906) to A591 New Bridge (506.863)
Grade IVd
No Portages
5 Kilometres
OS Sheet 97

Barry Howell's grade of III for the Lower Kent in his *Lake District
White Water* guidebook must have produced more heart murmurs
than all the sugar in the Kendal Mint Cake factory. There is much
here that is flat but there are a number of falls which a grade III
paddler would remember for the rest of his or her days.

Access to the left bank of the river is by way of a narrow track
which runs westward (towards Alavna Roman Fort) off the minor
road between Naitland and Kendal, just south of the K Shoe
factory. The first rapid of note is Scrogs Weir (IIb) which is a long
bouldery 'sloper', easily shot on the left – or anywhere else that
takes your fancy. Easy water then leads to Prizet Bridge (512.892)
near the village of Naitland. This bridge is an alternative access
point.

Below the bridge is the first of the gorges. The river drops
steeply through a narrow gap and continues between undercut
walls dripping with water and all manner of green things which
flourish on it. Near the bottom of this gorge is an old broken-down
weir forming a big two-tier rapid which is intimidating but not as
difficult as it first appears (IVd). After this rapid the river opens
out again and flat water leads down to a weir.

This powerful weir has an innocuous-looking tongue through the centre which is *not* as straightforward as it seems – a frightening experience in fact. If in any doubt, portage on the right and not through the immaculate garden of the house on the left. Above the next road-bridge, Sedgewick Bridge, the river chunters over a rock step and down through a narrow chute, reminiscent of the fall at Prizet Bridge. This is the start of the second gorge.

It is important to make sure that you can get out, and get swimmers out, *between* this slot and the fall which succeeds it underneath the Sedgewick Bridge. Sedgewick Bridge Falls (IVd) is an 'L'-shaped drop with the corner of the 'L' pointing upstream. It is most easily shot on the left and should be inspected from the left. The powerful stopper on the right will have no trouble in gobbling your boat if you enter it at less than full power.

Easier water now leads to an island where a sloping weir has been built across the river. This island should be taken on the left to line up for Force Falls (IVd). Force Falls is an intimidating 3-metre drop into a huge stopper which appears to have boulders in it; it doesn't! Taken left of centre it flushes through nicely but a grading of III still seems mean. Egress is on the right bank immediately below the concrete foundations of the A591 bridge (or continue for a relaxing 2 kilometres through Levens Deer Park to the A6 at Levens Bridge).

RIVER SPRINT

The Sprint is one of the best rivers in the Lake District. The canoeing is testing and continuous, with a number of continuous sections in tight gorges. Unfortunately, Longsleddale despite being long is also very thin, providing a limited catchment area for the Sprint; it is therefore very much a spate river. A good indication of the level may be gained at Garnett Bridge (524.993). If the rapid here is canoeable without a scrape, the river is up.

Sprint ***
Docker Nook (509.015) to Sprint Bridge (513.960)
Grade IVd

No Portages
6 Kilometres
OS Sheets 90 and 97

The Longsleddale road runs beside the Sprint above Garnett
Bridge. The river can be reached by a small track leading to
Docker Nook Farm (limited parking). Sprint it does not for the
first kilometre, the only notable feature being a broken foot-
bridge. The small weir at Murthwaite should read 2 or above to
make the river interesting, and it does become more interesting
after a further kilometre. There are three bridges at Dale End,
Cocks Close and Garnett. Below the second are the difficult 'S'
Bends (IVd), below the third the equally tricky Garnett Bridge
Falls (IVd), and in between a steep, shootable weir, Garnett Weir
(IIIc). 'S' Bends and Garnett Bridge Falls should be inspected
from the road on the way up.

The road now disappears and a feeling of isolation creeps over
the paddler as he or she tackles more difficult canoeing. Two
rapids are of note. The first is a narrow shoot through bedrock
plunging 2 metres into a pool. The second (Rock and Roll – IVd)
is a longer run, also through bedrock, with curling waves coming
in from right and left. A break-out is possible half-way down but
the canoe needs to be straight to shoot the last drop either side of
a boulder.

Below this excellent section is Gurnsall Bridge (521.975), a
possible egress point if it is getting late. But stay with it if you can,
for there is more. Some way below the bridge a broken weir is
shot on the right and then a good section of white water leads to
Sprint Mill Falls (IVd). This difficult rapid lies just above a bridge
carrying pipes. A final fall beside Sprint Mill Cottages and a small
weir will keep you guessing as far as Sprint Bridge. This is the last
before the Kent confluence and the best place to get out.

RIVER MINT

The Mint is the Sprint's sister tributary (of the Kent) but they bear

little more than this formal relation to each other. The Mint is far more abused and far less natural than the Sprint. There is some interesting canoeing in the lower half but typically the most difficult rapid is next to a works depot. The Upper Mint, between Bannisdale Low Bridge (A6) and Patton Bridge, has been canoed but cannot be recommended because of the amount of time spent on the bank, portaging first a big fall and then numerous low fences. There are also a few strands of barbed wire to negotiate on this unpleasant upper stretch of the river.

Mint *
Patton Bridge (557.974) to Laverock Bridge (536.952)
Grade IIId
1 or 2 Portages
5 Kilometres
OS Sheets 90 and 97

Access at Patton Bridge has the advantage of higher flows but the Lower Mint is still very much a spate run. It does not actually need to be raining to canoe from here (if you can canoe under Laverock Bridge the river is up) but it helps.

Below Patton Bridge easy water leads to a small drop above a left-hand bend, the start of a good rapid over bedrock steps (inspect). Two large tributaries enter from the left and swell the Mint. In between is Ivy Bridge, with a fence above it that forces a portage in high water.

Between Ivy Bridge and Meal Bank the valley sides are steeper and the rough water more continuous. A large weir Garlic Weir IVe) needs careful inspection and maybe portaging in high water; in low water it can be shot on the left. Meal Bank Rapids (IIId) are below the bridge in the village of the same name. The first rapid, a three-tier fall with a stopper in the top drop, is worth inspecting (from the works depot), because if you make a 'meal' of it, concrete steps and the occasional reinforcing rod lower down

Bouncing down the Mint in low water

will give an unpleasant swim. The second rapid, a little way below, is more straightforward. Easier water now leads to Laverock Bridge. Egress is to a lay-by just upstream of the bridge on the right bank.

The River Lune and its tributaries

The Lune flows through comparatively rich farming country, made richer by M6 compulsory purchase orders. It is land that gives off a self-satisfied air. The moss grows thick, rich and green on the river boulders and field walls, udder-full cows look contemptuously over downy shoulders, and PRIVATE is nailed deep into arms of sagging willows – NO ACCESS, NO FISHING, NO BOATING, NO CANOEING. When I was last there, underneath one such notice at Tebay Falls four dead moles hung on a fence, their heads neatly pierced by the barbed wire. The message was clear, but at whom it was aimed less obvious.

The Romans under Hadrian built a fort at the seaward crossing of the Lune and called it Lon Castrum (Lancaster). Lon, the Anglo–Irish word for the river, originally meant 'health-giving'. It was a place of rest and recuperation, but perhaps the accessibility of the valley and the very fame of its beauty – Turner, the great British landscape painter, painted the Crook of Lune 200 years ago – finally produced an unhealthy, if occasionally justified, suspicion of visitors.

If the Lune has lost some of the warm, unspoilt and welcoming beauty that so attracted travellers and tourists in the past, its major tributary, the Rawthey, is a reminder of what it must have been like. The Rawthey is an excellent run through beautiful country and far and away the best of the Lune's tributaries. It too has a couple of tributaries that are worth a look in high water. The Clough enters the Rawthey just above Sedbergh and has a hard gorge (Ve) between the A684 New Bridge and the confluence with the Rawthey. The Dee joins the Rawthey below Sedbergh, and high up in Dentdale offers some exciting canoeing over small narrow drops (IVd).

RIVER LUNE

The Lune divides the Lake District from the Pennines and, rich in water from both west and east, remains canoeable long after the

neighbouring hill country spate streams are dry. It would therefore be a popular white water touring river even if the M6 had not been built so close. The canoeing is interesting without being gripping. There are a number of narrow rocky channels (washed-out in high water) and near to the finish two weirs and some bigger water, but the technical difficulty is not continuous. Just as it is easy to get to the Lune, so you do not have to work too hard to get down it.

Upper Lune
Tebay Falls (613.028) to Crook of Lune (620.963)
Grade IIb (IVd)
No Portages
5 Kilometres
OS Sheets 91 and 97

Tebay Falls (IVd) and its subsequent smaller sisters in the short gorge a kilometre south of Tebay provide the hardest canoeing on the Lune. Access is above the old bridge, through which the Falls cascade. This is easily reached from the A685 a kilometre south of Tebay. Since, however, there is nothing much of further interest for 5 kilometres below Tebay Falls, most treat it as a 'one-off' and put in at the Crook of Lune.

Lower Lune **
Crook of Lune (620.963) to Killington New Bridge (622.908) or River Rawthey (629.895)
Grade IIIc (IVe)
No Portages
5 or 7 Kilometres
OS Sheet 97

The Kendal to Sedbergh road (A684) crosses the Lune at Lincoln's Inn Bridge thus dividing this section into two halves. It is normal to combine both halves since neither is long and the difficulties are comparable. If you want a shorter trip, it is best to finish at

Tebay Falls on the Upper Lune in very low water

Killington New Bridge after 5 kilometres; you miss some fun paddling, but also avoid the two weirs.

From the Crook of Lune Bridge (access left bank) there is fast, flat water for about 2 kilometres. Near Hole House the river becomes more constricted with a long rapid above a foot-bridge. Below the foot-bridge are two more pronounced stretches of narrows (except in very high water). The slots and drops are awkward for novice paddlers and photogenic for spectators. Lincoln's Inn's Bridge is seen from the second of these two slots 100 metres downstream.

The difficulties below Lincoln Inn's Bridge begin with the Strid (IIIc), a narrow rapid which also twists and drops. It is the most difficult (natural) rapid on the Lower Lune and is easily inspected (and if necessary portaged) on the left. More good rapids follow the Strid but the last one is full of boulders and quite tricky. Below lies Killington New Bridge which is a possible egress point for those wanting to avoid the weirs in the last 2 kilometres.

One hundred metres downstream of Killington New Bridge is Killington Weir (IIId). This can be shot (or portaged) on the right. A pleasant stretch of rocky rapids brings you to flat water above Strangerthwaite Weir (IVe). This, like Killington Weir, is more serious in high water. It can be shot on the right or left but the stopper is very powerful and has 'strangerthwaited' a number of canoeists. If in doubt portage.

Below Strangerthwaite Weir is a Div. 2 slalom site with some excellent play waves, followed by a flatter stretch of water and then a final wooded gorge. Surfing the standing waves as they march past the tree-lined shore, you could be forgiven for thinking you were in Scotland. Unfortunately, this splendid isolated world of white, brown and green does not last and changes completely when the River Rawthey enters from the left. Egress is also on the left just round the next bend where the road (A683) comes close to the river.

RIVER RAWTHEY

The Rawthey competes with the River Clough and the River Eden for drainage off Baugh Fell and Wild Boar Fell. It is not a big catchment area and heavy rain is necessary to bring the Rawthey into condition. If the sand bank below Sedbergh New Bridge (665.919) is covered then the river is up. Little more than a stream in its upper half, the Rawthey has the feel of the fells, wild, steep and untamed. It is a little more mature below Straight Bridge with the addition of the Clough but nevertheless has one or two pleasant surprises in store.

Rawthey ***
Rawthey Bridge (713.978) to confluence with Lune (629.895)
Grade IVd
No Portages
14 Kilometres
OS Sheets 98 and 97

The A683 first meets the river at Rawthey Bridge on the way to Kirby Stephen. A lay-by 100 metres downstream is a convenient access point. Small drops abound in the first 2 kilometres before the river loops away from the road. Where it comes back, the contours are tightly packed and the river drops steeply over a three-tier fall – Loup Falls (IVc). High Wardes foot-bridge is not far below.

   Continuously technical water from below the foot-bridge leads after a kilometre to Crook Holme Bridge. A further kilometre brings you to the start of Rawthey Gorge (IVd). The Gorge is lined and sometimes blocked by trees which adds a degree of seriousness to the four big drops. The river eases as you go left round an island and remains easy in a second inescapable rocky gorge. Hebbelthwaite Hall Ghyll enters down a culvert on the left at the end of this section of river.

   It is possible to get out just below at Straight Bridge (678.923). These first 8 kilometres are certainly the best of the Rawthey but the section below is not without interest or difficulty. The Clough enters from the left and then the river passes under Sedbergh New Bridge. In the next 3 kilometres there are three weirs, all needing care, and some bouncy water with well-defined eddies. After the

railway viaduct, the river drops steeply over a two-tier drop –
Railway Falls (IVd) – which should be inspected from the left. The
Rawthey then has a final fling before going under the A683 and
joining the Lune. Egress is at the A683 bridge or from the Lune to
the road on the left (see above).

The Duddon and other rivers of the Western Lake District

The River Duddon flows out of the south-central fells of the Lake District through a little frequented valley into Morecambe Bay. Duddon by name but not by nature, this river twists and turns, drops and dives, falling fast and free more like a swallow than a 'duddon' (surely a slow and dowdy thing!). Wordsworth thought the Duddon was the most beautiful river in the Lake District, and it would be hard to fault his judgement if he had also said it was the most exciting.

Apart from the Esk, which is described below, the other canoeable rivers of western Cumbria flow out of low-lying lakes. They have a good head of water but their gradual gradient means they are of no great interest to the white water canoeist. The Irt and Ehen flow almost flat out of Wastwater and Ennerdale Water to the Irish Sea. The Cocker flows north into the Derwent out of Crummock Water, and is a little more interesting particularly as it enters Cockermouth–Southwaite Bridge (130.283) to Derwent Bridge (116.306), 4 kilometres, IIIb.

RIVER DUDDON

The Duddon may be conveniently divided into two sections: the Upper Duddon from Birk's Bridge to Ulpha Bridge, and the Lower Duddon from Ulpha Bridge to Duddon Bridge. The upper section is only canoeable during or just after heavy rain. In exceptionally heavy downpours or during snow-melt the river above Birks's Bridge can provide good sport (IIb). In such conditions the rest of the Upper Duddon provides wild, wild water, so take plenty of 'put-in paper'. The best place to judge the level of the river is at Duddon Bridge which takes the A595 over the river. The concrete platforms supporting the two bridge-pillars should be well covered to make the river worth paddling.

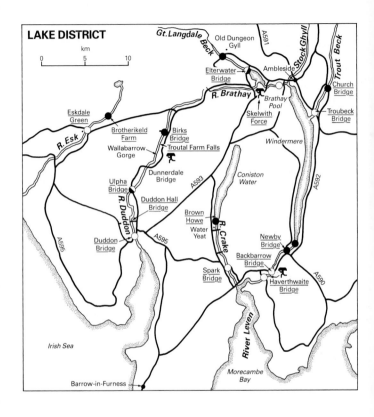

The Duddon, Great Langdale Beck and Leven and other rives of the Western and Central Lake District

Upper Duddon ***
Birk's Bridge (234.594) to Ulpha Bridge (196.930)
Grade IVd (Ve)
No Portages
9 Kilometres
OS Sheet 96

The narrow slot just above Birk's Bridge (Vf) is a straight run but only 1 metre wide and very dangerous due to boulders on the river-bed under which the water sumps. Most people launch in the pool immediately below Birk's Bridge.

Half a kilometre of relatively straightforward canoeing leads to a nasty surprise – Troutal Farm Falls (Ve). A series of small drops precede the falls, and a 20-metre high crag on the right leers over it from the right. Prior inspection from the road is the only sure way to locate this naughty little number. Take care if you are canoeing on sight, and portage on the left if you don't like what you see.

Troutal Farm Gorge, which follows, is continuous and difficult (IVd) but well supplied with eddies. From here the best route may be judged and the soft scenery of mountain and moorland relished. A wire spans the river – used by walkers to steady their progress across stepping-stones – two islands are passed in a wider section of river and then, on the right, the hillside rears up in rocky battlements, a warning of Wallowbarrow Gorge (Ve) just below.

Wallowbarrow Gorge is best inspected from a footpath on the right bank. Get out for this sphincter-tightening experience where a stile goes over a wall and a fence comes down from the crags. Do not worry overmuch about missing this marker since an enormous boulder nearby (the first of many in the gorge blocking the view downstream) will encourage you to get out and have a look. High water is best, blocking out the desperately tight turns and drops; one particularly mean fall in the middle of the gorge is often portaged (on the right) because of the pinning rocks below.

The gorge gradually eases in difficulty until an arched foot-bridge (carrying a path from Seathwaite and often used for prior

inspection) marks its final demise. Shortly thereafter Long House Gill enters from the left which is a large tributary providing a short, interesting paddle in its own right (IVd).

The confluence with Long House Gill marks a dramatic change in the nature of the Duddon. Twice the weight it was previously, the river flows down half the gradient and expands into a broad, green and gentle valley. After 1 kilometre there is Dunnerdale Bridge, and after 2 kilometres a metal foot-bridge and Waterworks Weir – best taken on the right. The river continues for a couple more kilometres through small gorges with some tight little problems – Jill's Folly (IVc) on a sharp left-hand bend is noted for unseating paddlers – and on down to Ulpha Bridge.

Lower Duddon **
Ulpha Bridge (196.930) to Duddon Bridge (180.883)
Grade IIIc (IVd)
No Portages
6 Kilometres
OS Sheet 96

Ulpha is the Viking for Wolf Hill but on the section of river below the town only Duddon Hall Falls is likely to produce any baying. The Duddon is now less continuous and more of a pool-drop river, although in flood there are long sections of fast-moving water. The road loops away from the river (now on the left) and wooded banks close in. Two islands must be negotiated before the road returns for a brief visit (after 2 kilometres) and further interesting but not too difficult canoeing leads (after a further 2 kilometres) to the most dramatic rapid on this section of the river, Duddon Hall Falls (IVd).

Two telegraph wires high above serve as warning that the Falls are approaching. They lie immediately below an island and immediately above Duddon Hall Bridge, from which they may be inspected. The Falls, taken on the right, are a spectacular plunge into white froth.

High on the Upper Duddon

Two weirs follow Duddon Hall Falls, the second much more powerful than the first. Easier water leads to the last interesting and quite long rapid round the right-hand side of a series of islands. The final kilometre down to Duddon Bridge is flat and a useful wind-down before the lorries on the A495 jolt you back to industrial reality. Egress is easiest immediately below the bridge on the left.

RIVER ESK

Emerging from the ground around Esk Hause, the Esk shares with the Duddon the accolade of being one of the Lake District's most impressive rivers. Like the Duddon it is not lake fed so it needs heavy rain to bring it up. Unfortunately, there is no road over Esk Hause, the Lakeland's highest pass, so canoeists must carry their boats some way up the river if they want to paddle all the way down it.

Ample compensation for the inconvenience of a long carry is provided by the wild scenery and wildlife. Esk Crag and Scafell provide a dramatic arena for the wagtail, dipper, ring ouzel and the occasional heron and kingfisher. Otters still fish in the pools and are joined – and now sometimes displaced – by the North American mink.

Esk **
Brotherikeld Farm (212.013) to Eskdale Green (149.995)
Grade IIIc
No Portages
8 Kilometres
OS Sheet 89

It is possible to carry up the Esk to put in above Brotherikeld Farm. A path follows the left bank – pick your spot. Below Brotherikeld the difficulties are continuous but nowhere extreme. The river drops continuously but there are no huge falls, and there

One of the final rapids on the Upper Duddon

is a notable absence of weirs and other man-made intrusions. The liveliest spots are just above Doctor's Bridge after 3 kilometres, and ½ kilometre further down where there is a short gorge. The water only eases off completely in the last kilometre to Eskdale Green. Egress is at the bridge below this village, 200 metres from liquid refreshment of another kind!

Great Langdale Beck and other rivers of the Central Lake District

Great Langdale Beck and the Brathay, of which it is a tributary, have the undeserved reputation of being dangerous rivers. Undeserved but nevertheless educational, because a video-recorded epic on Pillar Falls on Langdale Beck did more to promote white water safety in general, and keyhole cockpits, chest harnesses and paddle hooks in particular, than all the instructors in the BCU put together. And on the Brathay, inspecting the dangerous Skelwith Force will teach canoeists more about the hydrography of waterfalls than any number of books.

Their dangerous reputation is undeserved because anyone in a modern boat and with an ounce of common sense can canoe this combined stretch of 12 kilometres quite safely. Moreover, the reputation inflates the adrenalin level of those paddling these rivers to the extent that they may be disappointed by the reality.

Those seeking heart-stopping excitement should consider the smaller streams in the area. Ambleside and the central Lake District are surrounded by mountains, and the streams which rush down them are difficult to catch in condition and to canoe. The best is the Troutbeck (see below) but Stock Ghyll and Little Langdale Beck are also worth considering.

Stock Ghyll joins the Brathay in Ambleside and four or five times a year provides a short (1 kilometre) and very difficult waterfall run (Ve). A road parallels the stream some distance away on the right bank and you can decide on the day where you want to start.

For those wanting a real adrenalin rush, the awesome Colwith Force (VIf +) on Great Langdale's little sister, Little Langdale Beck, has probably yet to be done. The river as a whole, however, is too easy and hard by extremes to warrant more than this mention: ford (029.306) to road-bridge (330.030), Grade IIb (one portage), 3 kilometres. A small weir after a sharp left-hand bend serves as warning of Colwith Force – get out above the weir.

GREAT LANGDALE BECK

The Great Langdale Beck flows out of arguably the most scenic and certainly the most famous mountain valley in England, and therefore has much to offer besides good canoeing. White water there is, but only Pillar Falls is really serious and that succumbs easily enough with bank security. The first 4 kilometres of the stream are of little consequence in the white water stakes, but there are crags upon hills, knotts, fells and hows, becks charging white down ghylls and over dows and banks, everywhere curves and steepness, enough to please the most jaundiced eye. The beck may be flat and artificially straightened, but nothing around it is.

Great Langdale Beck *
Old Dungeon Ghyll Hotel Bridge (285.060) to Elterwater Bridge (327.047)
Grade IIIc (IVd)
No Portages
6 Kilometres
OS Sheet 90

If it is possible to paddle from the bridge opposite the Old Dungeon Ghyll then the Great Langdale Beck is up. It quickly picks up more water from the valley sides but only starts to drop at Baysbrown Bridge (alternative access 317.053). There are then 2 kilometres of exciting white water leading to the bridge in Elterwater. Towards the end of this section is Pillar Falls (IVd) which trapped an unfortunate canoeist in his boat for 45 minutes in 1982 – the subject of the video-tape.

Pillar Falls is best taken close to the right or left banks. In the centre there are upward-pointing rocks which have pinned boats. The fall is best inspected (and if necessary portaged) on the right bank. A warning of its approach from the river is given by Chapel Stile Weir, a large 'sloper' that can be shot anywhere. Below Pillar Falls the slate walls of the time-share complex squeezes the river

Pillar Falls on Langdale Beck

into another good rapid, before flatter water leads down to the bridge.

A car-park on the left provides a convenient get-out in the village of Elterwater; or you can continue down into the beautiful lake of the same name. In Elter Water, Great Langdale Beck merges with Little Langdale Beck to form the Brathay.

RIVER BRATHAY

The Brathay is to the Lake District as the Llugwy is to Snowdonia: a river popularized by outdoor centre use. Only the short stretch between Brathay foot-bridge and Brathay Pool is regularly used, however, and the section above offers more isolated canoeing.

Brathay
Elterwater Bridge (327.047) to Brathay Pool (366.034)
Grade IIIb
1 Portage
6 Kilometres
OS Sheet 90

Put in at the bridge in Elterwater and canoe down Great Langdale Beck into Elter Water. This soon discharges into the Brathay which is flat as far as Skelwith Force (VIf). The Force is right beside the road and offers an alternative access point (341.044), and if it looks as though you are going to canoe the Force you should be able to quadruple the number of tourists in the time it takes you to get your canoe off the car.

Above Skelwith Force signs warn you of the approaching waterfall. This has been shot over the left-hand slabs in high water but at that level the stopper upstream tends to throw you off line. There are rocks in the fall and dangerous boils at the bottom awaiting anyone who gets the wrong line – which is the *only* line in low water. Common sense therefore suggests a portage (left bank). 10 metres downstream of Skelwith Force is an entertaining

The Brathay foot-bridge

stopper which is good for 'enders'. The stopper at the foot of the Force itself is good for permanent 'enders'!

Trees festoon banks and river on the next section of the Brathay. Finding a route between and round them can be awkward (IIIb). Below Skelwith Bridge the river is calmer again. It picks up speed after a kilometre and there is a little rapid above Brathay foot-bridge after 2 kilometres. For the one-car or lone canoeist the section from here to Brathay Pool offers a run of ½ kilometre. The last rapid, Brathay Falls (IIIb), is good in flood and the Pool often collects bodies and boats. Cars can be parked next to Brathay Pool.

TROUTBECK

The Troutbeck is a short, continuously difficult and serious river. It flows into Lake Windermere just 1 kilometre below Troutbeck Bridge and so does not hold the water it picks up in its limited catchment area. It needs to be raining *at the time* to paddle the river (a quick look over Troutbeck Bridge will settle any argument); not surprisingly, therefore, it is one of the least paddled rivers in the Lake District.

Troutbeck **
Church Bridge (413.027) to Troutbeck Bridge (403.003)
Grade IVe
No Portages
3 Kilometres
OS Sheet 90

Access is from the car-park, just upstream of Church Bridge. The two hardest sections on the Troutbeck should be inspected before you put-in, for there is little chance to stop once you are on the water. The first, half-way down the river, is Pipe Bridge Gorge (IVe) which can be inspected by getting down to the pipe bridge from the minor road on the right bank – the first time the road comes close to the river after the put-in. The second difficult section, Bobsleigh (IVd), is just above Troutbeck Bridge and can be inspected by walking up the left bank.

Although these are the most difficult rapids, there is much other technical canoeing above and between them, and the Troutbeck rates very highly as a white water run. So short yet so sweet, it is a pity that it is not more often in condition. Egress is either at Troutbeck Bridge or in Lake Windermere after following the bank to the left for 1 kilometre to the Millerground landing (402.987).

The River Leven and its tributary the Crake

The rivers described here drain two of the largest lakes in a district famous for them. They therefore stay 'up' longer than any other in the north-west of England and, for that reason if no other, are justifiably popular amongst white water paddlers.

RIVER LEVEN

In its entirety, the section between Windermere and Haverthwaite gives an excellent, albeit quite short, white water run. The shorter stretch between Newby and Backbarrow is the venue for the famous 'white water tests' and has been canoed by thousands. The Leven 'test course' runs from just below the weir downstream of Newby Bridge (368.864) to just above Water Close Weir at Backbarrow (356.853). This is the only section of river to have negotiated access at the moment. Details can be obtained from the Lakeland Canoe Club. Hopefully negotiations will soon give access to the longer and more satisfactory trip described here.

Leven **
Windermere (380.370) to Haverthwaite Bridge (345.836)
Grade IVc
1 Portage
6 Kilometres
OS Sheet 97

To warm up it is worth putting in near the Fell Foot Country Park on the south-east shore of Lake Windermere for a kilometre of flat water and fine hilly views. This takes you into the Leven under Newby Bridge. The bridge is an alternative access point (see above).

The first rapid is Brickchute which is best taken in the middle. From here the river continues down through wooded banks to the top of the Graveyard. This technical section of rocky river becomes a seething mass of white water in full flood (the test finish is at the bottom of the rapid on the left).

Below the Graveyard is Water Close Weir which can involve a solid landing. Backbarrow Falls (IVc) squeezes through the bridge below and is less dangerous but just as awkward as it looks. Bits and pieces can be collected in the gigantic pool below to the accompaniment of cheers and catcalls from the neighbouring buildings. Do *not*, however, attempt to give spectator sport on the weir immediately below Backbarrow Bridge, unless the water is very low. At levels when the rest of the Leven is fun, canoeing Backbarrow Weir (VIf) is reckless.

The second weir below Backbarrow Bridge is a more reasonable proposition if it is shot in the right place. It can be readily inspected from the left bank, after portaging Backbarrow Weir above. Standing waves lead to a low foot-bridge and an island. The waves grow in size as you pass the island and continue under the A590 road-bridge. Possible egress is on the right bank.

A big weir ½ kilometre downstream of the bridge is nicely angled and it is followed by another island. This also has the effect of constricting the river and building superb 'play' waves. The left-hand side of the island is safest. After the channels meet, easier water leads to a third island which can be passed on either side. The bridge at Haverthwaite is just below. Egress is to the left bank.

RIVER CRAKE

The Leven is too short to have anything in the way of good canoeable tributaries. Indeed, it is a small wonder of nature that the Leven itself is so good. Under pain of being excommunicated by local canoeists, however, I have been forced against my better judgement to include the Crake. In fact this river is not strictly a tributary of anything for it 'joins' the Leven at the tide.

Access to the Crake is on the west shore of Coniston Water at Brown Howe where there is public parking or, for very small groups, at the first bridge down the river – near Water Yeat

(291.881). Egress is well above the confluence at the third road-bridge.

Crake
Brown Howe (291.911) to Spark Bridge (306.849)
Grade IIIc
No Portages
7 Kilometres
OS Sheet 97

Crake is a mean little name for a mean little river. It is mean with its difficulty. There are just two technical rapids on the river – the first below Water Yeat Bridge and the second below the next bridge (Lowick Bridge) – Bobbin Mill Rapid. They are good value when the river is in full flood, but the rest of the river is uninteresting.

It is mean in its gentler moods. There are very few places in this narrow, broken river where the novice can relax and enjoy the cruise – he (or she) must always be avoiding trees, rocks, weir sills, weir spikes and on one occasion even barbed wire.

And it is mean with its views. Once you have paddled a kilometre down Coniston Water and entered the Crake, you can kiss goodbye to the southern lakeland landscape. Thick bushes and trees line the banks, and only when the river nears the get-out at Spark Bridge can you see much further than the average water vole.

So, why put it in the guide? Well, it is lake-fed so, like its much better neighbour the Leven, it stays up for longer than many other rivers in the Lakes; and locals like it – 'the most underrated river in the Southern Lake District' according to Barry Howell, and 'a swift and exciting run' writes Mike Hayward. There is only one way to find out for yourself.

The Swale and other rivers of the Northern Dales

Suddenly, round a river bend, Richmond Castle towers into view. A thousand years after its laborious construction, it still seems to block the entrance to Swaledale. In sunny summer weather the broken walls shimmer in the river's reflection; but should you want to preserve this gentle image do not venture inside the castle. There, in all its feudal splendour, is the rectangular keep standing monstrous and complete. Its 40 metre tall, 2 metre thick walls still dominate all those who stand and stare; a grim reminder of the Norman world of lord and fief.

If Swaledale and Richmond Castle are a reminder of our feudal past, Wensleydale, to the south, is a reminder of our feudal present. A little over a kilometre upstream of Wensley – a village which never recovered its premiership in the dale after an outbreak of the plague in 1563 – a 250-year-old private bridge crosses the River Ure to an enormous south-facing mansion. Originally built as a hunting lodge to the estate of Lord Bolton, it is now their home. And it is Bolton land as far as the eye can see; and the village of Wensley too, petrol station, pub, 13th-century church and all the perfectly matched brown stone houses.

Fortunately, the water of the Swale and Ure is sufficiently exciting (in parts) to make you forget these legacies of feudalism. Of the other Dales rivers (apart from the Tees – see page 153) this cannot be said. The Nidd running through Pateley Bridge to the south never rises above Grade IIb and, although beautiful, will never attract *white water* canoeists. The only other river regularly canoed in the northern dales is the Derwent, but this, like the Nidd, has little or no white water.

RIVER SWALE

The River Swale is one of the easiest and most popular rivers in this guide. For the white water tiger it has little to offer apart from the monstrous ragged horsehoe fall at Richmond, and some extreme spate possibilities above Muker. For the Canadian canoe buff, or the weekend kayak dabbler on the other hand, the Swale is a delightful run on fast water through gentle scenery and past easily accessible banks.

The Swale rises on Birkdale Common, flows east to Richmond and then swings south to its confluence with the River Ure near Boroughbridge. There is no white water below Great Langton Bridge. Above Langton the river depends on rain and/or snow-melt to bring it into canoeable condition. Moreover, because of the river's steep, albeit even, gradient, the run-off is fast, so do not go to the Swale after a dry spell.

The Swale is naturally divided into an upper and lower section by Richmond Falls; but anyone with a map and an ounce of imagination will see that there are many variations on the two trips described below. The river is frequently crossed by roads where the low banks offer ready access and egress. The Swale is a popular fishing river but there is also a long tradition of canoeing in the dale and the two sporting interests peacefully, if not always happily, co-exist.

Upper Swale ***
Gunnerside Bridge (949.978) to Richmond Falls (173.005)
Grade IIb (IVe)
No Portages
25 Kilometres
OS Sheets 98, 99 and 92

This long trip through Swaledale goes surprisingly quickly in high water. The shingle rapids and rocky channels do not encourage the paddler to stop and play, and the water is in a constant hurry to get from moor to valley floor. At lower levels, however, canoeists will want to gain the benefit of the additional water brought in by Arkle Beck by putting in at Grinton Bridge or even lower at Marske Bridge. This will give a trip of 15 and 10 kilometres respectively. In very high water it is worth investigating the Swale near its source above Muker; there are some exciting waterfalls in 'them there hills'.

The B6270 follows the Upper Swale in its descent from the hills and at Gunnerside Bridge it crosses from the south to the north bank. There is easy access to the river here and at other places along the north bank as far as Grinton Bridge. The river is fast with many small rapids and shallows.

Two kilometres below Grinton Bridge, beside Marrick Priory, is Staircase Rapid (IIb). This marks the start of more technical canoeing; the main problems are rocks (at medium water) and setting currents on the outside of bends (at high water). At Marske road-bridge and at the two islands which succeed it, right is right. Between Marske and Richmond the right bank is heavily wooded, and tree stumps and fallen trees on the outside of bends have impaled a number of canoeists.

The run-in to Richmond gives some interesting water, finishing in a deep pool on a bend. Richmond Falls (IVe), the 3-metre drop which lies below the castle, is awe-inspiring. It is regularly shot in a number of places, but the width of the falls makes bank security a problem and it is probably best to pre-position a boat downstream before attempting any of the middle shoots. Local paddlers avoid shooting the falls when it is impossible to land on the central rocks upstream of the lip. There may be obstructions lodged below the falls so whatever your eventual decision, inspection is essential. There is a public car-park immediately next to the fall on the left so you may be observed in your narrow-eyed appraisal by dog-walkers and check-trousered American tourists.

Lower Swale *
Richmond (173.005) to Great Langton (299.960)
Grade IIb
No Portages
18 Kilometres
OS Sheets 92 and 93

The section below Richmond is similar in difficulty to that above, but less continuous. Leaving Swaledale the river loses its constant gradient, dropping more in fits and starts. The first major 'fit', 2 kilometres downstream, is Eastby Abbey Weir which is shot or portaged on the left. This is soon followed by Eastby Slalom Site, a rocky rapid and island. Eastby Abbey dates from the time of Richmond Castle and it is rumoured that they are linked by a secret underground tunnel. Those less afraid of showing their intent have the pleasant alternative of canoeing, or walking, between them.

The confused water of Red House Farm Rapid is ½ kilometre below the slalom site, followed by still water running deep. There is more white water on the sweeping left- and right-hand bends as the river approaches Brompton-on-Swale. Below this village down to Great Langton there are only occasional gravel banks to interrupt the flow. Those wanting to finish, or start, at Brompton (10 kilometres above Langton) can get to and from the north shore of the river at a number of places upstream of Catterick Bridge (carrying the Old Great North Road – the A1).

A weir underneath Catterick Bridge carries a small stopper but apart from this – and the occasional tree in the river – there is little to exercise the grey cells on the trip down to Great Langton. Below this village, the road (B6271) comes down next to the water at Langton Wood. Here you should leave the Swale, unless slow meanders between high banks are your delight.

RIVER URE

The Ure is the major river of the northern Pennines. Like the Swale it too has a long history of untroubled canoeing. Unfortunately for the white water canoeist, however, most of the river is flat, suitable only for introductory canoeing (the section between Hack Fall and Slenningford is the best – check at campsite in Slenningford for access agreement). In fact there is only one good rough water section on the river starting at Aysgarth Falls and finishing at Wensley Bridge.

Ure
Aysgarth Falls (011.887) to Wensley Bridge (091.894)
Grade IIIc (Ve)
1 Portage

8 Kilometres
OS Sheets 98 and 99

The Ure here is only really worth doing in flood. It is canoeable at almost any level, so there is a grade for low water (LW) as well as high water (HW), but unless you want to try Aysgarth Falls, wait until the snow is melting on Giles Great Stone Hags, or Pen Hill has been hiding for days behind saturated stratus.

Aysgarth Falls is a four-tier drop but the first two are so close that they go together under the name of the Upper Fall (Ve LW, VIf HW). The Middle Fall (VIf LW and HW) and Lower Fall (Vf LW, VIf HW) are much bigger and more serious propositions. They are too shallow to be safe to shoot in low water and form monstrously powerful stoppers in high water. The sensible thing to do is to portage the lot. Park in the public car-park 200 metres along the road to Carperby and put in on the north shore between Middle and Lower Falls, crossing to the south bank to carry round the Lower Falls. The canoeable section between the Middle and Lower Falls contains a fairly meaty rapid over a bedrock sill – Don't Play With Fire (IIIc).

Three kilometres downstream the steep rabbit-warrened banks begin to squeeze the river, marking the approach of Redmire Force (IVc LW, Ve HW). This is best inspected (and if necessary portaged) on the left. The river continues to be interesting for another kilometre (IIb LW, IIIc HW), until flat water past Bolton Hall Bridge and down to Wensley Bridge (A684) leads the mind to other things.

The Wharfe and other rivers of the Southern Dales

The Southern Dales have always been a testing-ground in the fight for public access to Britain's wild country. An easy day-trip from the great conurbations of Manchester, Leeds and Middlesbrough, this beautiful hill-country is a great natural amenity for walkers, climbers and canoeists. It is also good farming and fishing country, and although the National Parks have often successfully mediated between farming and recreational interests, anglers have remained militantly obstructive against river use. Access agreements have been negotiated to the River Washburn for specified dates throughout the year, but this tiny river does not satisfy the big water lust of most white water paddlers. For them the Ribble and the Wharfe are the best touring rivers of the area: the first an outstanding spate run; the second a less continuous but more reliable pool-drop river.

After years of fruitless negotiation, Yorkshire canoeists lost patience with the tepid approach of the British Canoe Union (BCU) towards gaining access and, in 1986, formed the Campaign for River Access for Canoes and Kayaks (CRACK). CRACK received instant support from touring canoeists in every part of the country, and Yorkshire paddlers remain today at the forefront of the fight for fair and equal access to our rivers.

On the Ribble and Wharfe, canoeists have reported severe harassment from anglers, and on the Lower Wharfe even public access to the river is restricted. At the Strid, a beautiful and exciting gorge between Barden Bridge and Bolton Priory, a charge is now made for simply looking at the river – High Force on the Tees and Swallow Falls on the Llugwy have similar arrangements. One wonders whether canoeists in the future will be prepared to accept such a backward step as the price for enjoying their sport.

RIVER WHARFE

The waters of the Wharfe and its most famous (although not best or even biggest) rapid, Appletreewick, have been paddled (and swallowed) by canoeists throughout the country due to the annual white water races staged on the lower part of the Middle Wharfe. The race section has traditionally been the most accessible part of the river, but for white water canoeists it is certainly not the best and, were it not for the access problems, more paddlers surely would have experienced the unique gentle beauty of Langstrothdale and the excitement of Coniston Falls, Linton Falls, Ghaistrill's Strid and the Strid.

Upper Wharfe (Langstrothdale) *
High Bank (882.801) to Hubberholme (925.782)
Grade IVc
No Portages
5 Kilometres
OS Sheet 98

At Beckermonds, Oughtershaw Beck meets Green Field Beck to produce, in continuous heavy rain, a narrow and steeply inclined sliver of white. Access is a kilometre downstream of Beckermonds where the road is forced up against the river by the packed contours of High Bank. Upstream of the put-in is a largish waterfall. In high water it looks canoeable, and it must have disappeared completely in the floods of 1673 when the river left fish floundering in the pews of Hubberholme church.

The road follows the river along the valley of the Upper Wharfe – locally called Langstrothdale – so the whole section may be viewed from the car on the way up. The main difficulties lie in the first 2 kilometres but the stream is always fast so overhanging trees remain a problem to the end. Take out at the humpbacked bridge at Hubberholme, home of Hubber the Viking who settled here 1,500 years ago.

Despite the difficulty of getting to Langstrothdale one can see its attraction for Hubber. Dark dippers with white bibs bob above the water, herons tiptoe through the shallows, ducks and geese make raucous conversation, and still occasionally the rarest of British hawks, the merlin, rears its ferocious head. And then in spring, all along the riverside path which is now part of the Dales Way, the

Grass of Parnassus pushes its five stamens and single white flower 10 centimetres through the limestone topsoil.

Middle Wharfe (Wharfedale) *
Coniston Bridge (978.674) to Barden Bridge (051.574)
Grade IVd (Ve)
No Portages
16 Kilometres
OS Sheets 98 and 104

Within this long section several shorter trips are possible – access, or egress, at Grassington Footbridge (001.632), at Hebden foot-bridge (025.623) or at Burnsall Bridge (031.611). If you start at these bridges and get out at Barden, the trip is reduced to 11, 7 and 5 kilometres respectively. But, also respectively, you will miss Coniston Falls and Ghaistrill's Strid, Linton Weirs and Falls, and Loup Scar. In the unlikely event that 16 kilometres is not far enough, you can start at Hubberholme but there is no white water in the 15 kilometres between it and Coniston.

The Wharfe in Wharfedale has eroded an almost even gradient through the limestone countryside. Occasionally, however, harder rock, either naturally or artificially constructed, resists the river. This has produced six major rapids or weirs. With the lively River Skirfare from Littondale (canoeable despite several strands of barbed-wire across the river) joining the Wharfe just above Coniston, there is a serious weight and size to these rapids, particularly in flood. The Wharfe, with its large catchment area (over 1,000 square kilometres) and many feeder streams, floods easily. So do not let the broad valleys and rolling hills of Emmerdale Farm country, or the splish-splash of even paddle strokes lull you into a false sense of security.

Coniston Falls (IVd), marked simply as a Waterfall on the OS map, is a kilometre below the put-in. It is small by waterfall standards; about 4 metres over two tiers. It is best shot on the extreme right. A long flat section of 3 kilometres leads to

Consiton Falls on the Wharfe

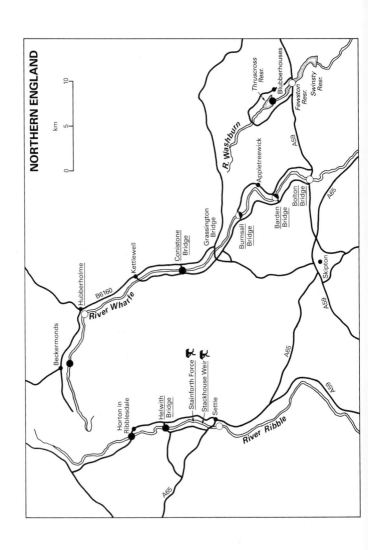

NORTHERN ENGLAND

km
0   5   10

Beckermonds

Hubberholme

B6160

River Wharfe

Kettlewell

Conistone Bridge

Grassington Bridge

Burnsall Bridge

Appletreewick

Barden Bridge

Bolton Bridge

R. Washburn

Thruscross Resr.

Blubberhouses

Fewston Resr.

Swinsty Resr.

A59

A65

Skipton

A59

Horton in Ribblesdale

Helwith Bridge

Stainforth Force

Stackhouse Weir

Settle

River Ribble

A65

A65

A59

Ghaistrill's Strid (IVc) which is a long rapid made easier and more fun by high water. It should be inspected from the left bank. A kilometre of easy water then leads to the seventeenth-century road-bridge (B6265) at Grassington.

Below the bridge are two weirs; the first is serious and easily portaged (IVe); the second more gentle (IIIc). The huge rapid which follows, Linton Falls (Ve), is probably even more serious. A foot-bridge immediately above it allows easy inspection from both banks and many will decide that the most sensible route is to portage down the left bank. However, the bottom wave does flush through if you get the right line at the top!

Below Linton Falls the river is entirely calm for the 3 kilometres to Hebden foot-bridge. Below that the water chops up a little and after a kilometre a big left-hand bend round a constricting limestone cliff peaks the water into huge waves. This is Loup Scar (IIIc) which soon quietens into a huge eddy, and runs out flat to Burnsall Bridge.

The 5 kilometres between Burnsall and Barden Bridge are used regularly for 'white' water racing. Apart from the rapid of Appletreewick (IVc), however, this would be more accurately described as an opaque water racing course. The river creeps down Wharfedale as lively as an oil slick. Then suddenly after 3 kilometres, as though a spark were thrown from the shore, the water is alight with wild movement. Long lines of dark firs marching down either bank accentuate the blazing white of Appletreewick; but a quick look at the rapid serves to show there is no danger when it is shot right of the island. Those wanting to inspect the rapid before a race should take the footpath from Hargill (left bank). This is much quicker (10 minutes) than walking up or down the river.

Lower Wharfe (including the Strid) *
Barden Bridge (051.574) to Bolton Bridge (071.528)
Grade IVe
No Portages

Rivers Wharfe, Washburn and Ribble

8 Kilometres
OS Sheet 104

Half a kilometre below Barden Bridge the dale country steepens and a resistant bed of millstone grit forces the Wharfe into sharp turns and narrow channels.

The Strid and its attendant rapids are a quite unique and spectacular feature of the Wharfe. High water is to be preferred for this stretch because the lower the river, the narrower and more dangerous the gorge.

The first indication of the Strid is a sweeping left-hand bend where the main channel pillows the water to the right of an island. This is Tankers Corner (IIIc), a heavy rapid with little chance of getting out before Little Strid (IIId). Here the course of the river turns right, offering a clear channel for those in control, but the main flow continues left, forming a sizeable stopper to catch the drifters. A hundred metres downstream is the Strid (IVe) which is very narrow and undercut in low water, and a mass of standing waves and diagonal stoppers in flood. The banks are easily accessible but the gritstone shoulders over and *under* which the water flows are worrying for swimmers.

Below the Strid the gorge gradually opens out into grassy pastures fringed with woods. After 4 kilometres the twelfth-century ruins of Bolton Priory – sometimes called Abbey although it never reached that status before being dissolved by Henry VIII in 1539 – are passed on the right. A foot-bridge and stepping-stones cross the river, causing, in addition to some ledges, small disturbances in the otherwise placid water. Bolton Bridge, carrying the A59 Harrogate to Skipton road, is not far below. Egress is on the right bank.

River Washburn

The Washburn is well worth a visit if you don't mind queuing for eddies. On a number of specified days in the year releases are made from Thruscross Reservoir for competition canoeing and on race days the Washburn may be run by touring canoeists. Race dates may be obtained from the BCU. A fee is charged for non-competitive use of the river but this includes a shuttle back from the bottom. The Washburn may be combined with a section of the River Wharfe for an enjoyable day or weekend out in southern Yorkshire.

Washburn *
Thruscross Reservoir (155.574) to Fewston Reservoir (168.553)
Grade IIIb
No Portages
3 Kilometres
OS Sheet 104

The Washburn depends on a release from Thruscross Reservoir to make it canoeable. Even then it is a tiny river with everything in miniature – small eddies, small waves, even small stoppers. It is an exciting *little* run.

Access is immediately below Thruscross Reservoir dam where there is a car-park on the right bank. The car-park is reached by a road running up the right bank of the river from the A59. The top part of the river is perhaps the most entertaining with a number of drops and rapids in a narrow channel. Lower down the river opens out somewhat but there remains some good white water. The river finally peters out into Fewston Reservoir. Egress is below the A59 road-bridge to a car-park on the right bank.

RIVER RIBBLE

The Ribble rises high in the Pennines on Gayle Moor and flows south through the rugged limestone country between Ingleborough and Pen y Ghent. Below Helwith Bridge and as far as Settle, the river flows through a gritstone area and in this boulder-filled valley lies the best rapid in England – Twin Bridges.

Ribble ***
Horton in Ribblesdale (807.726) to Settle (813.639)
Grade IVe

2 Portages (?)
10 Kilometres
OS Sheet 98

For the section between Helwith Bridge and Settle to be canoeable
the river needs to be in full flood. The 5 kilometre run-in from
Horton to Helwith Bridge is little more than a warm-up. There are
some pleasant rapids for ½ kilometre below Helwith and then the
fun really starts. Twin Bridges (IVe) can be inspected at a distance
from the road (B6479) on the way up, although if anticipation
ruins your digestion this is not advised. This superb kilometre of
continuous white water is not desperately difficult but you are on
your own in a wild sea running through two sets of railway-bridge
pillars between eddyless banks.

Below Twin Bridges the Ribble eases until Stainforth Bridge (a
2-metre wide seventeenth-century packhorse-bridge beloved of
watercolourists) warns of the approach of Stainforth Force (Vf).
The Force, which lies immediately below the bridge (inspect and
usually portage right), is dangerous in low water because of the
pot-holes immediately below the surface, and dangerous in high
water because of the powerful stopper and boils at the bottom. It
is sometimes canoed in medium water as a 'one-off' when the rest
of the river provides only mediocre sport.

Below Stainforth Force interesting rapids lead down to
Stackhouse Weir (IVe). This has a vicious tow-back, and has
'stackhoused' at least one canoeist; it is normally portaged. The
next weir, Settle Weir, is immediately above the A65 road-bridge
in Settle itself. The fish ladders on the left are tempting but quite
difficult and dangerous (IVe). Below the town bridge there is a
final rapid with a large rock in the centre – Municipal Falls (IVd).

This last rapid is named after the neighbouring North Yorkshire
County Council King's Mill depot, and the public foot-bridge just
below this, offers a convenient get-out. To reach the depot turn
south off the A65 at the town bridge on the east bank of the
Ribble; it is at the bottom of the fourth very small road on the
right. On the way you may pass the Naked Man, a pub sign that
changing canoeists should do their best not to emulate.

The Dart and other rivers of the South-West

The River Dart is a queen of rivers, amongst the half-a-dozen best in the land. Wild and rugged in its upper reaches, more gentle in difficulty and situation lower down, it is a beautiful and fascinating river throughout. It does rely on heavy rain to bring it into condition and it is a long way from almost everywhere. During the winter months, however, when the prevailing south-westerly airstream brings low pressure after low pressure spiralling in out of the Atlantic, rain is not in short supply on the moors of the south-western peninsula. So stiffen up the sinews and summon up the blood, for having canoed this river you will think the long drive a paltry price to pay for such enjoyment.

There is one other river which is always associated with the South-West, and, like the Dart, gives its name to the moor at its source and to the town at its mouth. The Exe, however, is not of interest to white water tourers for its steepness comes too early and its later fall in maturity is concentrated into weirs. These weirs, particularly Flower Pots, have achieved fame, or rather infamy, for their boat-wrecking lips in drought and man-eating stoppers in flood, and an annual race, the Exe Descent, ensures wide personal acquaintance with these undesirable traits. For racers, access to the Exe is just north of Tiverton by a school, foot-bridge and weir near the junction of the A373 and A396 (949.138), and for weir-doggers access is best near Head Weir and Flower Pots Weir next to the Mill on the Exe public house in Exeter (914.926). Egress is at Topsham near the Ferry (left bank) or to the canal (right bank) for a return paddle to Exeter.

Should you be within easy striking distance of the South-West or be lucky enough to live there, you will have ample opportunity to paddle the tributaries of the Dart and other spate rivers flowing out of the moors. Mentioned below are the Tamar, Tavy, Barle and the East Lyn. There are a number of spate rivers not described but worth investigating: the tiny Plym near the Dewerstone is reputed to be an exciting run in high flood, as is the

Erme as far as Ivybridge, and the upper reaches of the Fowey and Camel in Bodmin Moor are well worth a look. There also are the Avon, Teign, Bovey and Swincombe to consider, but still the fairest of them all is the Dart.

RIVER DART

Dartmoor, perhaps more than any other mountain and moorland area in Britain, is redolent with hostile imagery. It is the land of deceiving mist and treacherous bog, of hard granite and acidic peat, of dangerous prisoners and Danger Areas, of highway robbery and the Hound of the Baskervilles. If myth were ever to approach reality it would surely be at East Dart Head, the source of the River Dart, and the bleakest part of the moor. 7 kilometres from any dwelling or road, it is a most remote and rugged place.

The nature of an upland river can be judged in part from its source, and so it is with the Upper Dart. In flood it is a wild and frightening place, and like the moor to which it gives a name, attractive to adventurers. At Dartmeet, the West Dart joins the East Dart and together they roar and tumble over granite boulders in a deep and isolated glen. It is one of the most continuous and inaccessible sections of extreme white water in England.

Below Newbridge, the Dart gradually relaxes amidst oakwoods, bracken and royal fern. Still, however, there is excellent and this time more friendly white water. The Lower Dart is a good run in racing boats and touring canoeists of intermediate ability will find plenty to satisfy them. The level of the river may be judged at the start of this lower section at the packhorse-bridge at Newbridge which dates from the Middle Ages. If the river is only just canoeable here do not bother to go further upstream. Indeed, for both Upper and Lower Dart it is best to wait for heavy rain.

In heavy flood conditions three tributaries of the Dart are also worth canoeing. There is the East Dart which can be paddled from Postbridge (647.789) to Dartmeet at Grade IVd; the West Dart which goes at Grade IIIc from Two Bridges (608.750) to the same confluence; and the River Webburn which flows for 3½ kilometres at Grade IVd from below Ponsworthy (park at a lay-by – 705.734 – and get in on the western tributary) to the Lower Dart between Newbridge and Holne Bridge.

Upper Dart***

Dartmeet (671.731) to Newbridge (711.709)
Grade Ve
No Portages
10 Kilometres
OS Sheets 191 and 202

The Upper Dart seems to have been designed with the white water canoeist in mind. The East and West Dart meet just below the car-park at Dartmeet (a justifiably popular beauty spot for the wheel-bound) and then a kilometre of comparatively easy water allows for a warm-up. The drops gradually get harder as the river digs deeper into the valley and a number require bank inspection. There are no waterfalls but there are definite drops where the river disappears from view. Powerful stoppers often lie in wait at the bottom of these falls.

Reckoned to be a soft touch for its grade, the Upper Dart should not be underrated, particularly in high water. A footpath parallels the left bank and this is the only reasonable way out, up or down, should a canoeist blow it. The moor on either side, even if it could be reached up the steep hillside, would be a bleak and desolate place to search or wait for help. The atmosphere here is more Alpine or Corsican than English, and it would be a serious place to land in trouble.

There are several islands on the river and the route round them will depend, as it does also with the bedrock and boulder rapids, on the level of the river. This and the continuous nature of the canoeing make a detailed description of the Upper Dart superfluous. Near the end however, you will no doubt recognize Euthanasia Falls on the right hand side of a small island. It is possible to miss this ominously named rapid by going left of the island, but this is less satisfying. Further still there is the much larger Bell Pool Island, marking

the start of a pleasant final kilometre down to the get-out at Newbridge.

As if the paddling was not enough there is another sort of wildlife to enjoy. You share the pure waters of the Dart with caddisfly, dragonfly and mayfly larvae, on whom salmon and trout feed. Dippers also like this diet and these brown and white birds walk under water to catch their prey. Grey wagtails snap insects a few feet above and, if you are quiet, you may chance upon a heron fishing in the shallows. Mink regularly hunt along the banks and the occasional otter has been spotted by canoeists.

Lower Dart **
Newbridge (711.709) to Buckfastleigh (746.667)
Grade IIIc
No Portages
15 Kilometres
OS Sheet 202

In the twelfth century Dartmoor became the richest source of tin in Europe. The tin miners were so powerful that they had their own parliament, called the Stannary. For easier transport of the ore from the mines, packhorse-bridges were built on the Moor including Newbridge and Holne Bridge. The latter is a little short of half-way down this section of river, although, because the road climbs over a hill that the river meanders round, it is much less than half-way by car. Holne Bridge (730.706) is therefore a popular egress point for a shorter trip; all the more so because the best rapids lie upstream.

The named rapids (all IIIc in average water, rising to IVd in full flood), on the 7 kilometres between the two packhorse-bridges, are as follows. After 1 kilometre there is Washing Machine, an often narrow constriction sporting a powerful play-hole on the right. A further kilometre round a big right-hand bend brings Lovers' Leap where the water piles up against a cliff on the left. A

Should every white water river run dry, there is always the artificial slalom course at Holme Pierrepont, Nottingham

short graveyard section follows and then there is Triple Drop, whose name leaves little to the imagination. Towards the end there is the rapid the Spin Dryer leading into a large eddy under a retaining wall on the right. It is the last big rapid before Holne Bridge.

Holne Bridge spans a deep narrow section of river much frequented by bridge-jumpers wearing T-shirts reading 'No Brain, No Pain, No Problem'. Some way below Holne Bridge is the powerful Holne Weir, to be taken on the right. The River Dart Country Park and Holne Park Residential Centre follows on the right bank. Waterworks Bridge follows soon and then a long easy and quite beautiful stretch down to Furzleigh Weir which is a kilometre above the finish. This 8-metre, 45 degree weir should be inspected prior to any attempt. A way down on the right is possible or the salmon steps on the left can be taken.

Egress into Buckfastleigh is on the left between Old Dart Bridge and the new motorway-bridge. It is possible to continue further to Staverton Bridge (784.637), or even go as far as the tide at Totnes, but it would be almost as exciting and a good deal less tiring to follow the same route on the Dart Valley Light Railway. Better then to relax above Buckfastleigh on the 'oak tree stream' (the meaning of 'Dart') or take time to visit Buckfast Abbey built by monks (between 1906 and 1932) on the riverside site of the old Cistercian monastry pulled down by Henry VIII. I am told that the honey they distribute is an epicure's delight.

RIVER TAVY

The River Tavy flows south-west out of Dartmoor through the town of Tavistock and into the sea at Plymouth. It has some good canoeing with two contrasting sections: an upper, vigorous, shallow fast-flowing stream, and a lower, more gentle, powerful river.

Rivers Dart, Tavy, Walkham and Tamar

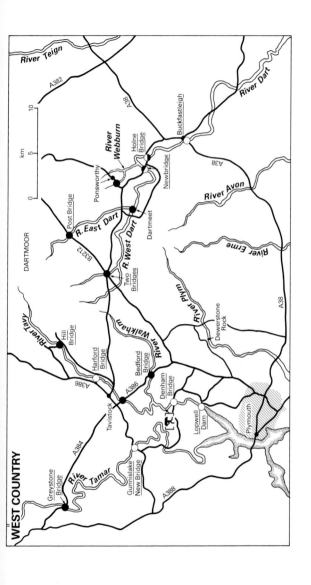

WEST COUNTRY

DARTMOOR

River Teign

A382

River Dart

River Webburn

Buckfastleigh

Holne Bridge

Ponsworthy

Newbridge

A38

Post Bridge

R. East Dart

Dartmeet

River Avon

R. West Dart

B3212

River Erme

Two Bridges

River Plym

River Tavy

Dewerstone Rock

Hill Bridge

A38

Harford Bridge

River Walkham

A386

Bedford Bridge

Denham Bridge

A386

Lopwell Dam

Tavistock

Plymouth

A384

Greystone Bridge

River Tamar

Gunnislake New Bridge

A388

km
0   5   10

Upper Tavy *
Hill Bridge (532.803) to Harford Bridge (505.767)
Grade IVc
No Portages
5 Kilometres
OS Sheet 201

This section of river may be increased to 11 kilometres by putting in at the confluence of the Tavy's two major tributaries, Rattle Brook and Amicombbe Brook (560.837). However, not only is exceptionally heavy rain necessary to canoe this narrow gully of a river but also exceptionally broad shoulders, for the confluence is 3 kilometres from the nearest road.

There is a weir and island at Hill Bridge which should be shot on the left. About ½ kilometre downstream is Creason Wood with the first of many drops on this continuous section of river. The west shore of the Upper Tavy is wooded for a good distance down to Harford Bridge and there may well be fallen trees blocking some parts of the river.

Lower Tavy
A386 road-bridge (475.737) to Lopwell Dam (474.649)
Grade IIIc
1 Portage (?)
13 Kilometres
OS Sheet 201

The Tavy below Tavistock is quite serious. The deep tree-lined valley through which the river flows would make access and egress difficult in an emergency. (A more exciting start to the last 7 kilometres of this lower section is the River Walkham from Bedford Bridge – see below.) Just after the confluence with the Walkham is Double Waters, an entertaining drop with a large boulder, fortunately well padded with a cushion wave. Two kilometres downstream of Double Waters is a weir with a powerful keeper. It should be portaged in high water.

RIVER WALKHAM

The River Walkham rises in south-west Dartmoor and provides an alternative and better start to the Lower Tavy. Combined with the alternative egress point given here it is also a shorter trip.

Walkham
Bedford Bridge (503.703) to Denham Bridge – on Lower Tavy (477.678)
Grade IIIc
No Portages
7 Kilometres
OS Sheet 201

The only notable fall on the Walkham is where the river emerges out of a wooded valley and enters the fields. Immediately on the left is a fence. Here the river drops suddenly down a shoot on the left. After this rapid the river picks up more pace with some continuous stretches of white water. Egress is 3 kilometres after the confluence with the Tavy at the first road-bridge – Denham Bridge.

RIVER TAMAR

The River Tamar is one of the longest rivers in the South-West and for much of its course forms the boundary between Devon and Cornwall. It rises just 7 kilometres from the north Cornish coast and then flows south for 70 kilometres to meet the Tavy at Plymouth. It is not a great white water river but the section described below is popular with novices.

Tamar
Greystone Bridge (368.804) to Gunnislake Newbridge (433.725)
Grade IIc
No Portages
20 Kilometres
OS Sheet 201

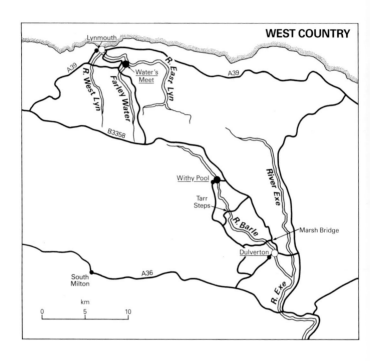

Rivers Barle and Lyn

Access to this section of the Tamar is at Greystone Bridge which was an 'indulgence' bridge – the medieval church persuaded people to contribute to the cost of the bridges by selling them indulgences for the remission of their sins. Egress is at Gunnislake at a crossing called 'Newbridge' simply because it was built after Greystone Bridge in 1520.

Between Greystone Bridge and Gunnislake the Tamar valley is steep-sided in places and densely wooded. Salmon find the deep pools good places to rest on their way up the river and the fishing is excellent.

This section is not difficult to canoe but it has one or two hazards that need watching. The first is numerous weirs. In low water all the weirs are shootable down tongues of water but watch out for stakes. In high water all the weirs, except the first, tend to be washed-out and can be shot safely. The second hazard is wire and planking washed down from fishing stands. These tend to lie in a tangled heap on the Devon (left) bank, but are submerged in high water, and a serious hazard to swimmers.

RIVER BARLE

The River Barle is a tributary of the Exe joining that river north of Tiverton. It rises in Exmoor a couple of kilometres from its parent river. For this section of the Barle to be in good condition for canoeing the water should be level with the right bank above Withypool Bridge. If it is only level with the bridge sill it will be a grade easier than described here.

Barle
Withypool Bridge (845.345) to Dulverton Bridge (912.278)
Grade IIIc
No Portages
19 Kilometres
OS Sheet 181

There are only three tricky sections on this long stretch of river

and some will prefer to start lower down at Tarr Steps (868.322).
From here to Dulverton Bridge is 10 kilometres.

The first section of white water is 3 kilometres above Tarr Steps.
It is a rock garden easily inspected from the left bank. 5 kilometres
below Tarr Steps is Dulverton Weir with a tree-covered island
awkwardly placed in the weir pool below. Finally just above
Dulverton Bridge is a drop with a big hole that tends to 'eat'
beginners. Egress is to the beach just upstream of Dulverton
Bridge.

RIVER EAST LYN

The East and West Lyn combined in the great flood of 1952 to
wreak havoc on the tiny North Devon coastal resort of Lynmouth,
an indication of the tremendous fluctuations in level possible on
this small river. Depending on the height of the East Lyn the
grade of the river varies between IVd and VIf. It should be fairly
obvious when the latter conditions prevail.

East Lyn **
Watersmeet (744.486) to Lynmouth (723.496)
Grade Ve
No Portages
3 Kilometres
OS Sheet 180

Negotiated access to the East Lyn is at Watersmeet although it has
almost certainly been paddled from Leeford. Watersmeet (so
called because the Lyn meets Farley Water here) is on the A39
coming in to Lynmouth from Barnstable, 1 kilometre below where
the road first starts to parallel Farley Water.

About half-way down this short stretch of river is a difficult
gorge (Ve) which should be inspected. Once committed to the
gorge it is very difficult to get out. The shallow pools have been
known to radically redesign the front ends of kayaks. The last fall
in particular drops you awkwardly into a big hole. Below the gorge

the Lyn remains rocky and technical particularly in low water. The whole river is an excellent run and it may well seem longer than it is. Egress is in the seaside village of Lynmouth where the last break-out is beyond the surf.

Wales

The Ogwen and other rivers of Northern Snowdonia

The highest peaks in North Wales are concentrated into four mountain chains. They are, from west to east, the Nantlle Ridge (with Hebog and Lefn); Snowdon (and its satellite peaks); the Glyderau; and the Carneddau. Heading north-west out of the valleys between these mountain ranges are three white water rivers. The Ogwen, running between the Glyderau and the Carneddau, is the best. Entering the Irish Sea at the other end of the Menai Strait is the Seiont which collects its water from the Glyderau and the Snowdon group. It is further from the mountains than the Ogwen and less steep but provides a continous middle-grade run of great quality. The Gwyrfai which runs into Caernarfon Bay out of the valley between Snowdon and the Nantlle Ridge is the least attractive of the three rivers but has its devotees.

If these three pall then there are always their close neighbours and tributaries to investigate – steep little streams which often involve as much legwork as armwork. The Anafon flows boldly out of the northern Carneddau past Aber and straight into Conwy Bay; in the same mountain range there are two tributaries of the Ogwen, the Caseg and Llafar. Then there is the unlikely Nantperis, the boulder-choked stream of Llanberis Pass and a tributary of the Seiont (via the two lakes, Peris and Padarn); and the incredibly steep Arddu, another tributary of the Seiont flowing through Llanberis into the junction of these lakes.

Afon Ogwen

The Ogwen drains the eastern Glyderau and the northern Carneddau. This is a high but relatively small catchment area, and the river flows for less than 14 kilometres from lake to sea. So, like many of the rivers in Snowdonia, the Ogwen rises and falls quickly and is only canoeable during or immediately after heavy rain. It is best to wait until the streams on the slopes of Y Garn, Foel Goch

and Pen yr Ole Wen are white. In very high spate the Ogwen can be a grade harder than given in this guide.

The best place to judge the level of the river is at Scout Hut Bridge, where the classic Fishermen's Gorge begins. If the boulders below the bridge are all covered this section will be grade Ve. Normally many boulders are clear, and it is then IVd. If you are unsure about whether you should tackle the river, a short walk down the right-hand bank from Scout Hut Bridge may settle your mind one way or the other.

At whatever level it is paddled the Ogwen is one of the finest white water trips in the country. Not the most scenic of rivers – it flows through the nineteenth-century slate mining shambles of Bethesda and the murky shadows of a wooded glen – but the intricate pattern of water movement in the Ogwen's gorges **is** supremely beautiful to the canoeist. In Fishermen's Gorge in particular, the flow of white water is more continuous at the grade than any other comparable British river. This section will draw you back time and time again. As the name suggests, fish and fishermen like it too, so it is best canoed between October and March.

To begin with there is no sign of the Ogwen's canoeing qualities. From Llyn Ogwen, the river falls over a steep waterfall into the Nant Ffrancon, a classic 'U'-shaped glacial valley that features in many geography textbooks, but whose even gradient ensures that it will never be in any white water guide books. It is only after 4 kilometres of flatness, just below Tyn-y-Maes (a farm on the other side of the river from the A5), that the Ogwen begins its descent to the Menai Strait, 10 kilometres and 200 metres below.

Upper Ogwen (Tyn-y-Maes and Bethesda Gorges) **
Tyn y Maes (632.642) or Ogwen Bank (626.653) to Scout Hut Bridge (610.677)
Grade IVc (Ve)
No Portages

Rescue on the Upper Ogwen in Tyn y Maes Gorge

1 or 4 Kilometres
OS Sheet 115

In high water it is normal to begin the Ogwen at Ogwen Bank
since Tyn-y-Maes Gorge is hard and easy by extremes. Access to
Tyn-y-Maes Gorge is by a small road off the A5 2 kilometres south
of Bethesda. The serious difficulties are just below Tyn-y-Maes
Bridge. There is first a tight fall which can pin canoes on the right
(IVc), and then a shorter, easier stretch leading to a divided drop
which can pin left or right (Ve). The banks are close in both places
so rescue can be effected providing that the river is not too high.

The river is then flat as far as Ogwen Bank Weir, not to be
confused with the much bigger and more serious drop that
succeeds it. The weir is easier than it looks since the plume of
water down the centre hides nothing more sinister than a sloping
shelf. Immediately below the weir is Ogwen Bank Falls (Ve).
Those wanting to portage, or start Bethesda Gorge here, should
put in from the left bank to the little pool below the Falls. Access
to and from the A5 is quick and easy with parking available
outside the entrance to Ogwen Bank caravan-park.

It is normal to combine Bethesda Gorge (IVc) with the next
section of the Ogwen, Fishermen's Gorge (IVd), but since the
former is less serious it may appeal as a shorter trip in its own
right. Access is either above or below Ogwen Bank Falls (Ve).
This metal-strewn waterfall is best taken on the right over a 2-
metre drop with a swing left down a long shallow, bone-chipping
ramp. In the small pool at the bottom swimmers should be
retrieved with all due speed lest they be 'shot' down the Gun
Barrel (IVc) below. This pool can also be used for access (as
suggested above).

The Gun Barrel (IVc) is an exciting shoot of water channelled
by the quarrymen in the last century. It ends in a steep rapid
containing some powerful stoppers – keep left past the last two to
avoid a hidden rock. Those wishing to avoid the Gun Barrel can

Looking down Fishermen's Gorge from the Scout Hut Bridge on the Ogwen
in canoeable low water

put in at the next road-bridge downstream carrying the B4366 over the river. To reach this access point turn left on entering Bethesda from the Nant Ffrancon and park on the road leading to Penrhyn quarry.

Easy water now leads to the start of Bethesda Gorge. The first rapid is on a sharp right-hand bend and is known as Bethesda Falls (IVc). A foot-bridge follows, and then a couple of steep drops which are washed-out in high water. The canoeing is not particularly serious, for each rapid is followed by a flatter section, but it can be quite tricky when the waves are rebounding off the bedrock walls. On leaving Bethesda the river flattens out with minor rapids and open banks as far as a broken weir 300 metres above Scout Hut Bridge. The latter marks the start of the classic Fishermen's Gorge.

Middle Ogwen (Fishermen's Gorge) ***
Scout Hut Bridge (610.677) to Half-way Bridge (607.689)
Grade IVd
No Portages
2 Kilometres
OS Sheet 115

The lead-in to Fishermen's Gorge (IVd) is just above Scout Hut Bridge and involves some steep technical paddling. To inspect get out on the right bank below the large white farmhouse – the scout hut is closer to the bridge. If you are starting a trip from here it is best to get in from a large eddy immediately below the bridge on the right.

Between Scout Hut Bridge and Half-way Bridge are two tree-covered islands. The first, immediately below the railway viaduct (itself just downstream of Scout Hut Bridge), is taken on the right; the second, above Dinas Farm camp-site, is fairly obviously shot on the left. About half-way between these islands there is a large fall ending on the left in a big stopper (inspection recommended). Below Dinas Farm the Ogwen relaxes slightly to Half-Way Bridge. If most of the boulders in Fishermen's Gorge are covered it will be Grade Ve.

It is normal to combine this classic stretch of the Ogwen with the 3 kilometres above, and the 2 (or 4) kilometres below. Certainly access and egress are easier on the longer trip. If you wish to get out at Half-way Bridge, climb steeply to a minor road on the left upstream of the bridge.

Lower Ogwen **
Half-way Bridge (607.677) to Expressway Bridge (600.703) or sea (614.723)
Grade IVc
No Portages
2 or 4 Kilometres
OS Sheet 115

Although not as continuous as Fishermen's Gorge, the Lower Ogwen has some interesting and difficult rapids. In its upper half the river braids through heavily wooded islands, and fallen branches and trees can prove a problem. Lower down there are a number of broken weirs and bridges where the right line is important. Nevertheless if you have canoed from Bethesda you should have few problems here.

After 2 kilometres you can get out on the left to a service road built round the foot of the North Wales Expressway bridge, but the Ogwen continues fast and white until well below the next railway and road (A55) bridge. So it is worth continuing down the last 2 kilometres to see the sea.

The river flattens off on entering Penrhyn estate with just a few safe weirs to break the flow. Suddenly round a corner, framed by a cast iron foot-bridge, is Puffin Island 10 kilometres across the sea. The final 500-metre paddle east along the shore of Conwy Bay is a suitably calming antithesis to all the fight and fury above. To reach the beach car-park by road turn north off the old A55 a kilometre east of Penrhyn Castle.

It is as well to make sure that the tide will be high when you use this egress point (ring Holyhead coastguard). Otherwise you may do a repeat of Caesar's retreat from Anglesey, when the Druids threw his legions squelching back across the Lavan Sands. If the

tide is going to be out, return another day and, like Caesar, finish the job in boats.

AFON SEIONT

The Seiont shares with the Ogwen the great attraction of being canoeable, without interruption, from the mountains to the sea. On neither river are there long, boring, flat sections, or, which is more common in the mountains, great waterfalls to bar the way. But where canoeists can go, trout and salmon can also, so it was perhaps inevitable that on one of these two great canoeing *and* fishing rivers, the simmering cold-war between anglers and paddlers would burst into flames.

For many years canoeists have been stoned and fish-hooked on the Ogwen and Seiont. Running the gauntlet of anglers was as dangerous as canoeing the water. Things got out of hand in October 1987, when Ben Wright, a local canoeist, was hit in the face by rocks while he was attempting to rescue a swimmer on the Seiont. The Campaign for River Access for Canoes and Kayaks (CRACK) responded by organizing a mass trespass on the Seiont in March 1988. In the short term this has made access to the Seiont more problematic; in the long term it probably did more to raise national awareness of the access problem in one afternoon than twenty years of letter writing by the British Canoe Union. Whether this new awareness will bring concrete results remains to be seen.

Seiont ***
Pontrhythallt (543.636) to Caernarfon Castle (476.626)
Grade IIId (IVd)
No Portages
11 Kilometres
OS Sheet 115

The purist will want to start the Seiont from its source, Llyn

Bryn Afon Steps on the Seiont

Padarn. This lake however, having almost recovered from the
ravages of Dinorwig, the largest slate quarry in the world, has now
lost a kilometre of its shoreline to the Central Electricity Board's
pump storage scheme. An equally good start for the canoeist
therefore is Pontrhythallt, 2 kilometres downstream; for unless
you like slate tips and turbine tunnels you will only be missing a
stretch of flat water.

Rhythallt Falls (IVd), the hardest on the river, comes ½ a
kilometre after Pontrhythallt. It may be inspected from either
bank, but a good view can be had from the course of the old
railway-line which runs parallel to the Seiont for the whole of its
length – close on the right bank at this point. There follows a
kilometre of water broken by small weirs. Continue under a road-
bridge and then into the Bryn Afon Steps, a series of small natural
drops through gorse and bracken country which are exciting even
when the river is low. A sharp right-hand bend leads through a
dismantled bridge on the old railway-line, and then the river
widens as it approaches Glanrafon Farm (522.641).

It is worth inspecting the weir below this farm, and the island
which follows, for it was on just such a stretch of the Seiont, where
the branches hang low, that a near fatal canoeing accident
occurred. In high water the penalties for a poor line of descent on
this river are out of all proportion to the technical difficulty of the
canoeing.

Next comes probably the best of the river: 2 kilometres of
Grade IIIc with a sharp left-hand bend and the
Caernarfon–Llanberis road-bridge marking the middle of this
section. After this, the river twists and turns each way, seemingly
trying to avoid the houses and factories which crowd its edge.
There is one bridge you will remember if the river is high for, after
avoiding a log blocking the left-hand channel, you must duck to
avoid its girders.

The largest weir on the river catches you unawares, on a flat
section ½ kilometre after the Glan Gwna housing estate. Possibly
for this reason, the back-tow in the stopper feels strong. That
done, there is only the broken weir at Pen-y-bryn to shoot, and
you are in salt water. This back entrance to Caernarfon harbour is

surely the most striking finish to any river trip in North Wales. One moment you are kayak king on a little river, the next a dwarf boat drifting amongst the rotting clippers and paint-bright catamarans. And where else could you draw your canoe out under the shadow of a thirteenth-century castle, its towers guarding the western end of the Menai Straits?

AFON GWYRFAI

Aquatic dinosaurs (long necks and no brains) will enjoy the Gwyrfai. Never has the twin-grading system been more useful – Grade III for the water, and grade d for the trees. In spate the river is dangerous because it flows through woods on either side and even in average flood there will be branches and trees across the river, forcing the occasional portage. Still, this river seems to hold a morbid fascination for local canoeists. So there is no reason why others should not find the trip equally 'interesting'.

Gwyrfai
Waunfawr Bridge (525.590) to Bontnewydd Bridge (482.598)
Grade IIId
1 or 2 Portages(?)
5 Kilometres
OS Sheet 115

The Caernarfon to Beddgelert Road (A4085) passes over the Gwyrfai at Betws Garmon and Waunfawr. Between Betws Garmon and Waunfawr the river is too small to canoe, so a small lay-by at Waunfawr Bridge is the best access point. The river is immediately technical (IIIc), and remains so until the small bridge below Plas Glanrafon (508.595). This bridge will decapitate, so it must be portaged; it has also on occasions proved a useful escape route back to the main road.

From Glanrafon to Bontnewydd, the Gwyrfai digs deeper into the valley and flows with greater power. There are no very big falls on the river, but this section is Grade IIId due to the potential obstructions and lack of break-outs. Some portages may be necessary, depending on the damage done by the winter storms. There is also a weir near Bontnewydd which some will want to portage. It is possible to put in again and canoe to the sea. After Bontnewydd, however, the river loses all technical interest, so the bridge in this village is the best egress point.

The Gwyrfai is a short trip – hardly 5 kilometres – but it is packed with interest. The technical interest indeed is so continuous that the canoeist will find it impossible to remember sections in any detail. So, should you want to canoe the Gwyrfai again, it will continue to hold plenty of surprises!

The Afon Conwy and its tributaries

With few equals among the rivers of Snowdonia is the Afon
Conwy. 'Con*way*' it was to the English who guarded its entrance
with their most powerful Welsh castle. Broad, flat and English it is
too in its lower half, where the flood plain provides rich farmland
and two golf courses. But just 20 kilometres from its mouth, above
the tourist town of Betws y Coed, where the London to Holyhead
road (A5) parallels the river, the Conwy shows its true descent
from the hills.

There is the 100 metre Conwy Falls and then the Fairy Glen, an
innocuous name for 2 kilometres of turmoil. There is nothing
English in this, nor in the somewhat easier 11 kilometres of the
Upper and Middle Conwy, twisting and turning in the contours
above. White where it falls, green as it eddies, this is the canoeist's
world, a series of progressively harder gorges isolated from the
world above.

At Beaver Pool, a major tributary enters the Conwy, the Afon
Lledr. Apart from the Llugwy, which is described on page 248, it
is the most canoeable of the Conwy's tributaries. The Afon
Machno entering near Conwy Falls has an impassable gorge, and
the Afon Merddwr coming in even further upstream is crossed by
too many barbed-wire fences to make it practical.

AFON CONWY

The Conwy has a stronger bladder than any other river in
Snowdonia, and the Fairy Glen in particular may be paddled after
two or three days of dry weather. The river's level may be judged
at Waterloo Bridge on the southern outskirts of Betws y Coed. If
the small boulders in the rapid below the bridge are showing but
there is some flow, the Fairy Glen is still canoeable. If the
boulders are all covered, the whole of the Conwy is worth doing,
although the section above the top A5 bridge (junction with
Merddwr) may be bony. If the river is brown you should leave the

Fairy Glen to another day. The rest of the river will be quite exciting enough!

Between Ysbyty Bridge and Conwy Falls there are two Sites of Special Scientific Interest and canoeists should minimize their impact on this fragile environment by using stiles provided at access and egress points and along portage trails. A widely used access point – the A5 road-bridge just below the junction with the Merddwr – has a sign and gauge (downstream right bank). The gauge should read above 12 for the Upper and Middle Conwy to be more than a bounce and scrape.

Upper Conwy ***
Pennant Farm (824.469) to Rhydlanfair (827.524)
Grade IIIc (IVc)
1 Portage
9 Kilometres
OS Sheet 116

After heavy rain it is possible to canoe from Pennant Farm (off the B4407) to the A5 and the confluence with a major tributary, the Afon Merddwr. Most, however, will prefer to start just below this confluence from a lay-by and bridge on the A5 north of Pentre-foelas, because of more reliable water and easier access. Below this bridge the river runs into the first and easiest of its gorges.

Two kilometres below Pennant Farm, and near the dwelling of Pandy Uchaf, there is a *dangerous* fall presently blocked by a tree (839.843). It is fairly obvious on the run-in, and is best portaged on the right bank. It is followed by a steeply inclined weir (IIIc), and a long rapid above the bridge at Ysbyty Ifan. Ysbyty Falls (IVc) is intimidating in big water, and can be inspected from either bank. The only other time you will want to leave your boat before the A5 road-bridge (alternative access point) is to look at Hargreaves Folly (IIIc), an awkward slot below Bryniau Defiad Farm.

After picking up the water of the Merddwr, the Conwy digs deep with its new-found power. Rock sills and protruding cliffs make the water more technically and continuously difficult. After

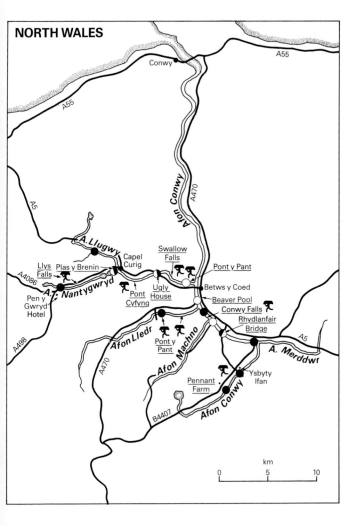

The Afon Conwy, Lledr, Llugwy and Nantygwryd

½ kilometre in this new vertical world, a huge house on the right
momentarily shatters the illusion of isolation. This is the Voelas
estate; the windows of its myriad rooms are opaque and disturbing
when viewed from the companionship of the river.

The gorge, however, soon takes you into its arms again,
whisking you down, under bridges (first the Voelas track, then the
A5), over shelves, round house-size boulders, through narrow
channels, and, after a kilometre, to Bryn Bras Falls (IVc). This
comparatively long rapid can be inspected from the road on the
way up. The way down is fairly obvious; first right, then left, then
right again to finish through a stopper at the bottom.

Now the river relaxes and after a kilometre you will pass under a
rickety foot-bridge. This marks the end of the rapids on this
section, and, a further ½ kilometre below, the bridge taking the
road to Rhydlanfair appears round a corner. Egress is on the left
bank. Finish here if IVc is what you came for, because now the
river drops more steeply as it heads towards Conwy Falls.

Middle Conwy *
Rhydlanfair (827.524) to Conwy Falls (812.533)
Grade IVd (Ve/VIe)
No Portages
2 Kilometres
OS Sheet 116

This is a serious section both because of the two very difficult falls
dividing it, and because it ends immediately above the portage of
Conwy Falls. This has been shot, but not at a level you could paddle
the rest of the river. Nevertheless, even if the two falls are portaged,
and you find it impossible to relax in the final 100 metres, there are
many other interesting rapids to enjoy in this broad and leafy gorge.

Immediatel below the put-in at the bridge there are three or
four good rapids over bedrock shelves. A flatter section leads to
another good rapid wiggling down river right. Some way below, a
large fallen tree (left bank) heralds the start of Waterfall Rapid

(Ve). This is canoed on the left down a series of steps, a difficult and serious proposition.

Below Waterfall Rapid a few smaller drops lead to the Gobbler (VIe). This desperate problem has unseated a number of notable paddlers, but always flushed them out at the bottom! Most people prefer to squelch through the leaf mould on the left bank, or, after climbing down a wooden ladder, seal launch spectacularly off a 4-metre cliff into the plunge pool below. The rapid immediately below the Gobbler has been partially blocked for some time by a log – a not uncommon problem on this tree-lined section of the river.

Half a kilometre downstream is the bridge taking the road to Penmachno. Do *not*, however, go as far as the bridge or you will be committed to paddling the Conwy Falls. The bridge is hidden from the river until the last moment, particularly when the forest is in leaf. The get-out is an eddy on the left bank about 50 metres below a large pink rock in midstream. So go gently, or even better check the egress point before starting the trip.

Lower Conwy (Fairy Glen) ***
Conwy Falls (807.537) to Beaver Pool (798.547)
Grade Vf (VIf)
No Portages (?)
2 Kilometres
OS Sheets 116 and 115

This is one of the best, most difficult and most serious sections of white water in Wales. The river rages down a narrow channel in a small but steep gorge, carving outrageous sumps and pot-holes. In addition to these mantraps, there are sections of the gorge where it would be impossible to escape without the aid of a rope. The hardest rapid – Fairy Falls (VIf) – is easily portaged, but some of the others are very difficult to avoid. Yet despite, or perhaps because, of all this, the Fairy Glen draws you back again and again.

Park at Conwy Falls café on the A5, go through the turnstile,

and follow a path that leads to the bottom of Conwy Falls. There are five hard falls in the first part of the Fairy Glen, and five or six others graded IVd. All are concentrated in a just a kilometre of river. Inspection is definitely the better part of valour, and no amount of description will take the place of a good look.

After an initial section of rapids the first big drop is the Doors of Perception. This is somewhat easier than it looks although still serious due to a siphon on the left. The Doors are followed by a surprisingly strong stopper, and then there is Left Wall, a narrow double-drop beside the left bank. Left Wall has serious pinning potential and is not possible in low water. The third major drop is Henry Moore which is shot left to right to avoid the natural rock sculpture on the left. In high water there is a powerful stopper here. The fourth and next drop should also be shot on the right to avoid bottoming, and runs into the final long rapid, the Gates of Delirium. The Gates should be taken left of centre, to avoid being pushed into No Through Eddy half-way down on the right. The Glen now opens out to give two less serious drops, and the gentle run-in to Fairy Falls. This rapid marks the start of the second part of the Fairy Glen.

Fairy Falls (VIf) is a desperate and dangerous rapid. It has been canoed a number of times, but it is normally portaged on either bank. It is possible to escape from the Fairy Glen at this point by carrying a short way down the right bank, but, if courage and energy have not deserted you, it is well worth doing the final four falls.

Immediately below Fairy Falls is the Elbow, a double-fall needing careful inspection; a number of people have been pinned on the left near the bottom. An easy run down to the right then takes you to Pipeline, a complicated rapid especially in low water. The Weaver is the penultimate rapid, another twist and turn job. Finally there is See No Evil, a 4-metre waterfall over a slab of rock right across the gorge. It is impossible to get out of the Fairy Glen between the Weaver and See No Evil, so you cannot inspect this

Just above Gates of Delirium on the Lower Conwy (Fairy Glen)

final fall. Take it just left of centre, thus avoiding the huge rock on
the right and the boulders on the extreme left – a worrying drop!

The Fairy Glen now eases to a continuous grade IIIc. On the
right is a steep path much frequented by tourists and
photographers. This is a possible access point for those wanting to
do this last tantalizing taster of the Glen – the Fairy Steps. Tight
little rapids lead down to the final gap of the Fairy Steps and so to
Ivy Pool and the confluence with the Lledr. The combined waters
of these two rivers now rush in a final spurt of energy under the
A470 road-bridge before collapsing into the murky depths of
Beaver Pool. Get out on the left bank below the bridge.

AFON LLEDR

The Lledr (pronounced 'cledder') runs east from the Moelwyns
into the River Conwy above Betws y Coed. High in the Moelwyns,
where a bridge, Pont y Coblyn (719.514), carries the A470 up and
away to Blaenau Ffestiniog, there is a short section of Grade IVd,
but, sweet though it is, this stretch is only short, and it is followed
by a long flat section through Dolwyddelan. Most therefore will
want to start downstream of that village, at Pont y Pant where the
Lledr takes its first dramatic plunge towards Betws y Coed.

Lledr *
Pont y Pant (755.538) to Beaver Pool (798.547)
Grade IIIc (Ve)
1 Portage
5 Kilometres
OS Sheet 115

Access is just below, or if you are feeling exceptionally brave, just
above Pont y Pant Falls (VIf). If the rooster tail rock in Lower
Pont y Pant Falls is showing, the river below will be too low. On
the other hand this may be the time to tackle Pont y Pant Falls and
the other grade VIf rapid, Viaduct Gorge.

There is only one really hard section of river if you start below
Pont y Pant Falls and portage Viaduct Gorge. This is Rhiw Goch

Gorge, and a warning of its approach is given a kilometre below
Pont y Pant Falls by Double Drop (IVc), an exciting and
appropriately named rapid on a left-hand bend. The first waterfall
in Rhiw Goch Gorge is difficult and enclosed, but the remaining
drops are accessible from both banks – if the precarious
fishermen's catwalk is used on the left. A huge cliff, from which
the gorge takes its name, looms out of the forest on the left bank
as you clear the last rapid.

One and a half kilometres of easier water leads to Viaduct
Gorge (VIf), only paddled when the river is a dribble. The railway
crosses the Lledr immediately above this rapid, and the large
viaduct is obvious from the river – portage on the right. The final
kilometre is increasingly interesting, finishing with tight technical
paddling (IVc) above and below a humpbacked bridge and into
Ivy Pool.

From here the Conwy takes over from the Lledr leading their
combined waters down a bouncy rapid under the A470 bridge and
into Beaver Pool. If you haven't yet had enough 'fight or flight'
stimulation, try the unpowered variety – jump off the downstream
side of the road-bridge into Beaver Pool.

The Afon Llugwy and its tributary the Nantygwryd

The Llugwy is the most popular touring river in North Wales. In particular, the section from Plas y Brenin to the A5 road-bridge has probably seen more paddle and breast strokes than the local swimming baths. This is primarily because of the lack of access problems. And therein lies a story with a moral.

The mighty Swallow Falls has now been canoed and has even been rafted, but it still prevents game fish from breeding in the upper Llugwy. So there is little money to be gained from renting fishing rights on the upper half of the river. One local riparian owner thought, however, that he could make money out of canoeing, and proposed charging for every boat that went across 'his' water, with a special price for local outdoor centres.

This was tempting to the local outdoor educationalists, for they rely on the Llugwy for teaching white water canoeing and without it their courses would be less attractive. If they *had* gone for the easy option a dangerous precedent would have been set. Other owners would have jumped on the bandwagon, and canoeing, like game fishing, would have become the preserve of those who could afford to pay (the National Centre for Mountain Activities, Plas y Brenin, has created just such an inflationary rod for other people's backs by paying for access to the Dee near Llangollen).

Unfortunately for the owner in question, there was a good case in law for a public right of navigation on the Llugwy resulting from 25 years' uninterrupted and unchallenged use of the river. The centre directors refused to pay, continued canoeing (as did the public) and after a while the owner sold up and went away. It was a notable victory for canoeists.

It is perhaps worth remembering then, when you join the happy weekenders at Jim's Bridge, or Cobdens, or Forestry Falls, or even when you venture onto the more testing and as yet uncontested sections above Brown's and below Swallow Falls, that the Llugwy can be enjoyed without a fight, perhaps even as a right, because for once someone *other* than the ambushed paddler on the bank has stood up for free public access to Britain's rivers.

AFON LLUGWY

Jim's Bridge opposite the only petrol station in Capel Curig is an easily accessible spot to judge the level of the river. If the midstream rock downstream of the forestry bridge is covered the river is up; if the right-hand bridge arch is canoeable, the river is high, and the Lower Llugwy in particular will be in good 'nick'; if the river is flooding the field between the road and the river (this happens two or three times a year), Cobden's Falls will be Ve (or more), and the Upper Llugwy (apart from Brown's Falls) or the Nantygwryd (see p.255) will be the best choice.

Upper Llugwy *
Nant y Gors (698.596) to Brown's Falls (720.571)
Grade IVc (Ve)
No Portages
4 Kilometres
OS Sheet 115

From Ffynnon Llugwy reservoir the Llugwy rushes into the Ogwen valley to be joined by a myriad streams as it heads towards the small village of Capel Curig. During or shortly after *heavy* rain it gives an exciting paddle starting at or below the junction with the Nant y Gors coming out of Gallt Yr Ogof, 3 kilometres west of Capel Curig. Below this confluence the A5 runs convenienty close to the river, although parking is difficult.

Flat at first, the Llugwy soon becomes strewn with boulders, technical, shallow and not very serious. A stand of pines on the other side of the A5 is passed on the left after 1 kilometre, and the canoeing becomes more difficult, although still quite escapable. One rapid in particular needs careful inspection to avoid entrapment. The technical difficulties continue until an old girder (invisible from the road) marks the lead-in to Brown's Falls 100

metres below. Those wishing to portage this difficult drop can get
out just above the falls to the field on the right.

Brown's Falls (Ve) is in Capel Curig, and may be readily
inspected from behind the climbing shop of the same name. The
best line is down the right-hand side in medium to low water.
There remain only a succession of standing waves and a sharp left-
hand bend, before the Llugwy goes under the A4087 and is joined
by the Nantygwryd. If you are intending to finish with this section
of river it is better to get out immediately below Brown's Falls.

Middle Llugwy **
Plas y Brenin (716.577) to Ugly House (756.574)
Grade IIIc (IVd)
1 Portage
6 Kilometres
OS Sheet 115

The access point for this section, Plas y Brenin (PYB), is in fact on
a tributary of the Llugwy, the Nantygwryd. Nevertheless, it is the
logical starting point for the Middle Llugwy. Get to the river from
the A4086 down a public footpath to the west of PYB. The bridge
at the eastern end of the twin lakes produces a good introductory
rapid at almost all levels.

The Nantygwryd is then flat as far as its confluence with the
Llugwy. The combined river then flows strongly over shingle
rapids and round two tight bends to the rapid at Jim's Bridge
(IIb), opposite the petrol station in Capel Curig. Below Jim's
Bridge the rapid peters out, and flat water leads to Cobden's Falls
(IVd). To inspect this awesome-looking rapid (opposite the pub of
the same name) and the little drop which precedes it, the Slot
(IIIc), get on to the forestry track and footpath on the right bank,
which leads to the foot-bridge below Cobden's.

The Slot catches many unawares and swift action is necessary to
prevent an unoccupied boat from proceeding over Cobden's. It is
possible to get out below the Slot on the left bank, and climb

Cobden's Falls on the Middle Llugwy at a good canoeable level (IVd)

through the A5's retaining wall by some steps. Cobden's is best shot over the central slab which should be well covered. The water tends to take you right down a mean little gully, but that route is only advisable in high water. In very high water the big stoppers can be missed by going down the left-hand side (Ve).

A sharp right-hand bend below Cobden's leads to a pleasant little rapid beside another watering-hole, the Tyn y Coed Hotel. If you have come to grief above, and you prefer to drown yourself rather than your sorrows, then proceed down the next rapid which is the lead-in to Pont Cyfyng Falls. The first two drops of Pont Cyfyng Falls have been canoed a number of times in very low water, and even the last corkscrew drop has been given a bashing (VIf), but in levels that you would want to paddle the rest of the river most consider the Falls are a portage. Fortunately flat water precedes the Falls so there is plenty of time after you have seen the bridge and rapid to get out and carry along the track on the right bank.

Below Pont Cyfyng access to the river is down a muddy path beside the Worsley Wardley Outdoor Pursuits Centre Cottage. From here down to the Ugly House (A5 road-bridge) the rapids are frequent, but never hard. Notable is the Graveyard (IIIb), a long boulder-filled rapid near the beginning, and, at the end, Forestry Falls (IIIc), a bouncy run down either side of an island meeting in a friendly haystack at the bottom. Egress is to a small road on the right 100 metres below Forestry Falls, or at the road-bridge lower down, where a right of way (downstream left bank) leads to the Ugly House car-park.

Lower Llugwy *
Ugly House (756.574) to Pont y Pair (790.566)
Grade IVd
2 Portages
6 Kilometres
OS Sheet 115

Pont Cyfyng Falls on the Middle Llugwy

Less than a kilometre below Ugly House, and the A5 road-bridge, lies Swallow Falls, a noted tourist attraction. Like Pont Cyfyng, this has been canoed a number of times in very low water (VIf). This says as much about the advent of plastic kayaks, as the rise in standard of white water canoeing; nevertheless the first descent in 1985 was an important psychological advance. The next challenge is to paddle Pont Cyfyng Falls and Swallow Falls at a level when the rest of the river is fun. Most will prefer to portage!

Get out above Swallow Falls on the left bank in plenty of time. Carry (or lower) down the steep bank pausing to gawp, with the fee-paying tourists on the opposite shore, at the three-tier 100-metre waterfall. Put in below the last drop, and you are immediately involved in technical canoeing. This continues for 3 kilometres in a broad open gorge surrounded by forest. The canoeing is best when the water is high, filling the river from bank to bank and covering all the boulders. Below an obvious narrowing is Bench Falls (IVd) ending in a powerful stopper. Get out on the right bank below this drop at some wooden benches, and portage round the Mincer (VIf). This mean rapid has been canoed. The problem is that the only line is blocked by a boulder.

Immediately below the Mincer is Miner's Bridge Rapid (IVd), a narrow run under the bridge of the same name. Although it is at the top end of its grade, the rapid is not as a hard as it looks, so it is worth carrying upstream to the pool below the Mincer. Below Miner's Bridge, the Llugwy remains technical and interesting, particularly in high water. It eases considerably before cascading over Pont y Pair Falls (VIf), thus allowing the wary or weary paddler to reach the car-park on the left before taking the plunge.

Pont y Pair Falls has been canoed in high water over the central rock, and in low water down the left-hand channel. In the first case a vicious stopper awaits the paddler who makes the bridge, in the second case there are pinning pot-holes just below the surface. It is not a choice that most people like to make. Below Betws y Coed there is little of interest to the white water paddler before the Llugwy joins the Conwy for a sedate journey to the sea. Better then, if it is chucking it down, to return to Capel Curig for a blast down the Nantygwryd.

AFON NANTYGWRYD

The Nantygwryd depends on heavy and prolonged rain to bring it
into condition. At first glance this stream appears to drain the
eastern slopes of the Snowdon massif, but in fact that is the
watershed of the Glaslyn. The Nantygwryd has only a small cwm
on the southern slopes of the Glyders to feed it, and as soon as the
tap is turned off the river runs away. Whilst on the run, however,
it is a lovely little river. There is a steep gorge at the top and a big
fall at the bottom, the views of the surrounding mountains are
unrestricted, and the whole scene can be enjoyed at leisure in the
final paddle across the twin lakes, Llynnau Mymbyr.

Nantygwryd *
Pen y Gwryd (663.559) to Plas y Brenin (716.577)
Grade IIId (IVd)
1 Portage
6 Kilometres
OS Sheet 115

Access is by a bridge carrying the A4086 over the stream just
below the Pen y Gwryd Hotel. An exciting kilometre – the Pool
Slide (IVd) – leads to Llys Falls, a small waterfall 100 metres
below the Nant y Llys, the first major tributary entering from the
right. Further warning of the approach of Llys Falls is given by a
fallen concete stanchion and then the remains of an iron bridge
just above the fall itself. It is best to get out immediately above or
below the concrete stanchion on the right, and certainly do not go
beyond the iron bridge which decapitates at some levels. Llys Falls
has been canoed, but take a good, long look before you try! I
recommend a portage.

Below Llys Falls, the Nantygwryd becomes progressively easier,
until Garth Falls (IVd), a big rapid underneath the bridge going to
the farm of the same name. It is easily seen from the main road on
the way up, and needs much water to blot out some large boulders
and bedrock steps. A route under the right-hand arch is advisable
and easier than it looks.

After Garth Falls, the Nantygwryd flows into the twin lakes, Llynnau Mymbyr, and out again as a small rapid under Pont y Bala, the foot-bridge below Plas y Brenin. Either continue down the Middle and Lower Llugwy, or egress to the road on the left by a public footpath from Pont y Bala.

The Glaslyn, its tributaries and other rivers of Tremadog Bay

The Afon Glaslyn originates in the heart of Snowdon at Llyn Lydaw. The outflow of this lake is fed through a pipeline into one of the oldest hydro-electric stations in the country at the head of the Gwynant valley. At Llyn Gwynant and Llyn Dinas, the Glaslyn picks up more water from tributaries out of Snowdon and the Moelwyns. It is canoeable between and below these lakes after heavy rain.

In the little village of Beddgelert, the Glaslyn is joined by the good although less popular Afon Colwyn. The combined waters of the Colwyn and Glaslyn then descend through a steep gorge called Aberglaslyn. It is a hairy ride in a canoe, the scene of numerous epics. Below there remains only reclaimed esturial flats to the sea at Porthmadog. It is, however, a matter of minutes from the bottom of the Aberglaslyn Gorge to another tributary of the Glaslyn, the Afon Nantmor. It is a good deal further to the lonesome Afon Artro south of Porthmadog, but then it is slightly more likely to be in condition. In between is the fierce little Afon Goedol, the hardest, if not the best, river of them all.

AFON GLASLYN

The Glaslyn flows through the dramatic scenery of Snowdonia's heartland, so eloquently described by George Borrow in his nineteenth-century classic *Wild Wales*:

> Before me lay the meadow of Gelert with the river flowing through it towards the pass. Beyond the meadow was the Snowdon range; on the right the mightly Cerrig Llan; on the left the equally mighty, but not quite so precipitous, Hebog. Truly the valley of Gelert is a wondrous valley – rivalling for grandeur and beauty any vale in either the Alps or the Pyrenees.

It would be hard to find a more inspirational setting for wild water canoeing.

Upper Glaslyn
Llyn Dinas (613.413) to Old Railway Bridge (591.473)
Grade IIb
No Portages
4 Kilometres
OS Sheet 115

The A498 carries gawping tourists on the Snowdon circuit, so change on the lakeside of your car at the Llyn Dinas lay-by. From there a short paddle leads past an old boat-house and into the river. It is quite straightforward, occasionally making a lazy turn as though wanting to present new angles for the canoeist viewing the beautiful hill country until two bridges announce the village of Beddgelert. In Beddgelert itself there is a small rapid where the water is constricted by bridge arches and accelerated over gentle drops – Gelert's Rapid (IIb).

Gelert, a faithful dog stabbed to death by his master under the mistaken assumption that he had attacked a baby, could probably have swum down the rapid named after him. He might well have managed the next kilometre as well, for the Glaslyn is bigger but no harder for the addition of the Colwyn. Even this brave wolf-slayer, however, would have had problems in the Aberglaslyn Gorge. So if you are a habitual swimmer and unless you want a village named after you (Beddgelert – grave of Gelert), it is best to get out where the old railway-bridge crosses the river, ½ kilometre upstream of the gorge.

Lower Glaslyn (Aberglaslyn Gorge) ***
Old Railway Bridge (591.473) to Pont Aber Glaslyn (594.461)
Grade Ve
No Portages
1 Kilometre
OS Sheet 115

The Glaslyn carves its dramatic path from the mountains to the sea in just a kilometre, less than a minute's drive by road. Short, but so sweet, the river is more alpine than British in its ultimate fling. So peek over the road's retaining wall, if you will, or gaze hesitantly from Pont Aber Glaslyn at the bottom, or inspect brazenly from the catwalk on the left bank, and imagine yourself in there. You will join many others who have looked . . . and left it for another day.

The start of the Aberglaslyn Gorge is ½ kilometre below the put-in. There is a marked narrowing of the rhododendron-covered gorge, and the water immediately falls steeply between large boulders – if it is going over them it might be better to come back on another day. The Gorge broadens out before the biggest fall, the Breaker, which is taken through the stopper on the right. This fall is invisible from the road being tucked under the high retaining wall, a position which makes it hard to protect from the bank. Unless you are far right, the Breaker is a mean drop, and as its name suggests, it has done a good deal of damage to boats and people over the years.

Below the Breaker, the Gorge is still hard, but the best, or worst, is now over. There is continuous white water to the bridge and then . . . nothing. All the Colwyn's and Glaslyn's remaining fluid ounces of energy have seemingly been spent in the turmoil above. Get out at the bridge on the left, or relax in the placid meanders for a little, until it is possible to scramble to the road (A498) on the right. Should there be a wind peaking small wavelets against the flow, it is not hard to imagine the slapping hulks of the eighteenth-century sailing ships beating upriver. For before Porthmadog embankment was built, they brought goods and people to Pont Aber Glaslyn, the gateway to the mountains.

AFON COLWYN

The Afon Colwyn drains the south-western slopes of Snowdon, and the eastern side of the Nantlle Ridge, and is best paddled from below the junction of the tributaries flowing out of these

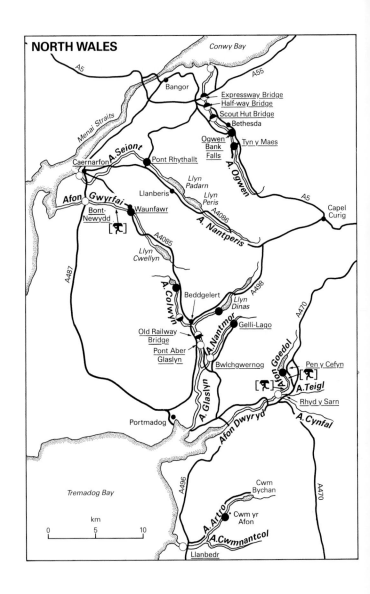

watersheds. It flows into the Glaslyn at Beddgelert and can therefore be combined with the Aberglaslyn Gorge to form one of the best white water trips in North Wales.

Afon Colwyn **
Hafod Ruffydd Isaf (575.498) to Warws (587.482)
Grade IVe
No Portages
3 Kilometres
OS Sheet 115

The Colwyn is an exciting, albeit short, pool-drop river, with some serious paddling needing close inspection. The A4085 Caernarfon to Beddgelert road, south of Rhyd-Ddu, runs parallel to the river and access, although not inspection, is easy to and from it. A forest track (metalled) leads west off the A4085 to Hafod Ruffydd Isaf, close above the confluence of the Colwyn's two main tributaries. Put in on the eastern tributary where the track crosses it.

A kilometre of tight, technical paddling over bedrock steps leads to the Forestry Commission camp-site (right bank) and an exciting rapid, Forestry Bridge (IVd). Three hundred metres below Forestry Bridge is the two-tier fall, Paddle Test (IVe), preceded by a nasty little drop on a left-hand bend with a submerged boulder blocking the main channel. Paddle Test is serious but not highly technical, requiring more bottle than brains.

The river continues through some tricky narrow gorges into Beddgelert. At the entrance to the town is the third road-bridge (585.482) and just below it the meanest rapid of them all, Dragon's Tail (Ve). The bridge and rapid are just above the Warws, a prominent shop on the road out of Beddgelert towards Rhyd-Ddu. The rapid may be inspected from the bridge, and looking upstream a gauge is visible. A good level for the Dragon's Tail, and the rest of the river, is 4.

The Afon Glaslyn, its tributaries and other rivers of Tremadog Bay

The Colwyn becomes progressively easier below *Dragon's Tail*, until it has become flat where it joins the Glaslyn. If you do not want to continue down that river it is best to get out to the car-park behind the Warws.

AFON NANTMOR

If you can bring yourself to take seriously a 3-metre wide stream that has the same technical grade as the Findhorn or the Ogwen, then this river is a must. It is spate canoeing *par excellence*; low bridges, even lower trees, and tiny gorges with continuous Grade IV water.

The Nantmor rises in the Moelwyns, a group of low-lying hills much used by outdoor centres to teach mountain navigation. Perhaps the erosion that has occurred on the popular routes as a result of this use has increased the surface run-off from the Moelwyns. Whatever the reason, after *very* heavy rain, the stream on its eastern fringe – the Nantmor – becomes canoeable.

Afon Nantmor
Gelli-lago (632.483) to Bwlchgwernog (611.452)
Grade IVe
1 Portage
4 Kilometres
OS Sheet 115

Between Llyn Gwynant and Llyn Dinas, 4 kilometres north-east of Beddgelert, a small road branches off to the south-east. This leads after two gates and a 90 degree right-hand bend to the small dwelling of Gelli-lago, opposite an old quarry (parking) and on the other side of the mighty torrent which is the Nantmor. Access is below Gelli-lago's Bridge, since it is impossible to canoe under it.

The first gorge (IVd), ½ kilometre below Gelli-lago (and some 300 metres below the bridge taking the road across to the left

The wave – a worthy opponent

bank), is preceded by a strand of barbed-wire across the river – usually a portage. A short interlude precedes the second and more serious gorge (IVe). The stream divides at the top, with the better left shoot difficult to get.

The remainder of the Nantmor is easy, but also serious due to the overhanging branches, fallen trees, and barbed wire fences. Egress is below a large house on the right (rope course across the river) at Bwlchgwernog Bridge which takes a minor road towards Pont Aber Glaslyn. Alternatively, it is possible to continue down the Nantmor, eventually reaching the placid waters of the Glaslyn.

AFON GOEDOL

This short river, running south from Blaenau Ffestiniog into the Afon Dwyryd (and thence into Tremadog Bay), is largely dam-controlled. The chiefs at Tan y Grisiau power station will not say when it is releasing, but it usually is after heavy rain. The amount of water varies, and this is critical for some of the drops. Decisions over portaging will therefore vary from day to day, and some portages are to be expected at every level. The lower gorge section on the Goedol is an SSSI (Site of Special Scientific Interest), and canoeists should be sensitive to this.

Goedol
Pen y Cefyn (689.445) to Rhyd Sarn (689.421)
Grade VIf
Some Portages
3 Kilometres
OS Sheet 124

The river consists of a series of waterfalls interspersed by flatter boulder-fields. A strong team is necessary for this extremely technical and serious river. Access is best from the lay-by on the B4414, by dragging the boats down the steep bank to the foot of the waterfall.

Interesting paddling leads to the first of many falls, Power

House Falls (Ve). Easier canoeing now leads to an impressive series of drops, Rhaeadr Cymerau (Ve). The river eases again until a boulder-field is reached (Vd). This is followed by a narrowing of the valley and the start of the lower gorge (VIf). Below it is the footbridge at Rhyd Sarn, the recommended egress point. If you have not yet had enough, take a look at the next two tributaries downstream of the Goedol, the Afon Cynfal and the Afon Llennyrch (Maentwrog Gorge). The former is a little futuristic, but the latter has been paddled on a dam release (VIf+).

AFON ARTRO

The Afon Artro drains the western Rhinogs into Tremadog Bay. It can only be reached along the A1496 coast road, and so may be sensibly combined with the Glaslyn, Goedol, or Mawddach. It is a smaller river than the Glaslyn, and, because it is also closer to the sea, it needs even more rain to bring it into condition. In spate conditions it has a tributary, the Afon Cwmnantcol, which can be canoed including a short gorge of Ve.

Artro *
Cwm yr Afon (621.298) to Llanbedr (585.268)
Grade IIIc
No Portages
5 Kilometres
OS Sheet 124

Mischievously dubbed the 'Raging River of the Rhinogs' by a paddler recently returned from Nepal, the Artro *is* surprisingly fast for such a small river. It starts gently enough through wooded slopes and hedged fields, but after Pen y Bont (607.281) – a possible access point for a shorter trip – it drops steeply through a narrow gorge.

The road from Llanbedr follows the right bank of the Artro up into Cwm Bychan. Access, just below Cwm yr Afon, is by a small stone bridge. The river passes under three more such bridges, on the way to Llanbedr, and the difficulties, such as they are, lie between the third (Pen y Bont) and the fourth. At the fourth bridge a tributary, the Afon Cwmnantcol, enters the Artro. Get out at the fifth bridge in Llanbedr.

The Afon Mawddach and its tributaries

The source of the Mawddach is just 2 kilometres the other side of a hill from the source of the Dee, and 10 kilometres south of the source of the Tryweryn. The hills of this watershed are insignificant compared to their neighbours to the north in Snowdonia, but they certainly contain some magic for they give birth to an excellent canoeable tributary of the Mawddach, the Afon Eden.

The Lower Eden and Lower Mawddach taken together provide a classic white water run. The Lower Eden is very continuous at the grade, and the Lower Mawddach is one of the biggest volume rivers in North Wales. There are no portages to interrupt the trip, and the Coed y Brenin forest provides a splendid sense of isolation from the neighbouring road (A470), not to mention shelter from the disagreeable weather in which the rivers must often be paddled. An alternative start to Lower Mawddach is the Upper Mawddach, a much harder proposition even if the three portages are used.

The Mawddach and all its tributaries in the Rhinogs and Arenigs rise and fall like a cistern because of their proximity to the sea. However, the Rhinogs and Arenigs are small compared to the mountains further north, so orographic precipitation is less. This is a good place to be when other rivers in North Wales are too high. Then the Eden becomes a superb yet still 'easy' helter-skelter; the Upper Mawddach's boulders and shelves are covered with cushions of water; the Lower Mawddach thunders brown down its motorway; and its smaller tributaries, notably the Gamlan and Wnion, rush roaring over steep ledges and down narrow gorges.

AFON MAWDDACH

The best place to judge the level of the Mawddach is at Public Toilet Falls at the small village of Ganllwyd on the A470. These falls are a severe narrowing of the river containing an enormous boulder. In low water the boulder is visible, in medium water it forms a large stopper, while in high water it is entirely hidden by a huge, brown tongue of water.

The sections below are graded for medium water. In full flood the Lower Mawddach (and Lower Eden) is a superb roller-coaster of big holes and stoppers (Vd), but the Upper Mawddach becomes much more serious (Vf). In low water the Lower Mawddach is still worth doing (IIIc), but the Upper Mawddach is too bony for good sport.

Just 20 kilometres below its source at Llanelltyd, the Mawddach becomes tidal and of no further interest to white water canoeists. There are however two exciting little spate streams that enter the Mawddach estuary and are canoeable after very heavy rain. On the Afon Cwm-Mynach, which enters from the north, the canoeing is continuous from the Stepping Stones (689.200) down to the estuary with falls at the top end of Grade Ve. Egress is at Pen y Bryn (690.191) just before the river enters the estuary. On the Afon Gwynant, which enters from the south, the canoeing is not quite so hard – IVe (Ve) – but there are two portages. Access is at Kings (682.161), and the biggest fall (Ve) not too far below. It is succeeded by a tree choke which must be portaged; the box weir between the next two road-bridges is also a recommended portage. Egress from the Gwynant is at the second (main) road-bridge (678.171).

Upper Mawddach *
Pont Aber-Geirw (768.290) to confluence with Eden (728.247)
Grade Vd
3 Portages
8 Kilometres
OS Sheet 124

Like many rivers in Britain, the Upper Mawddach feels more serious than it is. In your canoe you seem to be surrounded by a wall of firs; there are no houses, no comforting obtrusive sounds of traffic, no obvious way out except downriver. Look at a map,

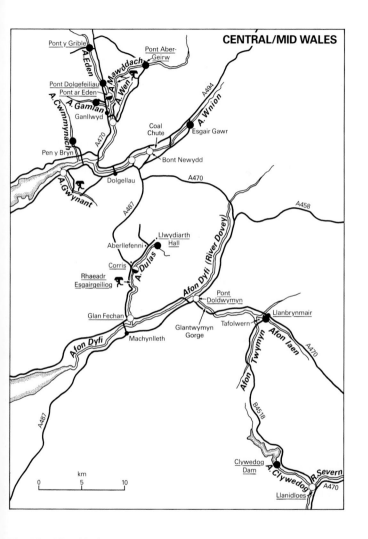

The Afon Mawddach, Twymyn and surrounding rivers

however, and you will see a web of forest roads, two of which parallel the lower half of the river on either bank, and up any of which, in an emergency, a four-wheeled-drive vehicle could go.

There is difficult canoeing to be had on the Upper Mawddach, even if (and this is normal) you portage the three waterfalls. The first waterfall (3–4 metres) is about 2 kilometres after the start – the small bridge Pont Aber-Geirw – in an otherwise relatively straightforward section of river. After another kilometre the hills begin to close in and a second waterfall appears round a bend (4–5 metres). Not far below is a working gold mine, and next to it is Rhaeadr Mawddach a huge (10-metre plus) double-drop with a nasty landing. It says something for the standard of modern canoeing that all these waterfalls, including this last big one, have now been shot.

The waterfalls are easily portaged (right bank). As you get in below Rhaeadr Mawddach look right to an even more awesome drop, Pistyll Gain. This has not been canoed, although the excellent small river above has – Afon Gain, Grade IVd with two sections of Ve. (Access is up the road behind Rhiw Goch ski slope to a ford. Increasingly difficult canoeing leads to a 3 tier fall below a forestry bridge. Shortly after this the Gain plunges over Pistyll Gain. Portage on the right to the Mawddach).

Below the confluence with the Gain, the Mawddach is bigger and more difficult. This point can be reached up a forest road on the true right bank, with parking at a picnic spot. There is a kilometre of Grade IIIc followed by three big drops (IVd or Ve). Half a kilometre of easier water precedes a second difficult section (IVd or Vd). This ends in a spectacular drop over the right side of a huge boulder.

Lower Mawddach ***
Pont ar Eden (727.248) to confluence with Afon Wen (733.224)
Grade IVd
No Portages
3 Kilometres
OS Sheet 124

The emerald waters of the Eden are muddied by the murky waters of the Mawddach as they churn together over the sizeable Ganllwyd Weir. This forms a powerful stopper in flood and should be shot in the centre. Not far below is Public Toilet Falls (IVd), named after the public convenience in Ganllwyd. If the boulder in PTF is showing, a route to the left seems favourite. If it is covered, a central line is possible.

Below PTF a foot-bridge is followed by a smaller rapid (larger in HW) and the Afon Gamlan pouring in from the right. Three hundred metres downstream is Hand Roll (IIIc), an innocuous-looking drop on a left-hand bend. Smaller rapids lead down to a road-bridge which provides access to left bank of the Lower and Upper Mawddach.

Below is the Tyn y Groes bend, with the hotel of the same name high above the retaining wall on the right. This marks the start of the Graveyard (IVd), a superb kilometre of boulder-filled rapids, with powerful stoppers and holes in high water. This is the best rapid on the Mawddach and in flood provides some very heavy white water.

The last rapids of the Graveyard peter out above an obvious right-hand bend. The remaining 5 kilometres down to Llanelltyd are flat, so the white water canoeist will want to take out here. Just upstream of the Wen confluence on the left is a footpath leading up to the minor road which parallels this bank. This in turn leads back onto the A470 by the bridge above the Tyn y Groes bend.

AFON EDEN

The best place to judge the level of the Eden is at Pont Dolgefeiliau. If the island rapid above this bridge looks bony then it is best to leave the Upper Eden to another day. If the rapid *below* the bridge looks like a bounce and a scrape, then there is little fun to be had anywhere (except perhaps on the very channelled Afon Gain – see above). If small stoppers are forming below this lower rapid then the Upper Eden (and Upper Mawddach) will probably be good.

Upper Eden
Pont y Grible (708.304) to Pont Dolgefeiliau (720.269)
Grade IIIc (IVd)
No Portages
5 Kilometres
OS Sheet 124

The recently strengthened bridge at Pont y Grible is reached from
the A470 by a gated 'no-through-road'. The river is gentle at first,
but look out for barbed-wire fences strung across the river. After 2
kilometres a bridge and a major tributary entering from the right
(Afon Crawcwellt – canoeable at Grade IVd-Ve) herald the start of
more interesting water in the Coed y Brenin forest.

Two Morals Rapid (IVd) is preceded by a tiny weir with a black
box water gauge on the left. This is obvious from above, but Two
Morals is difficult to read from the river. Below it the Eden
becomes wider and strewn with boulders. This provides interesting
canoeing in flood, but a frustrating blunder and bash in anything
else. A small island precedes the bridge – Pont Dolgefeiliau.

Lower Eden **
Pont Dolgefeiliau (708.304) to Pont ar Eden (727.248)
Grade IIIc
No Portages
2 Kilometres
OS Sheet 124

At Pont Dolgefeiliau the main Ffestiniog to Dolgellau road (A470)
crosses the river from left to right bank, and remains on that side
of the river for the remainder of the trip. The Eden is still wide
and rocky after the bridge, but is more channelled than above. A
forestry bridge soon appears (unmarked on the OS map), and a
little way further a broken weir forms a pronounced drop.

After 1 kilometre an old stone barn on the left, and some houses
high on the right, heralds the start of Tyn-y-newydd Gorge. The
gorge is neither steep, deep, nor particularly imposing, but there is

a distinct narrowing of the river with some quite exciting drops. This section becomes significantly harder and more serious in high water (IVd, occasionally Vd). The gorge is narrow enough to be blocked by a tree! The last rapid is just before Pont ar Eden, and egress is below the bridge on the left. Most people however will want to continue over the small weir and into the Lower Mawddach.

AFON GAMLAN

The Gamlan is a ferocious little river flowing out of the Rhinogs and into the Mawddach at Ganllwyd. It is possible at most water levels, but is something of a stunt in low water and extremely difficult and dangerous in full flood. The level can be checked from Ganllwyd where the main road crosses the river. If, when looking upstream from the bridge, there is water coming over the obvious slab, the Gamlan is canoeable. If the slab is a mass of white, the river is probably too high.

Gamlan *
Foot-bridge (719.244) to Ganllwyd (726.242)
Grade VIf
No Portages
700 metres
OS Sheet 124

To reach the access point drive a little way up the left bank of the river and then walk up to a foot-bridge about 700 metres above the confluence. All the drops on the river starting with the *bottom* fall just above this foot-bridge have been canoed in medium to high water. The canoeing is utterly relentless, but outstanding value for distance if you are water-hungry.

It is possible to canoe the Gamlan from further upstream, but beware the *top* fall above the foot-bridge. This is a 15-metre rocky waterfall (portage), and not to be confused with the second canoeable 10-metre slab. The land round the Gamlan is owned by the National Trust who do not object to canoeing provided that

paddlers are sensitive to the environment. This should go without
saying whoever owns the land.

AFON WNION

After the Eden, the Wnion is the major tributary of the
Mawddach, joining that river just below Dolgellau. The Bala to
Dolgellau road (A494) runs alongside the right bank of the Wnion,
and much of the river may be inspected from it. Access is possible
at a number of places, but the small road-bridge (just off the
A494) leading to Esgair Gawr is probably the best.

Wnion **
Esgair Gawr (807.229) to Bont Newydd (770.201)
Grade IVd
No Portages
6 Kilometres
OS Sheet 124

The river, small at first, is soon swollen by tributaries from north
and south. It passes under the disused railway four times before
Pont Llanrhaiadr (795.209), the half-way point and the start of
more difficult canoeing. The falls under the bridge are a one-shot
wonder, but after a kilometre the river visibly drops away at a left-
hand bend. From here there is a kilometre of very exciting
canoeing in a shallow gorge.
    The first part of the gorge is relatively open, containing a set of
three distinct rapids: Milky Way (IVc), Milk Shake (IVc) and
Vinegar Stroke (IVc). The second section of the Wnion gorge –
Coal Chute (IVd) – follows after 100 metres. It is a very long, fast
funnel of water bounded by 7-metre sheer rock walls. The Coal
Chute becomes Grade Ve in very high water. It is worth looking
(from the road on the way up, perhaps) to see if there are any
trees blocking this superb section of river, for once committed it
would be very difficult to escape. After the Coal Chute the river
relaxes for the last kilometre to Bont Newydd. Egress is on the left
bank.

It is possible to continue for another 2 kilometres on easier water to the next road-bridge, or a further 4 kilometres into Dolgellau itself. Alternatively this last 6 kilometres offers a much easier alternative trip to the one described above.

The Tryweryn and other rivers near Lake Vyrnwy

The Tryweryn is internationally famous as the site of the 1981 world championships. Whether you think it lives up to this reputation probably depends on whether you are a slalom paddler or not. This competition-minded breed are able to ignore the boredom of endlessly repeating the same section of river by concentrating on technique. And for the practising slalomist, or course organizer wanting predictable water, or indeed any white water-hungry southerner, the Tryweryn is ideal. It is dam- and BCU-controlled, so all you need to do is get on the blower, jump in the motor, pay the geezer, siphon the python, and, Bob's your uncle, you are on the water.

Unfortunately for the touring canoeist the BCU only owns access to the slalom site, which is the top fifth of the river from the dam down to Tyn y Cornel Bridge. Below that point the BCU have had little success in sorting out the usual access hassles, so the price of your ticket only secures guaranteed access to the Upper Tryweryn. In point of fact, Bala Mill Falls is the only rapid on the lower section of river that compares in quality to the slalom site, but a touring canoeist likes to travel, as well as play, and the rest of the Tryweryn has some good, if fairly easy and discontinuous white water.

So go to the Tryweryn for some social fun, but do not expect much that is natural or free. If that is what you want, and it has been raining, try the Wnion just down the A494 from Bala (see the chapter on the Afon Mawddach p.267), or go further south to a couple of rivers near Lake Vyrnwy. There is the little frequented Vyrnwy itself, or the Dugoed a river on which you are less likely to meet other paddlers than almost any other river in this book. The inescapable irony of guidebook writing is that this very recommendation may change all that.

Finally there is a little spate stream called the Twrch, hardly worth describing because the difficulties are so short and so easily inspected, but worth mentioning because there is no end of fun to be had during torrential downpours on such a mountain torrent as

this. The Twrch flows into the top end of Bala Lake and has been
canoed from Talardd (894.269) to Llanuwchllyn (880.298) at
Grade IIb for the first 3 kilometres and at Ve (two 3-metre drops)
for the last kilometre.

AFON TRYWERYN

Access to the Tryweryn is the responsibility of the Canoeing
Management Officer, and when the dam is releasing he or his
representatives will answer queries or leave a message on the
phone at the National White Water Centre (0678 520826) situated
beside the slalom site. If the answerphone gives levels of 'very low'
or 'low' do not bother to go. On 'one third volume release' the
slalom site is a very rocky IIIb and the rest of the river is
uncanoeable. On 'two thirds volume release' the slalom site and
Bala Mill are IIIc. At 'full volume/release' these sections are IVc
and the rest of the river IIIb. Since it costs you the price of a
couple of gallons of petrol even after you get there, it is probably
worth waiting for a full release.

Upper Tryweryn (slalom site) ***
Llyn Celyn Dam (881.398) to Tyn y Cornel Bridge (895.399)
Grade IVc
No Portages
2 Kilometres
OS Sheet 125

The true 'upper' Tryweryn, flowing like a drain for 3 kilometres
into Llyn Celyn, has been paddled in torrential rain (IIIb), but it is
the section below the dam which is known to all and sundry as the
Upper Tryweryn. Access is below the fish-pass under the dam,
reached from the A4212 by a turn-off at Ciltalgarth, 5 kilometres
north-west of Bala.
    The first series of drops appears round a left-hand bend, 300
metres downstream of the dam. This marks the start of the
Graveyard (IVc), a boulder field of 100 metres. Below the
Graveyard are a couple of angled and artificially enhanced

stoppers, followed by the start of the International Slalom Course. At full release the water laps the concrete apron on the left.

Fedwrgog Falls (IVc), under the bridge below, is the meanest rapid on the river, and has caused a number of black eyes. The left-hand bridge arch is blocked by boulders forming a big eddy, and below the right-hand arch lies a powerful stopper. Either take this on the extreme left and into this eddy or, easier, keep close to the right bank past a big boulder.

Some 200 metres downstream, a difficult 'S' bend is best broken in the large eddy on the right. Standing waves and a shoot with angled stoppers follow, and then a double fall with a notable haystack wave – Scaffolding Bridge Falls. Finally in this section there is a steep weir, Chapel Mill Falls. The weir is easy, in a straight line, but is difficult to 'play'.

And so to the bottom of the International Slalom Course. Many will want to exit on the right to a field above Tyn y Cornel Bridge, carry their boats back up and across the scaffolding bridge, and put in again above Fedwrgog Falls. This is the best section of the Tryweryn for slalom or white water practice.

Middle Tryweryn **
Tyn y Cornel Bridge (895.399) to Factory Pool (920.367)
Grade IIIb
No Portages
5 Kilometres
OS Sheet 125

Below the slalom site the river broadens and flattens into 5 kilometres of technically interesting but less serious river. The banks are always accessible and the difficulties are well spaced. In the middle of this section a couple of rapids are difficult to see from the river so inspection is useful.

Towards the end, the banks become higher and more rocky – a sign of the approach of Bala Mill Falls (IVc). If you do not intend to canoe this rapid, get out in Factory Pool where the road comes

Buried in Fedwrgog Falls on the Upper Tryweryn

close to the right bank, or portage round Bala Mill Falls on the right bank and continue to the egress given below.

Lower Tryweryn *
Factory Pool (920.367) to Pont Tryweryn (929.362)
Grade IVc
No Portages
1 Kilometre
OS Sheet 125

This section is very short and consists of one difficult rapid followed by a short section of Grade IIb. Although Bala Mill Falls (IVc) is a one-shot wonder, it is a little bit harder in the straight run than anything on the Upper Tryweryn. White water racers usually take a chicken shoot on the left of the main fall, but this misses the point if you are touring in a 'rockered' boat.

The problem with the big drop on the right is that all the water pushes onto the central rocks. It is perhaps best to break-out on the left above the main fall, and then re-orientate for the big drop. Whatever you decide, there will be plenty of people watching or taking pictures from the overhanging tree on the right, and occasionally a thoughtful person holding a throw line in the pool below!

The river eases quickly below Bala Mill Falls, and egress is to a car-park in Bala below Pont Tryweryn (A494 road-bridge). Bala Mill Falls can be reached on foot from the A4212 (right bank).

RIVER VYRNWY

The River Vyrnwy (Afon Efyrnwy) drains Lake Vyrnwy (Llyn Efyrnwy), a reservoir created by Liverpool Corporation in the 1880s. The birdlife round the lake and on the river bank is profuse, encouraged and protected by extensive natural forest and plantations. The pied flycatcher, arriving from Africa in April, nests amongst the oak trees; the rare crossbill lies in the deep

Cruising Bala Mill Falls on the Lower Tryweryn

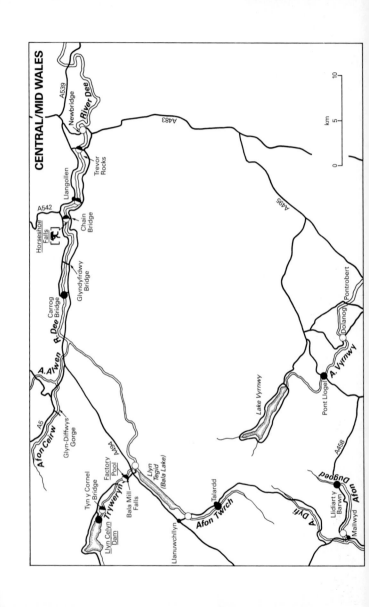

CENTRAL/MID WALES

A539
River Dee
Newbridge
A483

Llangollen
Trevor Rocks

A542
Horseshoe Falls
Chain Bridge

Glyndyfrdwy Bridge

R. Dee
Carrog Bridge

A. Alwen

A5
Afon Ceirw
Glyn-Diffwys Gorge

Tyn y Cornel Bridge
Factory Pool
A494
Bala Mill Falls
Llyn Celyn Tryweryn Dam

Llyn Tegid (Bala Lake)

Llanuwchllyn

Afon Twrch
Talardd

Lake Vyrnwy

A495

Dolanog
Pontrobert
A. Vyrnwy
Pont Llogel

A458
Dugoed
Afon
Llidiart y Barwn
Mallwyd
A. Dyfi

km
0   5   10

shade of mature conifers and black grouse are often seen in the younger plantations.

Vyrnwy
Pont Llogel (031.153) to Pontrobert (107.128)
Grade IIIc (IVd)
1 Portage
11 Kilometres
OS Sheet 125

Access to this section of the Vyrnwy is at the bridge in Llwydiarth carrying the B4395. For a shorter trip get in below the portage at Dolanog (064.126) on the B4382. The 6 kilometres below Dolanog are the best of the river, consisting of a steep-sided gorge, a difficult fall immediately afterwards (IVd), and much other interesting canoeing. Above the portage at Dolanog, the Vyrnwy is less interesting although scenic and quite isolated. The river is best canoed in high water. A telephone call to Lake Vyrnwy dam may determine whether and how much it is releasing.

AFON DUGOED

The Dugoed is a small tributary of the Afon Dyfi (Dovey). It needs to be brim full to make it worth canoeing. In these conditions Mallwyd Gorge is a serious undertaking.

Dugoed
Llidiart y Barwn (903.124) to Mallwyd (861.127)
Grade IIIc (Ve)
Occasional Portages
6 Kilometres
OS Sheet 125

The A458 Welshpool to Dolgellau road parallels the right bank of the Dugoed as it runs down to the hamlet of Mallwyd and the

The Afon Tryweryn, Vyrnwy, Dugoed and River Dee

confluence with the Afon Dyfi (road junction with the A470). At the house of Llidiart y Barwn it crosses a small tributary, the Afon Clywedog (not to be confused with its bigger southern neighbour), and access to the river is down a track into this tributary and so into the Dugoed.

The river is small and technical with some tree danger. At the bottom it drops very steeply for ½ kilometre through Mallwyd Gorge (Ve). This may be easily inspected by walking up the left bank from the A470 bridge. In the gorge, as in the river above, trees force the occasional portage.

The River Dee and its tributaries

The Afon Dyfrdwy, or, as the Saxons called it, the River Dee, is the best known of all the Welsh white water rivers. For long it has been a popular touring river, canoeable even after drought from Bala (confluence with the Tryweryn) to Connah's Quay, a distance of 140 kilometres. More recently three stretches of the Dee in the Vale of Llangollen have become popular with white water enthusiasts.

The cream of the Dee cake has to be the stretch from Horseshoe Falls to Llangollen, which hosts the annual invasion of the Mike Jones Rally. If all the canoeists and canoes in the Mike Jones Rally were placed end to end you could probably walk on water from Bala to Connah's Quay. Better then to go on another day to appreciate this classic run, with big waves, stoppers and exciting drops, in the famous rapids of Serpent's Tail, Tombstones, Factory Falls, and Town Falls. Medium to high water is preferred.

Above Horseshoe Falls is the beautiful upper valley of the Dee, called in Welsh Glyn-dyfrdwy. It is well worth a visit for a scenic and relaxing paddle. Below Llangollen too there is an easy yet nonetheless enjoyable section of river, containing the historically famous Trevor Rocks Rapid, other more minor disturbances, and fast sections between.

The Dee, in the Vale of Llangollen, is a relatively mature river flowing through gently rolling country, so it is not over-endowed with canoeable tributaries. However, just below its source, Bala Lake, is the excellent Tryweryn (see p.276). The two other major sources of water for the Dee near Llangollen are the Alwen and the Ceiriog.

The Ceiriog looks interesting on the map, but I have no knowledge of it. The Afon Alwen is canoeable from Bettws Gwerfil Goch (029.464) to Pen y Bont (044.436) at Grade IIIc, but look out for barbed wire in its upper half. The Alwen in its turn has a canoeable tributary, the Afon Ceirw. The Ceirw has a very difficult (VIe) gorge just below the hairpin bends at Glyndiffwys on the A5.

RIVER DEE

Whichever section of the Dee you choose to paddle, you will never be faced by a dry river bed, for the Dee is kept topped up from Bala Lake and Llyn Celyn (via the Tryweryn) to provide drinking water at Chester. The best place to judge the level of the river is the Serpent's Tail; if there is no stopper at the bottom, it is very low; if the rocks on the left bank are all covered, it is very high. The more water there is in the river, the harder and more serious the middle section becomes, but the Upper and Lower Dee do not alter appreciably in difficulty.

The Dee is one of the great game fishing rivers of Wales and legal access to the sections described is limited and difficult to obtain.

Upper Dee **
Carrog Bridge (114.437) to Horseshoe Falls (194.433)
Grade IIb
No Portages
11 Kilometres
OS Sheet 125

Turn off the A5 at Llidiart y Parc and you are soon at Carrog Bridge. This is the start of a beautiful and relaxing stretch of mature river. From Carrog to the bridge at Glyndyfrdwy (150.430) shingle rapids are interspersed with flatter sections, but in high water this stretch of 3 kilometres passes surprisingly quickly. More interesting water lies below Glyndyfrdwy. All around the hills start forming a spectacular ampitheatre. This is a special place in autumn when the bare brown and green slopes are glimpsed through rust-coloured leaves, and the low sun dapples the water with shadows. One drop, called Lunchtime Weir because of the conveniently-placed seats on the left bank, has an excellent play wave in low to medium water. Other longer rapids lower down the river are better in high water.

After 8 kilometres, the road on the left bank runs right beside the river offering the chance to shorten the trip if so desired. Fun rapids remain, however, including the Berwyn Chicane (IIb). The elegant curving weir of Horseshoe Falls marks the end of the trip. It is not all that obvious round a right-hand bend, but unnaturally still water above and a dull roar from below should be warning enough. Egress is above the weir on the left bank.

The really energetic may extend the Upper Dee trip by a further 5 kilometres by putting in above Carrog at Corwen where the A5 crosses the river. Access is downstream of the bridge on the left bank. If the islands below the bridge are covered the river is high.

Middle Dee ***
Horseshoe Falls (194.433) to Llangollen (216.420)
Grade IVd
No Portages
3 Kilometres
OS Sheet 117

Horseshoe Falls (designed by Thomas Telford) is the main weir feeder for the Shropshire Union Canal which follows the left bank of the Dee to Llangollen and beyond. When full the canal offers a pleasant return trip for the unshuttled driver. The weir may be shot on the left-hand side by a broken double-drop (IIIc), but the uniform central and right-hand side is very dangerous (IIIe). Having parked in the Chain Bridge car-park, most put in below Horseshoe Falls on the left bank.

Easy water leads past an island, under the road-bridge and down to Chain Bridge Rapid (IIIc). Below the Chain Bridge the main flow leads down right to the Serpent's Tail (IVc), although in high water a succession of stoppers forms over ledges and sills on the left. A tricky but safe rapid, the 'Serpent' spits swimmers into its 'tail' with monotonous regularity. It is an excellent place to perfect rolling, and in high water the expert will enjoy the powerful stopper and glutinous eddies at the bottom.

After the final meanders of the Tail a flat section, much used for collecting bodies and boats, leads to a broken weir (IIIc). This is best shot on the left where a sharp eddy cut sets the canoeist for some exciting upstream crosses – beware the iron spikes in low water.

Another smaller rapid precedes the railway bridge, and then there is Half-way Weir (IIIc) shot either on the left, or, in high water, by a tongue in the middle. Half-way Weir can be seen from the back road (on the left bank) into Llangollen.

The next rapid, Tombstones (IIId), is quite serious due to the remains of concrete stanchions in the main flow of the river. This broken weir is usually shot on the extreme left, but routes down the middle and right are exciting in high water. Tombstones marks the start of the 'Nomad Slalom Site', accessible from the A5 and the only part of the river which has negotiated access available throughout the year (contact the owner at the site).

Shortly after Tombstones is a perfectly-formed stopper which will hold boats (broadside) but not swimmers. Those 'playing' in this stopper may find the following excuses useful – 'I would have rolled but the paddle was torn out of my hand', 'I was just setting up when my spraydeck was ripped off', and 'I was nearly sucked out of my boat'.

Those 'torn', 'ripped', or 'sucked' may end up swimming over Factory Falls, which marks the end of the Nomad Site, and is the last rapid before Town Falls. Factory Falls (IIIc) is on a bend to the left of an island (the factory, now used by Nomad Canoes, is to the right), contains big standing waves, and, at most levels, has an excellent play hole (see above for excuses).

The lead-in to Town Falls (IVd) is lengthy, allowing plenty of time to egress on the right bank for inspection – get out when the bridge comes into view. It is both difficult to choose and to find the right line down Town Falls. It is a long and complicated rapid with three distinct drops. The first is a weir easily taken in the middle by a little spout. The second, called the Pot, can be shot anywhere but most easily right of middle. The Pot leads to the falls proper which are to the right of an island and just above the bridge. A route close to the island, or the right bank, seems preferable, but you may have little choice in the matter. In high water it is

possible to go to the left of the island through big waves and
stoppers.

One hundred metres below Town Falls is Town Weir, broken
and easily shot on the left (IIIc), but forming a very nasty keeper
on the middle and right (IVf). Prompt action below Llangollen
town bridge is required from friends and strangers alike to prevent
the damp and dispossessed from swimming into, and not
necessarily *through*, this weir. Egress is on the left bank below
Town Weir; a concrete path leads up to a much-used watering hole
at the end of the bridge.

Lower Dee
Llangollen (216.420) to Newbridge (287.417)
Grade IIIb
No Portages
9 Kilometres
OS Sheet 117

The 5 kilometres between Llangollen and Trevor Rocks will not
inspire you to poetry, but in high water it can be a fast and
exhilarating paddle. Trevor Rocks (IIIb), lying just above a road-
bridge (the first below Llangollen), is easily accessible and may be
preferred as a put-in. It gained something of a reputation after
being selected in 1939 as the site of the first slalom competition
held in Britain and, as late as 1956, Alec Ellis in his *Book of
Canoeing* thought it 'very bad', recommending that you should
'stand up in the canoe and inspect the approaching rapid'. By
modern standards it is a doddle as long as you don't try standing
up in your canoe.

Between Trevor Rocks and Newbridge the rapids are
entertaining for the novice paddler. The Dee passes under the
canal (after ½ kilometre), the railway (after 3 kilometres), and
then the road – this 'new' bridge marks the egress point. To reach
the A483 it is best to scramble steeply up the right bank.

The Twymyn and other rivers of Mid-Wales

Mid-Wales' weather is a little less kind than that of the southern Alps, but since Brits cannot rely on snow-melt to fill their rivers, the west-coast monsoon climate is to be welcomed. And now that the ozone layer has been punctured we often get warm winters as well. So there is much to recommend a weekend or week spent in the hinterland of Cardigan Bay, paddling the better known rivers, and exploring other plastic boat benders.

If the Twymyn is the classic of the area, the Dovey's (Dyfi) other major tributary, the Dulas North (there is another *southern* tributary also called the Afon Dulas), comes second only because of its lack of continuity at the grade. Variation in difficulty is not a problem in the Rheidol or Ystwyth gorges; they are unredeemingly hard, and for that reason are the preserve of an élite. Today's élite, however, have a habit of creating the norm for tomorrow, so perhaps these rivers will not seem so difficult or serious in the light of more widespread knowledge. Finally there is the dam-controlled Clywedog, too short in difficulty to be a classic, but a useful little number when all else is dry.

AFON TWYMYN

The Afon Twymyn is an excellent little white water river which can stay in condition for 48 hours after heavy rain. The source of the Twymyn is in the bleak hills south-west of Machynlleth, but there is little to interest the white water paddler until the river reaches the small hamlet of Tafolwern near Llanbrynmair. Here the Twymyn is joined and revitalized by the Afon Iaen for the run down to the Dyfi.

Twymyn **
Llanbrynmair Bridge (898.028) to Pont Doldwymyn (825.046)
Grade IIId

Glantwymyn Gorge on the Afon Twymyn

No Portages
10 Kilometres
OS Sheet 135

Access is possible at Tafolwern, but it is probably best to put in on
the Afon Rhiw-Saeson (a tributary of the Iaen) at Llanbrynmair
Bridge (downstream left bank). These two little rivers provide a
pleasant route into the Twymyn and if they are canoeable then the
Twymyn will be up. From Tafolwern, the Twymyn flows for 8
kilometres at continuous Grade IIb through idyllic and peaceful
countryside. The picnic-site by the A470 marks the end of this
section and is an alternative access point (853.030).

Just downstream of the picnic-site the river livens up and
continues to be interesting into Commins Coch. One kilometre
below Commins Coch a bouncy rapid below a railway-bridge
heralds the run into the final harder section. A long, low dry-stone
wall on the right marks the start of Glantwymyn Gorge (IIId).
Those wishing to inspect it should get out here, as once past this
point the trap is sprung and escape would be difficult.

There are three falls in the gorge, with difficult boils, cross-
currents and eddies in between. The first fall is straightforward and
becomes washed-out in high water. The second is taken on the
right and in medium water can provide good pop-outs. There is
little choice where to take the third, since the gorge is less than 4
metres wide at this point, but there is a big catchment pool below.
The gorge continues for a couple of hundred metres until a large
calm pool is reached by the railway viaduct at Cemmaes Road.
Egress is at the road-bridge just beyond, up a steep bank on the
right.

AFON DULAS

The (Northern) Dulas is a river of contrasts both in terms of
canoeing and scenery. The Upper Dulas from Llwydiarth to Corris
is a fast mountain stream flowing steeply through bleak slate
quarries. The Lower Dulas flows from Corris to Glan Fechan in
the lush flat expanse of the Dyfi valley. Here it is deeper, stronger

and, with one or two exceptions, more continuous than its upper half. It is also more often canoeable, since the upper catchment area is well drained.

Upper Dulas *
Llwydiarth (779.104) to Corris (754.078)
Grade IVd
No Portages (?)
5 Kilometres
OS Sheet 124

After heavy rain those making the effort to drive up past the slate quarries of Aberllefenni will be rewarded with some interesting and technical canoeing. Access is at the bridge across to Llwydiarth Hall.

One kilometre below Llwydiarth is Rhaeadr y Pwll Du (IVd). The Fall of the Black Pool is an excellent series of four drops invisible from the road: the first fall ending in the reputedly bottomless Black Pool. From here to Aberllefenni only the odd tree or fence will cause any concern, and occasionally a portage. Below Aberllefenni the canoeing is still good, but never as hard as above. The most serious rapid before you reach the bridge in Corris is Pont Newydd Falls (IIId). This is beneath the left arch of a forestry bridge 1 kilometre below Aberllefenni and has a holding stopper lurking at the bottom.

Lower Dulas *
Corris (754.078) to Glan Fechan (751.024)
Grade IIId
1 Portage
8 Kilometres
OS Sheets 124 and 135

Access and egress in Corris are at the bridge in the village not far from the Slaters Arms. After about a kilometre a caravan-site marks the start of an excellent stretch of white water. There is an interesting rapid called Think Small (IIId) just above the road-

bridge, a weir a few hundred metres downstream, and some nice
standing waves leading into Esgairgeiliog village. Great care is
necessary here as a few metres downstream of the foot-bridge is
Rhaeadr Ceirws (VIf). Unless you are feeling very good, or are
blessed with a lack of imagination, portage on the right.

The Lower Dulas continues to be interesting all the way to Glan
Fechan. There are two large falls of note: the broken Llwyngwern
Weir, easily seen from the A487, is best shot right of centre, and a
short way downstream is the aptly-named and entertaining Coal
Yard Fall. Egress is possible at Pantperthog, but having come this
far it is probably worth continuing on the relaxing run down to Glan
Fechan.

AFON RHEIDOL

The Rheidol Gorge is one of the most serious rivers in this guide.
The atmosphere in the heart of the Gorge is more Alpine than
British with huge boulders littering the river bed in a deep 'V'-
shaped tree-lined valley. The canoeing is highly technical and
potentially very dangerous (many sumps) with the added problem
of complicated portages (50 metres of rope necessary). A long day
is necessary to complete the whole river because of the amount of
inspection and safety-cover required. Some may prefer therefore
to start or finish at Parson's Bridge.

The river is dam-controlled and rarely has much water released
into it. Should there be a big release, the river described below
would be a different 'ball game'. The level can be checked at
Ponterwyd. If the weir visible from the bridge has more than 4 or 5
centimetres of water coming over it, it may be best to leave the
gorge until another day. At the normal low release level open
sections of the gorge will be a bump and scrape. The Rheidol is
one of the few rivers in the guide where this characteristic is
sought after.

There is an easier, but rarely canoeable trip on the Rheidol, starting at Nant y Moch dam (754.861) and finishing at Ponterwyd. This
is Grade IVd for the first kilometre and then much easier for the next
4 kilometres. The long flog through Dinas reservoir spoils this trip.

Upper Rheidol *
Ponterwyd (748.808) to Parson's Bridge (748.790)
Grade Ve
No Portages
3 Kilometres
OS Sheet 135

The A4120 meets the A44 at Ponterwyd. Here the man-made weir
can be shot on the right-hand side (IVc), but it is probably better
to put in just below. Just out of sight round a bend is Ponterwyd
Gorge (Ve) which is the gateway to the rest of the river. The
initial 3-metre drop into the gorge is followed by a very rocky
section of 200–300 metres. A large waterfall coming in from the
right marks the end of this difficult section.

For a while the river then eases to grade IIb. A 5-metre twisting
drop called Frank's Falls (Ve) then marks the start of another
difficult section. To portage this rapid requires a 6-metre seal
launch. A long boulder field, the Somme, succeeds Frank's Falls
with the river finally easing again before Parson's Bridge Gorge.

If you are having second thoughts about the river it is possible
with some difficulty and a long rope to escape from it at the
Parson's Bridge. From the bridge walk east to Ysbyty Cynfyn on
the A4120.

Lower Rheidol *
Parson's Bridge (748.790) to foot-bridge (727.781)
Grade Vf
3 Portages
6 Kilometres
OS Sheet 135

Parson's Bridge Gorge (Ve) is the third hard section below
Ponterwyd. It marks the start of 3 kilometres of continuously
technical and dangerous canoeing. The initial drops are very tight
and rocky. Once through them the river calms down until a left-hand
bend round a boulder. Past the boulder there is a 6-metre twisting
drop, Hesitation Falls, with a pot-hole on one side and an undercut

wall on the other (Vf). The Rheidol then flows through a 7-metre wide gorge which empties over a 10-metre waterfall, Y Rhaedr Fawr (portage or VIf).

The river is a little easier now (IVd) except for one dangerous drop which most will want to portage (VIf). A fall from the right then m arks the top of Gyfarllwyd Falls - an awesome waterfall onto rock which *must be portaged* by abseil (50 metre rope required). The pool at the bottom of the fall runs into a boulder-choked sump, so continue the portage.

The river now flattens off, and after the confluence with the Afon Mynach, with the famous Devil's Bridge high above, there are only two falls of note (IIId). Egress is by some disused mine buildings below the second fall, about two kilometres after Devil's Bridge. If you want a last fling, continue down river or road for 3 kilometres to Rheidol Falls (Ve), a nasty 5-metre sting in the Rheidol's tail.

AFON YSTWYTH

Six kilometres south-east of Devil's Bridge a minor road breaks off the B4574 into the valley of the Afon Ystwyth, climbing past first Cwmystwyth, then Blaenycwm, before crossing the watershed into the valley of the Wye. The Ystwyth down to Blaenycwm is an excellent adrenalin rush in high water. The river below Cwmystwyth is more serious and better done at lower levels. Access is at the bridge in Cwmystwyth village, or in higher water 5 kilometres upstream at Blaenycwm, or in full flood 3 kilometres still further upstream either on the Ystwyth itself or on its tributary the Afon Diluw (from the ford near Lluest-dolgwiail - 843.773).

Upper Ystwyth **
Watershed (852.757) to Cwmystwyth (789.738)
Grade IVd
No Portages

8 Kilometres
OS Sheet 135

The steep boulder-filled river down to Blaenycwm is a brilliant high spate run with no eddies. Access is where the road from Rhayader first runs beside the river – pick your spot. Below Blaenycwm there is more good paddling, particularly between Cwm Ystwyth lead mine and Cwmystwyth itself. If these two sections are well up, then the river below Cwmystwyth is probably better left to another day, since Dologau Gorge becomes progressively harder the higher the river.

Lower Ystwyth *
Cwmystwyth (789.738) to Pontrhydygroes (741.797)
Grade Ve
No Portages
7 Kilometres
OS Sheet 135

The main feature of this section of river is the difficult and committing Dologau Gorge starting 2 kilometres downstream of Cwmystwyth and finishing just below Dologau Bridge. There is a dam at Dologau which has a hole through it, shootable in medium water but impossible in high water (portage). Immediately below the dam is another fall with a big stopper. An 'S' bend, with a bridge in the middle of it, half a kilometre downstream of Dologau, provides the last of the difficulties before the village of Pontrhydygroes (3 kilometres). Egress is in the village.

   The short, sheer-sided gorge immediately below Pontrhydygroes - gradient 30m/km - is at the very upper limits of difficulty and seriousness - VIf and portages. It has been attempted but until the log jams are removed it will be of little interest to most people.

AFON CLYWEDOG

The Clwedog is a dam-controlled river with regular releases all the year round (phone the dam for information). Full release on this river is an impressive sight, especially when you realize that half release is equivalent to full release on the Tryweryn. Like the Tryweryn, however, the big waves and holes hide no nasty surprises so, as national slalom coaches have discovered, it is a good place to practise 2/3/4 stroke break-outs or mentally rehearse gate strategies – or just 'play'.

Clywedog *
Clwyedog dam (912.868) to Llanidloes (954.847)
Grade IIIc (IVc)
No Portages
6 Kilometres
OS Sheet 136

To canoe the whole river one has to start from the foot of the dam. Access is from Bryntail Mine car-park. Immediately downstream is the hardest rapid on the river, Bryntail Fall (IVc). A powerful stopper guards the exit to this fall which is at the top of a shallow gorge. From here on the gorge becomes easier (IIIc).

Half a kilometre after the start is the road-bridge which is an alternative access point for those wishing to miss Bryntail Fall. An easy kilometre leads to Brithdir Falls (IIIc), a bedrock step taken left or right in low water and anywhere in high water. After another 2 kilometres Clywedog Caravan Park Weir appears. The only safe route is through the central notch although in very high water even this route is suspect because of the enormous uniform stopper.

Trees and weirs decorate the run-in to Llanidloes and bank inspection is occasionally needed. Egress is most convenient at the confluence with the Severn in Llanidloes. Either get out at the causeway immediately opposite the confluence on the right bank, or continue down under the arches of Long Bridge. There you may choose between playing on a large wave (left arch), or in a big but safe stopper (right arch).

The River Wye and its tributaries

The Wye (Afon Gwy), thought the much-travelled Borrow, was probably 'the most lovely river which the world can boast of'. Exaggeration though this may be, there can be no denying that the Wye carves an idyllic 214-kilometre course through the Welsh and English landscape. Below Glasbury, the Wye is a public navigation, suitable for novice canoeists, and much frequented by touring campers because of its rural nature. By the time the river crosses into England at Hay, it has become 'ole man river', a steady, meandering plod. The Welsh Wye is younger, more vigorous, more to the liking of white water canoeists.

Should you be in search of something harder, and are prepared to drop everything when it rains, consider one of the tributaries of the Wye. They are numerous and of sufficient quality to be regularly paddled by local enthusiasts. The Claerwen, Upper Irfon, and Edw, in particular, deserve attention.

RIVER WYE

The Wye between Builth Wells and Glasbury is popular with canoeists of moderate ability and limited experience, and I have called this the Lower Wye. Some 20 to 30 kilometres upstream of Builth, in the district of Rhayader, the Wye is more continuous, and of greater interest to the white water paddler. Properly called the Upper Wye, I have divided this section, for the purposes of this guide, into the Upper and Middle Wye.

As with all good white water rivers, the level of the Upper and Middle Wye fluctuates dramatically. If the gauge upstream of the bridge in Rhayader shows above 3 the river is canoeable; 5–6 is a good level; if it is above 10 then most of the river is washed out and Rhayader Town Falls becomes IVd – this only happens two or three times a year on average. The Lower Wye benefits from two major tributaries, the Ithon and Irfon, and is therefore more often canoeable. Only when the Wye is seen to be very shallow under Builth Bridge is this section impractical.

Upper Wye **
Pant y Drain (915.763) to Marteg confluence (951.714)
Grade IIIc
No Portages
7 Kilometres
OS Sheet 147

Since the Wye is flat below Llangurig it is best to put in from the
A470 3 kilometres to the south, where a farm track crosses the
river at Pont y Drain. Between here and the little foot-bridge (2
kilometres) are, in descending order, Bedrock Rapid, Son of
Bedrock, Island Rapid, and Circulating Eddy Rapid. There is then
Foot-bridge Rapid, whose location you will probably guess,
followed by a small boulder-field, before the Wye relaxes down to
Glyn Gwy Gorge (IIIc).

Glyn Gwy Gorge is an exciting 2 kilometres of river. The A470
is squashed next to the left bank by the steep contours above and
the river drops continuously over many small falls. These are
washed-out in very high water but then the boils gives the gorge a
different kind of excitement. The Gorge ends at the junction with
the Afon Marteg where there is a bridge and car-park.

If, at the end of all this, you are looking for even more intense
excitement, drive up the north bank of the Afon Marteg and put in
at an old railway-bridge (959.714). The canoeing is at first easy but
near the Marteg's junction with the Wye is a ferocious 200-metre
gorge called Y Ffrwd (Ve). In high water this is an excellent
adrenalin pump.

Middle Wye **
Marteg confluence (951.714) to Llanwrthwl (976.639)
Grade IIIc
No Portages
11 Kilometres
OS Sheet 147

This section, as far as the town of Rhayader, is used for white
water races. There are three major rapids including Town Fall in

Rhayader. Below Rhayader is a less confined but nonetheless interesting section of river.

After the Marteg confluence the river is pushed to the west by the steep crags and hillside of Gamallt. The speed and gradient of the river are thus increased, producing two notable rapids: Gamallt Falls (IIIc) and Cwmcoed Falls (IIIc). The first is a straight shoot in all water levels, with big waves extending 50 metres downstream in high water. The second rapid can be shot anywhere in high water but in low water should be taken on the right. The river is then easier down to Rhayader. Marteg to Rhayader can be paddled in 21 minutes in a white water racer!

Town Fall (IIIc), otherwise called Rhaeadr Gwy (Wye Fall), was blasted out in the nineteenth century to make a weir for a woollen mill. Prior to that it was a much bigger rapid. A three-tier drop, it now reaches IVd only in very high water. Egress is possible on the right below the fall.

Below Rhayader there is a pleasant section down to Llanwrthwl. There are pipes over the river taking drinking-water to Birmingham, with white water beneath them over bedrock steps. The river is then flat for 3 kilometres down to an old railway-bridge. Quarry Falls (IIIc) consists of two rapids, one just above and one just below the bridge. This ends in a big salmon pool at the confluence with the waters of the Afon Elan – or at least that portion of it which is not being drunk in Birmingham. The remainder of the Wye down to the new bridge in Llanwrthwl is not without interest particularly in high water.

Below Llanwrthwl (egress at the bridge) the Wye continues at Grade IIb for a kilometre, and then is flat as far as Newbridge (9 kilometres). From Newbridge down to Builth Wells (11 kilometres) is entirely flat except for Builth Rocks (IIIc), a meaty rapid 1 kilometre upstream of Builth. Most canoeists prefer, therefore, to miss this section of the Wye. The Lower Wye (as described) starts at Builth Wells.

Lower Wye
Builth Wells (042.511) to Llanstephan Bridge (112.416)
Grade IIIc

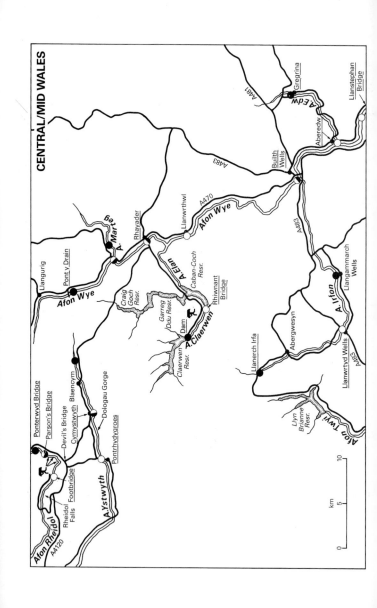

CENTRAL/MID WALES

Ponterwyd Bridge
Parson's Bridge
Devil's Bridge
Footbridge
Rheidol Falls
A.Ystwyth
Afon Rheidol
A4120
Cymystwyth
Blaencym
Dologau Gorge
Pontrhydygroes

Llangurig
Pont y Drain
Afon Wye
Be
A. Marte
Rhayader
Craig
Goch Resr.
Garreg
Ddu Resr.
Claerwen
Resr.
Dam
A.Claerwen
Caban-Coch Resr.
Rhiwnant
Bridge
A.Elan
Afon Wye
Llanwrthwl
A470

Llanerch Irfa
Abergwesyn
Llyn
Brianne Resr.
Afon Tywi
Llanwrtyd Wells
A483
A. Irfon
Llangammarch
Wells

Builth Wells
A483
A481
Aberedw
A.Edw
Gregrina
Llanstephan
Bridge

Afon Wye
A470

0   5   10
km

No Portages
16 Kilometres
OS Sheets 161 and 147

This section of the Wye is perhaps the most popular easy stretch of white water in the guide. There are three rapids of note and a number of other shallows and reefs. It is a long trip, but in high water and high summer the kilometres flow by in a warm blur of lush, green scenery. It is also a popular stretch among fishermen, not all of them against canoeing. I always remember the comment of one Wye fisherman, an instructor of the sport no less, who, after cheerily waving a party of canoes through, said to his students: 'Remember lads, a disturbed fish is a hungry fish'.

Three kilometres below Builth Wells there is a section of rocky reefs which must be negotiated. This is Llanfared Rapids (IIIb) and a girder lies in the water here at the bottom of the rapids, covered at most levels. After 8 kilometres the Afon Edw enters from the left. A kilometre downstream are the Erwood Rapids (IIIb), with deep narrow channels and bedrock steps in low water, or big waves in high water, stretching over a kilometre. Erwood Bridge is some way downstream (12 kilometres downstream of Builth), and, just below, the tiny Nant yr Offeraid flows into the Wye offering spate possibilities similar to the Nantmor in North Wales.

Between Erwood Bridge and Llanstephan Bridge are the most famous rapids on the Wye, Llanstephan Rapids with Hell Hole (IIIc). The rocks here slope upstream making for an uncomfortable swim, but at normal levels Hell Hole is a 'play' stopper. Only in high spate is there a keeper of sufficient force (on river left) to justify comparisons with the underworld (IVd).

Below Llanstephan Bridge (recommended egress point) there is one small fall before Boughrood Bridge (alternative egress point) and then the river is almost flat as far as Glasbury. The extra 4 or 10 kilometres are only worth the effort in exceptionally high water.

AFON CLAERWEN

The Afon Claerwen is a tributary of the River Elan – the latter is
canoeable (if water is flowing over Caban Coch dam) at Grade IIb
from Elan Bridge (924.644) to its confluence with the Wye
(966.656). Together these two rivers drain over 45,000 acres of
sparsely-populated, peaty, sheep-grazed land. Left to itself all of
their water would flow into the river Wye and thence into the
Bristol Channel. Instead 60 million gallons a day travel to
Birmingham, and from there into the Tame, Trent, Humber and
finally the North Sea. The Elan chain of dams – Craig Goch, Pen-
y-garreg, Garreg Ddu and Caban Coch – was completed in 1904,
with the mighty Claerwen Valley Dam a more recent addition in
1952.
    The Claerwen, like the Elan, is dam-released. It flows between
Claerwen reservoir and Caban Coch reservoir. It is easy to see
whether it is canoeable from the parking-place near Claerwen
dam. Moreover since the Claerwen runs through open country, it
can be inspected from the road on the way up. There are two
difficult rapids/portages in an otherwise relatively easy and
beautiful little river.

Claerwen *
Claerwen reservoir (870.633) to Rhiwnant Bridge (900.615)
Grade IVc (Vf)
1 Portage
4 Kilometres
OS Sheet 147

About 2 kilometres below the dam is Rhaeadr y Glaerwen. This is an
awesome fall over drops and through boulder chokes. It is best
portaged, and some may want to start the trip below here. A
kilometre of relatively easy water (IIIc) leads to a wooden
footbridge followed by a huge boulder on the right-hand side. Here
you should get out to inspect Rhaeadr Cwm-clyd (Vf), a 5-metre
drop followed almost immediately by a committing, rocky rapid. A
pool may enable you to collect your wits, or bits, before an excellent

little boulder-field (IVc). Egress is at Rhiwnant Bridge a kilometre
below Rhaeadr Cwm-clyd.

AFON IRFON

The Irfon is a major tributary of the Wye, but at the highest access
point it is little more than a stream. In spate the Upper Irfon
provides an excellent white water run. The Lower Irfon is much
less interesting, and if you want something more akin to the Upper
Irfon, drive west over its watershed into the valley of the Tywi.
Flowing out of the dam at the bottom Llyn Brianne reservoir are 3
kilometres of very exciting water – IVd or Ve, depending on the
water level. Egress is at the Bird Sanctuary. (Below the Bird
Sanctuary are some horrendous boulder chokes and sumps which
might just be possible in very high water – another 'last great
challenge'!)

Upper Irfon **
Llanerch Irfa (835.555) to Llanwrtyd Wells (878.466)
Grade Vd
No Portages
13 Kilometres
OS Sheet 147

At Llanerch Irfa the road crosses the Irfon by a ford. Below the ford
is a narrow gorge, Camddwr Bleiddiad, which has been paddled but
which ends in horrendous boulder chokes. Access is best therefore
downstream of the chokes.
    There are a number of hard rapids in the section before
Abergwesyn, including Rhaeadr y Twmffat (IVd). There are four
difficult rapids between Abergwesyn and Llanwrtyd Wells. The
first is Forestry Bridge Fall, narrow and very boily (Vd). The second
is Peter's Fall with a meaty stopper in very high water (Vd). Then
there is Andy's Folly, a 'backender', and finally an unnamed rapid
over bedrock steps. Below the river is easy down to Llanwrtyd
Wells. In that village there is a pipe over the river. The water should
be near the level of the pipe for the river to be canoeable-

watch out! Egress should be by the pipe rather than in the village itself.

Lower Irfon
Llangammarch Wells (935.472) to Builth Wells (031.510)
Grade IIb (IIIc)
No Portages
17 Kilometres
OS Sheet 147

The long Lower Irfon is canoeable from Llangammarch Wells to the confluence with the Wye above Builth Wells. The best egress is from the Wye at the bridge in Builth. The canoeing is straightforward apart from one large rapid (IIIc) about 2 kilometres above the confluence with the Wye.

THE AFON EDW

The Edw is another major tributary of the Welsh Wye although it needs a lot of water to make it canoeable. It is relatively straightforward, but has a number of interesting rapids, which make it attractive as an alternative start to the Lower Wye.

Edw *
Cregrina (123.521) to Aberedw (076.470)
Grade IIIc (IVd)
Occasional Portages (trees)
12 Kilometres
OS Sheets 147 and 148

The river is continuous grade IIb until, after 2 kilometres, a metal foot-bridge warns of the approach of Rhaeadr Rhulen (IVd). This should be inspected. The Edw then eases again down to the Common. Paddlers often get in here as an alternative start to the Wye (094.578).

  Downstream of the Common, the river enters a gorge and there are some good rapids, and one small fall which is worth inspecting for the right line (IIIc). Egress is easiest from the Wye, but it is possible to get to the B4567 just before the confluence and just after the railway embankment tunnel. This latter egress point is at the end of a continuous section of IIIb.

The River Usk and its tributaries

The River Usk (Afon Wysg) flows broad and even through a green and pleasant land. Everything seems to be in the right place and proportion for human habitation, unlike the craggy landscape of North Wales or the Scottish Highlands, or even the rugged moors of the Brecon Beacons. Rivers reflect and follow the pressures of the landscape through which they flow and so there is nothing wild, hard, or committing about the Usk. Should you tire of the soft open vistas of the Usk, you might consider one of its tributaries. None are very hard, but they certainly twist and turn more narrowly and continuously through the contours. But if it is extreme canoeing you are after, leave the valley of the Usk and head south over the Brecon Beacons and Black Mountains into the little valleys of South Wales. Here there is waterfall on waterfall, and enough white water to satisfy the most Desperate Dan (see chapter on the Tawe p. 316).

RIVER USK

The Usk is a pool-drop river suitable for intermediate paddlers, with a few exciting falls and much other pleasant canoeing. It is, with the Wye, the major canoeing river of South Wales, and the popular Lower Usk below Brecon is canoeable most of the year. The Lower Usk is particularly good in spate (defined as when the river is overflowing the banks at Talybont) and at this level a number of the rapids show a marked increase in difficulty and seriousness.

Upper Usk *
Pont Newydd (880.286) to Milestone Bridge (946.295)
Grade IIIc
No Portages
9 Kilometres
OS Sheet 160

The last big drop on the Upper Usk

For 20 minutes below the bridge at Trecastle (⅝ kilometre south of the A40, 5 kilometres west of Sennybridge) you have little more to do than wonder where the castle was – Trecastle means 'town of the castle'. The river is broad, pleasant, and even. But after 3 kilometres the Crai enters from the right swelling the Usk, and then a road-bridge (alternative access 903.291) marks the start of a steepish gorge. The river swirls this way and that, first beside the A40 and then away from the road, giving some interesting and technical rapids (IIIb). It returns again to pass under the road (a good place to judge the level of the river), flowing strongly into Sennybridge.

After the junction with the Senny, the Usk matures into a pool-drop river. There are three drops (IIIc) in the 3 kilometres between the last of Senny's bridges and the next road-bridge downstream, Milestone Bridge (so-called because there is a milestone on the road above). The first is quite a surprise; the river turns sharp right in a steep copse and immediately falls over itself. The last is the most serious, containing, in high water, a recirculating stopper on the left. In these conditions the rapid becomes Grade IIId.

For those with white water wanderlust it is best to get out at Milestone Bridge and skip on down to Talybont for the Lower Usk. The remainder of the river down to Brecon (11 kilometres) is much easier, albeit continuous at the grade (IIb). In high water all the small rapids are washed out, but you hardly have time to miss them. For novice paddlers this fast, fun run through gentle scenery is excellent value.

Lower Usk **
Talybont on Usk (119.230) to Crickhowell (220.176)
Grade IIIc (IVd in spate)
No Portages
15 Kilometres
OS Sheet 161

The Monmouthshire and Brecon Canal, restored to navigation in the late 1960s, parallels the Usk below Brecon, so it is possible, if rather tedious, for unshuttled paddlers to have a two-way trip. Access to the river from car or canal is at Talybont on Usk where a minor tributary (coming out of Talybont reservoir) is crossed by a minor road linking the B4558 to the A40. Parking is easier here than at any other suitable access point.

At first the river is flat, the only drop being an easily shootable weir, but things soon improve at Mill House Falls (IIIc medium water, IVc in spate). Then there is an island taken on the left, followed by a long rapid sweeping round a right-hand bend with standing waves at the bottom. The river passes under the remarkable seventeenth-century stone bridge at Llangynidir (possible alternative access) and into Llangynidir Rapid (IIIc medium water, IVd in spate), with, in medium to high water, a notable stopper – the Washing Machine. This is caused by water pouring over a ledge on river left, and, although fairly easily avoided, cannot be seen from above and therefore regularly gobbles paddlers.

The next rapid is Spuhler's Folly (IIIc medium water, IVd in spate) best shot down the left in medium water, and down the centre in spate. It is the last of the named rapids, but there remain some good play waves. The Glanusk estate owns the land on both banks for the last 2 kilometres above Crickhowell, so this is not a good place for a picnic. Egress is to a commodious lay-by off the A4077 1 kilometre below Crickhowell Bridge on the right bank. While changing you might wonder why the ancient stone bridge at Crickhowell has thirteen arches on the downstream side, but only twelve on the upstream side.

THE USK TRIBUTARIES

The tributaries of the Usk between Sennybridge and Abergavenny require heavy rain to bring them into condition. Because these streams are often confined, wooded banks, trees and occasionally barbed wire are a serious problem, and additional portages to those listed below may be required. The gradient of the rivers is surprisingly even, so detailed descriptions are superfluous. The seven tributaries – Afon Senny, Cilieni, Bran, Yscir, Tarell,

Honddu and Grwyne – are described in the order one would come across them if paddling down the Usk.

Senny
Abersenni Uchaf (9932.261) to Sennybridge (920.285)
Grade IIc
No Portages
3 Kilometres
OS Sheet 160

The Senny can be used as an alternative start to the Upper Usk. Trees are a problem, but there are no rapids of note, except for one just above the confluence with the Usk. The access point is reached by turning off the A4215 4 kilometres south of Sennybridge. The Senny joins the Usk in that town.

Cilieni *
Pentre'r Felin (920.303) to Usk Milestone Bridge (946.295)
Grade IIIc (IVd)
1 Portage
3 Kilometres
OS Sheet 160

This is an excellent albeit short section of river. Apart from trees, which are present early on, the major difficulties come at the end. Half a kilometre before the junction with the Usk there is a road-bridge. Above the bridge is a difficult fall (IVd) which should be inspected. Below the bridge the river is presently blocked by trees (portage on the left bank) but do not finish here as some exciting canoeing remains. Egress is at the first bridge on the Usk (after 1 kilometre).

Bran
Tir y felin (964.321) to Aberbran (984.296)
Grade IIIc

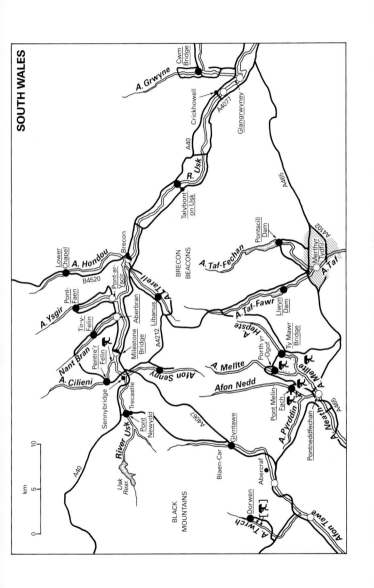

SOUTH WALES

No Portages
5 Kilometres
OS Sheet 160

The Nant Bran flows quite steeply through wooded country north of the Usk, and trees can often be a problem. Five hundred metres below Aberbran the Nant Bran joins the Usk. This can be followed for 8 kilometres to Brecon (IIb).

Yscir
Pont-faen (996.341) to Pont-ar-Yscir (003.302)
Grade IIIc
No Portages
6 Kilometres
OS Sheet 160

The Yscir parallels the Nant Bran and also has root and branch problems! A kilometre below Pont-ar-Yscir, the Yscir enters the Usk, which can be followed for 6 kilometres to Brecon. Above the recommended put-in at Pont-faen, the two tributaries of the Yscir (which meet there) are both canoeable in high water down to the confluence. The Yscir-fechan can be canoed for 5 kilometres from Pont Rhydberry (977.368), and Yscir-fawr for 6 kilometres from Merthyr Cynog Bridge (993.373).

Tarell
Libanus (995.250) to Brecon (039.288)
Grade IIIc
No Portages
7 Kilometres
OS Sheet 160

Trees are a major problem on the Tarell. The river joins the Usk in Brecon (egress point), and can be used as an alternative and much longer start to the Lower Usk. There are some interesting drops as the Tarell enters the town. The A470 parallels the river.

Honddu *
Lower Chapel (029.356) to Brecon (043.287)
Grade IIIc
No Portages
10 Kilometres
OS Sheet 160

The Honddu is perhaps the best of the Usk tributaries. It certainly has the longest reliable section of moving water, and there are a number of interesting rapids (after heavy rain), more particularly as the river is canalized down shoots and over weirs into Brecon. The Honddu joins the Usk in Brecon (egress point), and it is possible, if rather tedious, to continue 12 kilometres downstream to the start of the Lower Usk.

Grwyne *
Cwm Bridge (244.199) to Glangrwyney (238.163)
Grade IIIc
No Portages
6 Kilometres
OS Sheet 161

Below Cwm Bridge the Grwyne benefits from the junction of its two major arteries, the Grwyne Fawr and Fechan. It is still, however, a narrow stream easily blocked by trees. It joins the Usk 500 metres below the A40 bridge at Glangrwyney. It is a good, sustained run in interesting surroundings.

The Tawe and other rivers of South Wales

The *wild* rivers of South Wales are the spate streams of the southern Brecon Beacons and Black Mountains. The Tawe, Twrch, Taf, and Neath tributaries rise in open moorland, before descending through dense woodland (with the exception of the Tawe) into industrial valleys. Glacial activity steepened the sides of these valleys, and thereafter the rivers exploited natural fault lines in the rock to create some of the most impressive river scenery in Britain, narrow chasms, steep gorges and spectacular waterfalls.

South Wales' white water has traditionally been associated with the Teifi and more particularly the slalom sites at Llandyssul. The Teifi is in point of fact a comparitively poor white water river but it deserves a mention because its size ensures reliable water when other rivers in the area are too low.

AFON TAWE

In big water the Afon Tawe provides one of the most exciting runs in Wales, with 2 kilometres of sustained difficulty above and below Pen y Cae falls. In high flood this section can reach Grade Vf.

Tawe ***
Glyntawe (845.169) to Abercraf (815.125)
Grade IVe
No Portages
10 Kilometres
OS Sheet 160

In high water it is possible to begin 3 kilometres upstream of the recommended start, below Blaen-car (848.182). This is a difficult and committing stretch of water (Ve) with one portage (tree fall).

Put in from the track on the west side of the river in Glyntawe village. Continuously interesting but not too difficult water leads

for 5 kilometres and under two bridges to Pen y cae. Below the
second bridge is a four-tier rapid, Pen y cae Falls (IVe medium
water, Ve high water). The second and fourth drops on this rapid
are big natural shallow sloping weirs, which in high water can carry
enormous stoppers. Whatever the level this is not a pleasant place
to swim!

Below Pen y cae Falls there is a waterfall (IVe). Below again are
two sloping rapids; the second, on a left-hand bend, has a surging
'eddy fence' on the right-hand side. There is a man-made weir with
big spikes in Abercraf which is shootable. The river then passes
under the A4067 twice, and at the second of these big bridges is
the get-out. In between the bridges however is a 150-metre long
gorge to give you a final good memory of the Tawe.

It is possible to continue further downstream through Abercraf
over a number of interesting and shootable weirs. In this case it is
probably best to get out at the first bridge (765.081) below the
confluence with the Twrch; this adds another 9 kilometres to the
journey and is best done as a trip in its own right.

AFON TWRCH

A tributary of the Tawe, the Twrch needs a lot of water to make it
canoeable. In spate it is a fine, committing run.

Twrch
Dorwen (771.149) to confluence with the Tawe (765.081)
Grade IVd
2 Portages
8 Kilometres
OS Sheet 160

In high water the Twrch has been paddled from Dorwen. This
goes at IVd with two portages – the first a 5-metre sheer drop just
above Dorwen, the second on a right-hand bend below the first
gorge section. Both these portages have been paddled at Vf.
Access to Dorwen is up a rough private track (get permission from

farms *en route*) leading from Ystradowen off the A4068; egress is
at the first bridge after the confluence with the Tawe.

THE RIVER NEATH 'WATERFALL' TRIBUTARIES

In 1982/83 paths were created to link the nine waterfalls on four
tributaries of the River Neath – the Nedd, Mellte, Hepste and
Pyrddin. Two or three years later canoeists discovered falling over
waterfalls in plastic boats was possible and started to explore these
rivers. It takes five or six hours to walk the waterfall circuit, and I
recommend aspiring free-fall merchants to take the tour (while
you can still walk!).

The Neath is formed by the confluence of the Nedd and the
Mellte in Pontneddfechan. This is the common egress point for
these two rivers. The Pyrddin joins the Nedd 2 kilometres above
the latter's confluence with the Mellte. The Hepste joins the
Mellte 4 kilometres above the same confluence. I can get no
information on the canoeing potential of the Pyrddin. It is,
however, a pleasant walk and has two spectacular waterfalls.

Nedd *
Pont Melin-Fach (907.105) to Mellte confluence (902.073)
Grade IVd
2 Waterfalls/Portages
5 Kilometres
OS Sheet 160

This is an excellent stretch of river despite the two portages. The
Nedd is reached at Pont Melin-Fach, and from here to the
confluence with the Mellte, the Nedd is Grade IVd, except for the
two waterfalls, Upper Ddwli and Lower Ddwli. The upper
waterfall has been paddled, but the canoeist did not walk for a
year. Be warned, the landing is shallow!

Mellte
Porth yr Ogof (926.123) to Pontneddfechan (902.037)
Grade unknown

5 Waterfalls/Portages
9 Kilometres
OS Sheet 160

The Mellte is accessible from the Hepste, or further up at Porth yr Ogof. If choosing the latter, park at the cave entrance. Downstream of Porth yr Ogof are the two Clyngwyn waterfalls: Sgwd Uchaf and Sgwd Isaf Clyngwyn. Downstream of Sgwd Isaf is a slightly easier waterfall, Sgwd y Pannwr. Below the Hepste confluence the canoeing is Grade IIIc with two portages. All the waterfalls/portages have been paddled.

Hepste
Ty-Mawr Bridge (945.111) to Nedd–Mellte confluence (902.037)
Grade IVd
3 Portages (including 2 Waterfalls)
9 Kilometres
OS Sheet 160

The Hepste is accessible at Ty-Mawr Bridge, or below from the A4059 across the moors. Above Sgwd yr Eira the river goes underground – portage! There are two waterfalls/portages, Sgwd yr Eira (or Screwdriver) and Lower Cilhepste, with some big drops in between and below to the Mellte, and thence to its confluence with the Nedd (a further two portages – as above). Sgwd yr Eira was 'paddled' some years ago, with the canoeists claiming a 'world height record'.

AFON TAF

The Afon Taf rises in the Brecon Beacons as two heavily dammed streams the Taf-Fawr in the west and to the east the Taf-Fechan. After the confluence of these two streams in Merthyr Tydfil the Taf is of no further interest to the white water enthusiast.

Taf-Fawr
Llywn dam (012.114) to Merthyr Tydfil (028.079)

Grade IIIc
No Portages
5 Kilometres
OS Sheet 160

The 'big' Taf is easier than its smaller sister, flowing through a steep, but flat-bottomed valley. Nevertheless the scenery is impressive, with the brooding cliffs of Darren Fach on the left, and a green curtain of conifers swaying to and fro on the right, and the river is interesting enough, particularly towards the end. The Taf-Fawr is dam-controlled, and to avoid flooding on the Lower Taf there is a delay in releasing after heavy rain.

Taf-Fechan *
Pontsticill dam (059.114) to Merthyr Tydfil (033.080)
Grade IVd (Ve)
No Portages
7 Kilometres
OS Sheet 160

Of the Taf's two tributaries this is the harder and better, being if anything even more scenic. There are a number of moderate drops in the first 3 kilometres and then a more continuous gorge (IIIc) above the disused railway viaduct. At the road-bridge below the viaduct there is a difficult and dangerous fall (Ve). The river now leaves the road again and drops through a forested gorge (IVd). The river eases again into Merthyr Tydfil. It is best to get out in the town between the two road-bridges (A465 and A4102).

Bibliography

The following guidebooks will be found useful to white water
paddlers visiting particular areas in the country. They contain
descriptions of a number of rivers not included in this guidebook.
Some unfortunately are out of print (OOP) and hard to find.

HAYWARD, M., *Rivers of Cumbria*, Cordee, 1988

HOWELL, B., *Lake District White Water* (OOP), Cascade Press,
1982

LOCHEAD, I. AND TODD, A., *Scottish White Water*, British Canoe
Union, 1986

MEIKLE, A. AND ASHBY, A., *Guide to White Water of Scotland*
(OOP), Strathclyde University Canoe Club, c.1980

RAWSON, M., *Tayside River Guide* (OOP), Tayside Coaching Panel,
1987

MEMBERS OF THE SCOTTISH CANOE ASSOCIATION, *A Guide to Scottish
Rivers*, Scottish Canoe Association, 1989

STORRY, T., *Snowdonia White Water, Sea and Surf*, Cicerone Press,
1986

WOOD, G., *Canoeist's Guide to Yorkshire Rivers*, British Canoe
Union, 1984

The following three books may be found useful by those looking
for more sedate watery travel through the British countryside:

EDWARDS, L., *Inland Waterways of Great Britain*, Imray, Laurie,
Norie and Wilson, 1985

FOX, A., *Run River Run*, Diadem, 1990

BCU, *Guide to the Waterways of the British Isles*, BCU, 1961

Useful addresses and telephone numbers

British Canoe Union (BCU)
(Administration, *Canoe Focus* and
Coaching)

Mapperley Hall
Lucknow Avenue
Nottingham
NG3 5FA
(0602) 691944

BCU (Supplies)

The Elms
National Watersports Centre
Adbolton Lane
Holme Pierrepont
Nottingham
NG12 2LU
(0602) 817412

Holme Pierrepont National Water
Sports Centre (including Slalom
Course)

Address as for BCU Supplies
(0602) 821212

Canolfan Tryweryn Wild Water
Centre

Frongoch
Bala
Gwynedd
(0490) 2786

Scottish Canoe Association (SCA)

Caledonia House
South Gyle
Edinburgh
EH3 6AU
031 317 7314

Welsh Canoe Association (WCA)

Pen y Bont
Corwen
Clwyd
(0490) 2786

The Campaign for River Access for Canoes and Kayaks	c/o The Grove Inn Leeds LS11 5PL
Canoeist Magazine	4 Sinodun Road Appleford Oxon OX14 4PE

Index

Abbey Rapids, 158
Aberglaslyn Gorge, 257, 258, 261
Achlean Farm, 75
Achriabhach Falls, 103
Allan, river, 117, 121, 123–4
Allen, river, 144, 145, 147, 148,
149, 150–1
Allt Kinglass, 108
Alness, river, *see* Averon, river
Alt na Lairige, 114
Alwen, river, 285
Amicombbe Brook,218
Anafon, river, 227
Andy's Folly, 305
anglers, 40–6
Appletreewick, 202, 207
Aray, river, 105, 115–16
Archavady Gorge, 81
Arddu, river, 227
Ardle, river, 133
Ardross Castle, 63
Arkaig, river, 83, 89
Armathwaite Weir, 164
Artro, river, 54, 257, 265–6
Ashmore Gorge, 133
Averon, river, 61–4
Avon, river, 67, 68, 74, 75
Awe river, 105, 111, 113–14
Ayr, river, 135
Aysgarth Falls, 200–1

Backbarrow Falls, 195
Backdoor Man, 102
Bala Mill Falls, 276, 277, 279, 280
Banchor, 69
Barden Bridge, 205, 207, 208
Barle, river, 220, 221–2
Beaver Pool, 246, 247
Beddgelert, 257, 258, 261

Bedford Bridge, 218, 219
Bedrock Rapid, 300
Bell Pool island, 213
Ben Nevis, 88, 95
Bench Falls, 254
Berwyn Chicane, 287
Bethesda Gorge, 232
Big Rock, 108
Birk's Bridge, 179, 181
Blacksboat Rapid, 74
Blackwater, river, 63, 125, 126,
131, 133
Bobbin Mill Rapid, 196
Bobsleigh, 193
Bolton Priory, 208
Bonar Bridge, 65
Bontnewydd Bridge, 237, 238
Border Esk, river, 136, 139–40
Boughrood Bridge, 303
Brae Roy Lodge, 78, 81
Braemar, 133, 134
Bran, river, 312, 314
Brathay, river, 187, 190, 191–2
Breaker, the, 259
Brickchute, 194
Bridge of Avon, 75
Bridge of Isla, 123
Bridge of Orchy, 105, 107
Brithdir Falls, 298
British Canoe Union (BCU), 39,
40–3, 113, 202, 235, 276
Brothers Grimm, 81
Brown Howe, 196
Brown's Falls, 249, 250
Bryn Afon Steps, 234, 236
Bryn Bras Falls, 242
Bryntail Fall, 298
Builth Rocks, 301
Burneside, 165, 167

Burnsall Bridge, 205, 207
Bwlchgwernog Bridge, 264
Byreburnfoot Rapid, 140

Caernarfon, 236–7
Caledonian Canal, 75, 88, 94
Camddwr Bleiddiad, 305
Camel, river, 212
Campaign for River Access for
    Canoes and Kayaks (CRACK),
    39, 41–3, 202, 235
Campbell's Island, 138
Campsie Linn, 123
Capel Curig, 249, 250
Carloonan Mill Falls, 115–16
Carnage Corner, 70
Carron, river, 65
Caseg, river, 227
Catnish, 111
Cauldron, the, 87
Cauldron Snout, 153
Ceirw, river, 285
Chain Bridge Rapid, 287
Chapel Mill Falls, 279
Chapel Stile Weir, 189
Chesters fort, 146
Chicken Shoot, 108
Chollerford Weir, 145,146
Cilieni, river, 312
Circulating Eddy Rapid, 300
Claerwen, river, 299, 304–5
Cleghorn Bridge, 135
Clough, river, 173, 176, 177
Clunie, river, 134
Clyngwyn, 319
Clywedog, river, 290, 297–8
Coal Chute, 274
Coal Yard Fall, 294
Cobden's Falls, 249, 250, 251, 253
Cocker, river, 179
Coe, river, 95, 101-2
Colwith Force, 187
Colwyn, river, 257, 259–63

Common, the, 306
Coniston Falls, 203, 204, 205
Coniston Water, 195, 196
Constriction, 87
Conwy, river, 56, 57, 239–46
Conwy Falls, 239, 240, 242, 243,
    245
Corkscrew, 71
Cotherstone Bridge, 156, 158
Coupall, river, 97–8
Cown Head, 165
Crack of Dawn, 99
Crack of Doom, 99
Cragganmore, 74
Crake, river, 195–6
Crook of Lune, 173, 175, 176
Crunkley Gill, 153
Cupola Bridge, 150, 151
Cwmcoed Falls, 301
Cwm-Mynach, river, 268
Cwmnantcol, river, 265, 266
Cwmystwyth, 296, 297
Cynfal, river, 265

Dalbrack, Bridge, 127
Dalhastnie Bridge, 127
Dalmally Bridge, 111
Dalness, 100
Dart, river, 57, 211, 212–16, 217
Dee, river (England), 173
Dee, river (Scotland), see Royal
    Dee, river
Dee, river (Wales), 248, 267, 285,
    286–9
Derwent, river, 160, 163, 179, 197
Diluw, river, 296
Distillery Falls, 75
Dochart, river, 117
Docker Nook, 168–9
Dodd's Folly, 138
Dog Island, 140
Dologau Gorge, 297
Don't Play With Fire, 201

Doors of Perception, 245
Double Drop, 247
Double Waters, 218
Dragon's Tail, 261
Drumlanrig Bridge, 137, 138, 139
Duddon, river, 179–85
Duddon Hall Falls, 183, 185
Dugoed, river, 276, 283–4
Dulas (Northern), river, 290, 292–4
Dulsie Bridge,69
Dulverton Bridge, 221, 222
Dunblane Bridge, 124
Dwyryd, river, 264
Dyfrdwy, river, 56; see also Dee,
    river (Wales)

Eamont, river, 160
Earn, river, 123
Eas a Chataidh, 109, 110
Eas Urchaidh, 110, 111
Easan Dubha, 108
East Dart, river, 212
East Lyn, river, 222–3
Eastby Abbey Weir, 199–200
Eden, river (England), 160, 161,
    164, 176
Eden, river (Wales), 267, 268,
    271–3
Eden Lucy Falls, 164
Edw, river, 299, 303, 306–7
Effock Burn, 127
Eggleston Gorge, 155, 156, 158
Ehen, river, 179
Eing, river, 65, 66
Elan, river, 304
Elbow, the (Conwy), 245
Elbow, the (Falloch), 117
Elter Water, 189, 191
End of Civilization, 108
Ericht, river, 133
Erme, river, 212
Erwood Rapids, 303
Esgair Gawr, 274

Esk, rivers, 153, 185; see also
    Border Esk, river
Eskdale Green, 185, 186
Etive, river, 57, 95–101
Euthanasia Falls, 213
Exe, river, 211, 221
Expressway Bridge, 233

Factory Falls, 285, 288
Factory Pool, 279, 280
Fairy Falls, 243, 245
Fairy Glen, 57, 239, 240, 243, 244,
    245, 246
Fairy Steps, 87, 246
Fall of the Black Pool, 293
Falloch, river, 117
Falls of Aray, 115
Falls of Dochart, 117
Falls of Falloch, 117
Falls of Leny, 117
Falls of Orchy, 110
Falls of Shin, 64
Fedwrgog Falls, 278, 279
Feshie, river, 67, 74–5,76
Feshiebridge, 75
Fewston Reservoir, 209
Findhorn, river, 35, 53, 56, 67–72
Findhorn Bridge, 72
Fionn Ghleann, 102
Fishermen's Gorge, 229, 230, 232
Fishladder, 72
Flower Pots, 211
Foot-bridge Rapid, 300
Force Falls, 168
Force Gorge, 153, 155
Forestry Bridge, 261
Forestry Bridge Fall, 305
Forestry Falls, 253
Fort William, 88, 95, 104
Fowey, river, 212
Frank's Falls, 295
Furzleigh Weir, 216
Fyne, river, 105, 112, 114

Gain, river, 270, 271
Gairlochy, 88
Gamallt Falls, 301
Gamlan, river, 267, 271, 273–4
Ganllwyd Weir, 271
Gannachy Bridge, 128
Garbh Ghaoir, river, 117, 118, 120, 122
Garlic Weir,171
Garnett Bridge, 169
Garrigill, 147–8
Garry, river, 83, 89, 91
Garth Falls, 255
Gates of Delirium, 244, 245
Gaur, river, 117, 118, 120, 122
Gelert's Rapid, 258
Gelli-lago, 263
Ghaistrill's Strid, 203, 205, 207
Glantwymyn Gorge, 291, 292
Glaslyn, river, 255, 257–9
Gleann Glas Dhoire, 82
Glen Airlie, 137–8
Glencoe, 101–2
Glencoe Village Falls, 102
Glenferness House gorge, 69
Glenfintaig Lodge, 91, 93
Glenfyne Estate, 114
Glenshee, 131, 134
Gloy, river, 83, 91–3
Glyn Gwy Gorge, 300
Goat-Hole, 152
Gobbler, the, 243
Goedol, river, 257, 264–5
Grandtully Rapid, 122
Granite Falls, 112, 114
Graveyard, the (Leven), 194
Graveyard, the (Llugwy), 253
Graveyard, the (Mawddach), 271
Graveyard, the (Tryweryn), 277
Great Langdale Beck, 180, 187–9, 191
Green Field Beck, 203

Greta, river, 153, 157, 158–9, 160–3
Greystone Bridge, 219, 221
Grinton Bridge, 198
Grwyne, river, 315
Gun Barrel, 230
Gunnerside Bridge, 199
Gunnislake Newbridge, 219, 221
Gurnsall Bridge, 169
Gwynant, river, 268
Gwyrfai, river, 227, 237–8
Gyfarllwyd Falls, 296

Hack Fall, 200
Hagg Island, 140
Half-way Bridge, 232–3
Half-way Weir, 288
Haltwhistle, 147–8
Hand Roll, 271
Hargreaves Folly, 240
Head Weir, 211
Headbanger, 86, 87
Hebbelthwaite Hall Ghyll, 177
Hell Hole, 303
Helmsdale, river, 61
Henry Moore, 245
Hepste, river, 319
Hexham, 143, 145, 147, 150
High Bank, 203
High Force, 155, 202
Hog Bank Weir, 151
Hollow Mills Rapid, 140
Holme Pierrepont, 23, 32, 214
Holne Bridge, 213, 215, 216
Honddu, river, 315
Horseshoe Falls, 285, 286, 287
Hotel Fall, 137
Hubberholme, 203, 205
hydrograph, 51–5

Iaen, river, 290, 292
Imagine, 146
Inver, river, 61

Inveraray Pier, 116
Invercanny, 134
Inverchorachan,114
Invergarry, 91
Inverlair Bridge, 84
Inverness, 77
Invershin, 64
Irfon, river, 299, 305–6
Irt, river, 179
Irvine Rapid, 140
Island Rapid, 300
Itchen, river, 42
Ithon, river, 299
Ivy Pool, 246

Jaws O'Neath, 138
Jill's Folly, 183
Jim's Bridge, 249, 250

Kelso, 152
Kendal, 165, 167
Kent, river, 165–8
Keswick, 161, 163
Kiachnish, river, 95
Kielder Dam, 145
Kilchurn Castle, 111
Killington New Bridge, 176
Knockando, 74

Laggan Dam, 84
Lake Falls, 100–1
Langholm, 139–40
Langstrothdale, 203
Langton, 198, 200
Langwathby Bridge, 164
Laverock Bridge, 171, 172
Left Wall, 245
Leny, river, 117–19
Leonach Burn, 69
Letterbox, 99
Leven, river, 180, 194–5
Levens Bridge, 168
Levens Gorge, 69–70

Lido, the, 158
Lincoln's Inn Bridge, 175, 176
Linn of Dee, 133, 134
Linn of Tummel, 120
Linton Falls, 203, 205, 207
Little Langdale Beck, 187, 191
Little Strid, 208
Llafar, river, 227
Llanfared Rapids, 303
Llangollen, 285, 287, 288, 289
Llangynidir Rapid, 311
Llanstephan Rapids, 303
Lledr, river, 239, 241, 246–7
Llennyrch, river, 265
Llugwy, river, 202, 241, 248–54
Llwyngwern Weir, 294
Llys Falls, 255
Loch Actriochtan, 102
Loch Dochfour, 77
Loch Eigheach, 120, 122
Loch Etive, 113, 114
Loch Fyne, 105, 114, 116
Loch Garry Dam, 89
Loch Laidon, 120, 122
Loch Lee, 125, 127
Loch Leven, 102
Loch Lochy, 83, 88, 93
Loch Lubnaig, 117, 119
Loch Shin, 61, 64
Loch Tulla, 107, 111
Lochawe, 111
Lochy, river, 75, 83, 88, 94
Logie Bridge, 70
Long House Gill, 183
Loup Falls, 177
Loup Scar, 205, 207
Loups, the, 130
Lover's Leap, 215
Low Force, 155
Lower Cilhepste, 319
Lower Findhorn Gorge, 67
Lowther, river, 160
Loy, river, 83, 93–4

Lunchtime Weir, 286
Lune, river, 156, 166, 173–6, 177, 178
Lyn, river, 220, 222–3

Machno, river, 239
Mackerstoun, 152
Mains of Sluie, 72
Mallwyd Gorge, 283, 284
Mark, river, 127
Marske Bridge, 198
Marteg, river, 300
Mawddach, river, 29, 265, 267–71
Meal Bank Rapids, 171
Mellte, river, 318–19
Merddwr, river, 239, 240
Middleton Bridge, 156
Milestone Bridge, 310
Milk Shake, 274
Milky Way, 274
Mill Falls, 124
Mill House Falls, 311
Mill Race Rapids, 146
Milton Falls, 131, 133
Mincer, the, 254
Miner's Bridge Rapid, 254
Mint, river, 165, 167, 169–72
Monessie Gorge, 84–5
Monmouthshire and Brecon Canal, 310–11
Morie, loch, 61, 63
Mouse Water, 135
Mousemill Bridge, 135
Mucomir Power Station, 88
Muker, 198
Municipal Falls, 210
Murthwaite, 169
Mynach, river, 296

Nant y Gors, 249
Nant y Llys, 255
Nant yr Offeraid, 303
Nantmor, river, 257, 263–4

Nantperis, river, 227
Nantygwryd, river, 241, 249, 250, 255–6
National White Water Centre, 277
Neath, river, 316
Nedd, river, 318
Neptune's Staircase, 88
Ness, river, 67, 75–7
Netherton Rapid, 133
Nevis, river, 95, 102–4
Nevis Bridge, 104
New Bridge (A82), 93
Newbridge, 213, 215
Newby Bridge, 194
Nidd, river, 197
Nith, river, 135–9
No Through Eddy, 245
North Esk, river, 125–30
North Tyne, river, 143–7

Ogwen, river, 227–33
Ogwen Bank Falls, 230
Old Dungeon Ghyll, 189
Orchy, river, 29, 97, 105–11
Oughtershaw Beck, 203
Oykel, river, 61, 62, 65–6
Oykel Bridge, 65
Oykel Falls, 65–6

Paddle Test, 261
Parson's Bridge, 294, 295
Patton Bridge, 171
Pen y Bont, 265
Pen y Cae, 316, 317
Peter's Fall, 305
Pillar Falls, 187, 188, 189
Pipe Bridge Gorge, 192
Pipeline, 245
Pistyll Cain, 270
Plankey Mill, 150, 151
Plas y Brenin, 250, 255, 256
Plym, river, 211
Pont Aber Glaslyn, 259, 264

Pont ar Eden, 272, 273
Pont Cyfyng Falls, 252, 253, 254
Pont Dolgefeiliau, 272
Pont Llanrhaiadr, 274
Pont Newydd Falls, 293
Pont y Bala, 256
Pont y Pair Falls, 254
Pont y Pant Falls, 246
Ponterwyd Gorge, 295
Pool Slide, 255
Pot, the, 288
Pot Hole, 100
Potarch Hotel, 134
precipitation, 48–51
Prizet Bridge, 167, 168
Public Toilet Falls, 267, 271
Purners Bridge, 130

Quarry Falls, 301

Railway Bridge Falls, 85
Railway Falls, 178
rainfall, 48–54
Randolph's Leap, 35, 67, 69, 70,
    71, 73
Rannoch Moor, 107, 120
Rattle Brook, 218
Rawthey, river, 24, 173, 176–8
Red House Farm Rapid, 200
Redmire Force, 201
Relugas Bridge, 70
Rhaeadr Cenarth, 321
Rhaeadr Cwm-clyd, 304–5
Rhaeadr Esgairgeiliog, 294
Rhaeadr Gwy, 301
Rhaeadr Henllan, 321
Rhaeadr Mawddach, 270
Rhaeadr Rhulen, 306
Rhaeadr y Glaerwent, 304
Rhaeadr y Twmffat, 305
Rhayader Town Falls, 299, 300, 301
Rheidol, river, 290, 294–6
Rheidol Falls, 296

Rhiw Goch Gorge, 246–7
Rhiw-Saeson, river, 292
Rhythallt Falls, 236
Ribble, river, 24, 202, 206, 209–10
Richmond Falls, 199
rivers: baseflow, 56–7; drainage,
    54–7; grading, 29–30, 35–8;
    hydrology, 47–57; legal rights,
    39–46; pollution, 32, 39;
    portages, 30–1; water volume, 51
Roaring Mill, 104
Rock Hop, 162, 163
Rock Slide, 99
Rock Steps, 151
Rocks of Solitude, 128
Rokeby Falls, 159
Roller Coaster, 108
Rooster Tail, 80, 81
Roy, river, 78–82
Royal Dee, river, 125, 132, 133–4
Roybridge, 78, 82, 85
Rutherford Cauld, 152

St John's Beck, 160, 163
Salmon Ladder, 114
Sanquhar, 135, 137, 139
Sawmill Dam, 131
Sawmill Falls, 120
Scaddle, river, 95
Scaffolding Bridge Falls, 279
Scimitar Gorge, 103
Scout Hut Bridge, 229, 231, 232
Scrogs Weir, 167
Sedbergh New Bridge, 177
Sedgewick Bridge, 168
See No Evil, 245
Seiont, river, 42, 227, 234, 235–7
Senny, river, 310, 312
Serpent's Tail, 35, 285, 286, 287
Settle Weir, 210
Sgwd Isaf Clyngwym, 319
Sgwd Uchaf, 319
Sgwd y Pannwr, 319

Sgwd yr Eira, 319
Sheep Trolley Gorge, 108
Sheewater, *see* Blackwater, river
Shin, river, 61, 62, 64–5
Skelwith Force, 187, 191
Ski Jump, 99
Skippers, 140
Skirfare, river, 205
Slot, the (Findhorn), 72
Slot, the (Llugwy), 250
Somme, the, 295
Son of Bedrock, 300
Sore Tooth, 108
South Esk, river, 125, 126, 131
South Tyne, river, 143, 147–8, 150
Spark Bridge, 196
Spean, river, 83–8
Spean Bridge, 83, 85
Spean Gorge, 85–7
Spey, river, 67, 68, 72, 74
Spin Dryer, 216
Sprint, river, 165, 167, 168–9
Sprint Mill Falls, 169
Spuhler's Folly, 311
Stackhouse Weir, 210
Stainforth Force, 210
Staircase Rapid, 199
Stanley, 122, 123
Start Rapid, 138
Stepping Stones, 268
Stock Ghyll, 187
Stone Bridge, 78, 81, 82
Straight Bridge, 177
Strangerthwaite Weir, 176
Strid, the, 29, 176, 202, 203, 207–8
Swale, river, 157, 197–200
Swallow Falls, 202, 248, 254

Taf, river, 316, 319–20
Tamar, river, 217, 219, 221
Tankers Corner, 208
Tarell, river, 314
Tarr Steps, 222

Tavy, river, 216–18
Tawe, river, 316–17
Tay, river, 117, 121, 122–3
Tebay Falls, 173, 174, 175
Tees, river, 53, 147, 153–8, 202
Teifi, river, 316
Teith, river, 119
Teme, river, 56
Think Small, 293
Thirlmere, river, 160
Thistlebrigg, 122, 123
Three Bridges, 115
Thruscross Reservoir, 208–9
Thurso, river, 61
Tombstones, 285, 288
Torcastle, 88
Torrie Rapid, 119
Towler Hill Rapid, 158
Town Falls, 285, 288, 289
Treig, river, 84
Tremadog Bay, 260, 264, 265
Trent, river, 23, 32
Trevor Rocks Rapid, 285, 289
Triple Fall, 97, 99
Triple Drop, 216
Triple Steps, 71
Troutal Farm Falls, 181
Troutbeck, river, 24, 187, 192–3
Tryweryn, river, 276, 277–80, 298
Tummel, river, 117, 119–20
Tweed, river, 143, 144, 151–2
Twin Bridges, 209, 210
Two Morals Rapid, 272
Twrch, river, 276–7, 316, 317
Twymyn, river, 56, 269, 290–2
Tyn y Cornel Bridge, 276, 277, 279
Tyn-y-Maes Gorge, 230
Tyne, river, 143–50
Tyne Green, 150

Ugly House, 253
Ulpha Bridge, 179, 181, 183
Upper Ddwli, 318

Ure, river, 157, 197, 198, 200–1
Usk, river, 308–11

Viaduct Gorge, 246, 247
Victoria Bridge, 88–9
Vinegar Stroke, 274
Vyrnwy, river, 276, 280, 282,
    283–4

Walkham, river, 217, 218, 219
Wall of Death, 131
Wallowbarrow Gorge, 181
Warden Gorge, 143, 145, 146, 150
Washburn, river, 202, 206, 208–9
Washing Machine (Dart), 215
Washing Machine (Usk), 311
Water Close Weir, 194, 195
Water Yeat Bridge, 196
Waterfall, the, 99
Waterfall Rapid, 242
Waterworks Weir, 183
Waunfawr Bridge, 237

Weaver, the, 245
Webburn, river, 212
Wen, river, 271
Wensley Bridge, 200, 201
West Dart, river, 212
West Water, river, 125, 126, 130
Wharfe, river, 29, 202–8
Wharfedale, 205–7
White Bridge, 91
Whiteadder, river, 152
Whorlton Falls, 158, 159
Windermere, lake, 192, 193, 194
Wish You Were Here, 79, 81
Witches' Pool, 127, 128
Witches' Step, 110
Wnion, river, 267, 274–5
Wye, river, 56, 299–303

Y Ffrwd, 300
Ysbyty Falls, 240
Yscir, river, 314
Ystwyth, river, 290, 296–7